Hemingway: A Revaluation

Hemingway: A Revaluation

edited by

Donald R. Noble

The Whitston Publishing Company
Troy, New York
1983

Library of Congress Catalog Card Number 82-50413

ISBN 0-87875-249-8

Printed in the United States of America

DEDICATED TO THE MEMORY OF

MY FRIEND

JACK B. GILLIES

1903-1978

Eight of the papers in this volume were presented at the Third Alabama Symposium on English and American Literature, "Hemingway: A Revaluation," held in Tuscaloosa, Alabama.

Acknowledgements

Three of these essays have appeared elsewhere in somewhat different form. I wish to thank the editors of *The Saturday Review* for permission to reprint "Hemingway and the Search for Serenity," by Alfred Kazin; Jack D. Durant and M. Thomas Hester, eds., for permission to reprint "False Dawn: *The Sun Also Rises* Manuscript" by Michael S. Reynolds which appeared in *A Fair Day in the Affections: Literary Essays in Honor of Robert B. White, Jr.*; and Leonard F. Manheim, editor of *Hartford Studies in Literature: A Journal of Interdisciplinary Criticism* for permission to reprint "*Islands in the Stream:* Death and the Artist," by Richard B. Hovey.

I am grateful to a number of people for the support which made possible the original conference at which several of these papers were read. I wish to thank Dr. Douglas Jones, Dean of the College of Arts and Sciences, Dr. David Matthews, then President of the University of Alabama, The Office of Academic Affairs, especially Dr. Roger Sayers, and the Division of Continuing Education, especially Mr. Charles Adams, Mr. John Burton and my friend the late Ruth Tisdale Wilder.

I wish also to thank my friends Dr. George Wolfe and Dr. Dwight Eddins for their support and encouragement throughout.

For their help in the preparation of this manuscript I am grateful to Ms. Jan Wilson, Ms. Martha Rogers, Ms. Lisa Hodgens and Ms. Karen Miller.

CONTENTS

Introduction

by Donald R. Noble

In the face of the flood of Hemingway criticism which has swept over us all in the last few years, it seems reasonable perhaps to ask: is this book necessary? After all, we can hardly claim to be bringing to public light a worthy but too-long-ignored or recently-discovered literary figure. Hemingway is probably the most famous, most successful public literary figure in the history of the United States. Why then call this gathering of the clans?

There are, to my mind, two reasons. We need to pause periodically, to draw a breath, come together and in a sense think things over. We need to have, together, a look at the primary works and deduce, if we can, which ones we have overpraised and which ones we have undervalued. We need to have a hard look at the critical work which we commentators, scholars, critics, journalists, what-have-you have produced in the last twenty years and decide what is worthy of being kept and what ought to be consigned to oblivion, and on what grounds. We ought then to try to determine which areas of critical inquiry we have, through oversight or sloth or timidity, failed to explore and, of course, what kinds of mistakes we have been making; and, then we must resolve to make other kinds of mistakes in the future. All this so far is essentially retrospective.

Looking forward, there are two areas of challenge. First, we must come to grips with Hemingway's posthumous works. These works, *Islands in the Stream, A Moveable Feast* and others, present special problems and require special handling. Second, we must make our way into those critical areas which still need exploring. Fortunately, we in Hemingway studies have new navigational aids with which to find our way. At last the Hemingway papers have been collected, cleaned up and catalogued, and made available to students of his work. It will no longer be necessary or, one hopes, permissible, for scholars to proceed without consulting the relevant letters, notebooks, early drafts and revisions which are proving so valuable in these latest serious considerations of his work.

Jackson J. Benson leads off this volume by discussing these very questions. Benson has surveyed the sixty-seven books on Hemingway which he thinks worthy of consideration and has concluded that the great interpretive work has yet to be written. There are several fine ones, but by no means has the last word been said. More specifically, Benson cautions, works which might appear to have covered areas of inquiry have in fact fallen short. In spite of the existence of Killinger's *Hemingway and the Dead Gods* and Emily Stipes Watts's *Hemingway and the Arts*, work still needs to be done on the relationship of Hemingway to existential thought and aesthetic theory.

In surveying the periodical literature on Hemingway, Benson is, if anything, even more critical. Critics write on Hemingway without reading what has already been written; the result is massive repetition and duplication. Many of the dozens of articles per year tell us things we have long known. Many are either trivial or preposterous—especially so-called "influence studies." And many still commit the most attractive of errors in Hemingway studies: the biographical fallacy. Critics simply refuse to leave the man out of it and can resist no opportunity to publish a biographical anecdote, no matter how small or nasty it may be. In this regard, Benson says, the situation is getting worse, not better. Some commentators have even begun to treat the characters in Hemingway's novels, especially *The Sun Also Rises*, as if they were people, and have taken to criticizing *For Whom the Bell Tolls* for historical inaccuracies, as if it were a history text. We must, at the very least, treat the characters as characters, the fiction as fiction.

How we might go about this in the future constitutes the most valuable portion of Benson's remarks. Now that the Hemingway papers are available, we must avail ourselves of them. We must use them as tools in much more sophisticated studies of style and we must study the manuscript revisions from draft to draft in an attempt to discover what Hemingway's intentions were and how they changed as his work on a given book progressed. We must pay much more attention to language, Benson insists, for Hemingway always said what he meant, and we must take on hard questions, impossible without the manuscripts, such as Hemingway's philosophy of composition. If influence studies are still to be written, Benson urges, let them also be on the important questions. What did Hemingway really learn from Gertrude Stein, from Ezra Pound, from Sherwood Anderson? What did Hemingway learn from studying so carefully the landscapes of Cezanne? What about Hemingway's epistemology, his metaphysics, his ethics and, perhaps most challenging, his ideas of Time and the nature of reality? There is much work to be done. The subsequent essays in this volume meet some of Benson's challenges and indicate still more areas which would prove fruitful to the scholars of the next generation of Hemingway studies.

II

The three essays following Benson's, those by Stephens, Kazin and Gurko, are of a general nature, applying one or two ideas over the body of Hemingway's work.

Robert Stephens begins with a study of the comparative critical receptions given Hemingway in England and America. As Fitzgerald might have put it, British reviewers are different from you and me. They have a different set of expectations from American reviewers, a different aesthetic and come out of a different tradition of letters, all the while thinking of American literature as a branch of English letters.

Hemingway was well received but not overpraised in England in the early stages of his career. *The Sun Also Rises* did come out, after all, in the same year as *The Magic Mountain* and *To the Lighthouse*. After *A Farewell to Arms*, however, he was fully accepted by the British as the truly "modern" writer that he was. They perceived his nihilism early on.

In many ways, the British have taken a truer line on Hemingway than the Americans. They have concentrated on the work, while many American commentators have been distracted by the man and his legend. The English concentrated on the subjects of the books as "contributions to literary knowledge" while American reviewers focused on Hemingway's career. Is he improving? Can he keep it up? When will he write the legendary (and, in the history of twentieth century novels, abominable) Big One, the Great American Novel?

To Americans, writings other than novels have not counted for much, so the British have always been better prepared to appreciate works such as *Death in the Afternoon, The Green Hills of Africa,* and now memoirs such as *A Moveable Feast.* To the British, *Death* was a book on bullfighting; the American reviewers insisted on treating it as autobiography. The British wrote about the Hemingway hero; the Americans wrote about Hemingway. The British reviewers, Stephens concludes, have had a more sophisticated view of what constitutes a *career.* They understood that there are ups and downs and did not insist so strenuously on every book's being bigger, better, an advancement on all the previous.

Stephens also reviews the twin triumphs of *For Whom the Bell Tolls* (1940) and *The Old Man and the Sea* (1952) after the poor receptions of the thirties non-fiction and *To Have and Have Not* (1937) and *Across the River and into the Trees* in 1950. Twice the heavyweight champion of the world was perceived as being on the canvas on his back; twice the "sharks" thought he was finished; and twice he got up swinging, the second time winning the Nobel Prize.

One final aspect of Stephen's piece which may be of special interest to the second generation of Hemingway critics is his appreciation of the English critics' response to the posthumous works of Hemingway. The English are used to the publication of writers' memoirs, letters, papers in general and do not seem to have the same problems with them as American critics do. There seems to be less of a tendency in England to worry over what *Islands in the Stream* will do to Hemingway's overall reputation and more of a willingness to take the publications one at a time and judge them for what they are, not for what the critics wish they were, i.e., more Great American Novels.

Alfred Kazin follows with a discussion of the relationship between painting, peace and Hemingway's work. Hemingway had, Kazin argues, the clearest sense of any writer of his time of the "enduring injustice," "the fundamental wrongness at the heart of things." To Hemingway, "the world was as powerful a force as the unconscious or sex," and he had a keen sense of his own, man's own, vulnerability. He saw the chaos and violence in the world and formulated his own answer to it: we must stoically accept it and attempt to create an island of self-discipline and order in a sea of disorder and dissolution.

Hemingway did this, Kazin says, by creating, truly, life on the page: "his greatest gift was to identify his own capacity for pain with the destructiveness at large in our time. The artist works by locating the world in himself. Hemingway did something more: he located in himself his century's infatuation with technology, technique, instruments of every kind."

In his art, Hemingway sought to combine discipline, order and peace. In painting, especially in the composition, technique and serenity of the landscapes of Cezanne, he found his model. Gertrude Stein had taught him that "in the twentieth century nothing is in agreement with anything else." But she also advised him to "concentrate" and showed him the modern paintings on which he should concentrate. Stein was herself more interested in the painter's mind, in psychology, but Hemingway was interested in the rendering of the sensuous world. To Hemingway, the individual word could be equated with the individual brush stroke. If Stein worshipped the sentence, Hemingway went further and worshipped the word. Thus, like Goya or Cezanne, he makes us *see*.

At his height, then, in *Sun* and "Big Two-Hearted River" and *The Old Man and the Sea*, Hemingway was romantic, post-impressionistic about nature. He created in words a nature which is a possible source of serenity and order but which is also too big for man to comprehend. Nature can provide a respite from civilization, as it does in *Sun*, but it also "echoes the endless turmoil in the human heart." It can be a swamp as well as a clear-running stream.

Hemingway sought serenity all his life, his son Gregory tells us in his memoir, but he never found it—not in painting, not in writing, and probably not in death either, although he appears to have dared death to provide him with it on many occasions.

Hemingway was a seeker, Leo Gurko agrees. He searched for serenity in painting but also sought it in other places, especially in travel. "It wasn't change of scenery he was after, but a change of life," Gurko asserts, and takes a look at some of the many journeys in Hemingway's life and works and what it was he and his characters expected to get out of their constant traveling. Sometimes they search for the ideal place, often in nature. Sometimes they seek and, like Santiago, find, an intensification of consciousness. Sometimes it is a search for a rebirth such as Nick's in "Big Two-Hearted River."

In the first three novels (not counting *Torrents*) Gurko shows how the characters travel out and then, ultimately, back, not much changed by their experiences. In the last three novels, this is not the case. These protagonists "advance toward new ground" and are changed by their ordeals. Gurko, a respected commentator on the works of Joseph Conrad, shows how these journeys, like those of Conrad's heroes, take place in an empty universe and are part of "a manichean struggle between the forces of light and darkness." Changes of place make possible changes of state; physical movement makes possible emotional movement; journeys recharge the traveler and make him better able to endure the everyday.

III

The nine essays to follow are arranged in chronological order, by work, and are somewhat narrower in scope. Most address themselves to particular problems in specific works. In many cases, the manuscripts at the Kennedy Library have been consulted and often this has shed new light on some aspect of Hemingway's work. One must bear in mind throughout that revaluation does not invariably result in a work's being more highly treasured.

The Hoffmans begin with one of those areas Benson strongly suggests needs work: a more intense look at Hemingway's language. Using *In Our Time* as their object of scrutiny, the Hoffmanns examine how Hemingway learned to use words: as the equivalencies for events, as objective correlatives, as a means of overcoming time through reverberations with other words. They assert that *In Our Time* is novel-like, not merely by means of thematic threads but through the interrelationship of words, their rhythms and repetitions.

The Hoffmanns offer a fresh reading of "Big Two-Hearted River," showing not only how Nick overcomes his trauma through self-discipline and order, but how the reader is in a sense unconsciously led to recollect other stories ("On the Quai at Smyrna" and "The Battler" in particular) through the repetition of a number of connotatively loaded words, especially those having to do with roads and travel, water and walls, and death.

In an essay which may, like his *Hemingway's First War; The Making of "A Farewell to Arms,"* prove the model for much future Hemingway criticism, Michael Reynolds reports on his examination of the manuscript of *The Sun Also Rises*.

The Sun is now fifty years old, Reynolds reminds us, and the Modern Age which it helped to usher in, is dead. It is no longer sufficient to read and comment on the published text as if it were holy scripture. Now we must bring to bear these techniques of scholarship which will help to illuminate the text.

Reynolds discusses the correspondence between Hemingway and Fitzgerald concerning *Sun*. He examines the many working titles Hemingway considered. He believes we have not entirely understood the epigraphs from Gertrude Stein. In this novel, he believes, Hemingway consciously set out to beat Fitzgerald, to become the champ, and a part of his strategy was to abandon the vague, slightly sentimental hero like Nick Adams and portray instead, survivors.

These "survivors" were very much based on real people; in

the early chapters of the manuscript, they still have their real names. The temptation to think of the characters as real people is easily understood; it seems, that to a great degree, Hemingway thought of them that way.

Based on his study of the manuscript, Reynolds has reached several conclusions concerning how Hemingway composed. First, he must have "composed" a good deal in his head before sitting down; for Hemingway, much of the first draft was the last draft! When he revised he usually deleted, and usually whole paragraphs, pages or sections; he was not a putter-inner like Wolfe or a tinkerer like Joyce. We know now from Reynolds' study that, unlike Fitzgerald, Hemingway did not plot the entire novel before he started. He did not consciously know where he was going and this accounts in part for the disappearance of such fascinating characters as Count Mippipopolous, a victim of the unplotted novel.

Hemingway's first draft of *Sun* will also help us with our influence studies, Reynolds tells us. It seems that many references to Turgeniev were removed in revision. Other studies of other manuscripts may reveal more.

The most important discovery to come out of this manuscript study may be again related to Hemingway's most important theory of composition. That is, the most important fact or scene can be left out and it will still serve to energize the story if the rest of the story has been told truly. It may be, Reynolds surmises, that Hemingway's original plan was to base the character of Romero more obviously on Niño de la Palma, complete with his loss of nerve. Romero, of course, is never destroyed, but in a way, Jake nearly is. Because he is responsible for introducing Romero to Brett and thus endangering the young bullfighter, Jake loses the respect of Montoya and the other afficionados. He had already lost "manhood." Now he has lost the respect of men he respected. The scene which makes this explicit, Hemingway cut. We sensed it all the while: the character changed by the events of this novel is Jake. He was "lasting" with what he had. Now he will have to "last" with less.

Harry Stoneback, also writing of *The Sun Also Rises*, examines in detail the passages concerning the monastery at Roncevaux and the story of Roland and finds in them clues to understanding the character of Jake and, in fact, another dimension of the meaning of the novel.

Roncevaux, the site of Roland's last stand against the Moors in 778 AD, has, for Hemingway, heavy symbolic value. Roland is, in his folly, courage, loyalty and prowess, a paradigm for Jake. Stoneback stresses that this novel is a quest story, a quest for lasting, spiritual values. This quest motif, Stoneback argues, is not properly understood if the scenes at Burguette and San Sebastian are *contrasted* to the scenes at Paris and Pamplona. What we should understand is that the pilgrimage to Santiago de Campostela begins on the Rue St. Jacques in Paris, a street on which Hemingway, pointedly, has Jake walk.

Jake is, thus, a pilgrim. Stoneback argues that, unlike Brett and the others, Jake has faith, and that he, like St. Augustine, understands that it is God's will, not his, that will be done. Like Ignatius Loyola, Jake has been wounded in battle; he tries to be a spiritual guide to Brett and others; he prays often and reaffirms his belief in God. He is genuinely moved by the monastery at Roncevaux and visits other churches.

Stoneback spends some time, too, discussing Falkner's use of Roland and Roncevaux in *Flags in the Dust*, suggesting many similarities between Bayard Sartoris and Jake Barnes. Both are haunted men, seeking spiritual values in a utilitarian, mechanized world. Sartoris is finally killed in an airplane, the scene of Jake's wounding. Both are true, modern-day knights.

The conclusion to this essay, however, offers some strong contrasts to Reynolds'. Whereas Reynolds sees Jake as a big loser in *Sun*, Stoneback sees him as something of a winner. He is more than a survivor; he holds on to his spiritual values in a world where most men have none.

Scott Donaldson has taken as his subject the much discussed but still misunderstood personality of the young Lieutenant Frederick Henry. By studying the text itself and, more importantly, the manuscripts of *A Farewell to Arms*, Donaldson has reached some new conclusions concerning the hero's character.

Frederick claims throughout the novel to be the victim of forces too powerful to fight. He often laments his impotency. All this, Donaldson argues, is basically fraudulent, a pose Henry has adopted to avoid responsibility for his actions.

Frederick Henry has deserted the army, made his separate peace with war, and impregnated his girl friend. While no one is pointing accusing fingers at him for these deeds, his conscience is bothering him. In several deleted passages, Hemingway makes this explicit. In the text itself, he leads the reader to feel Henry's uneasiness; it is one of those important things Hemingway felt a good writer could and should leave out. His motivation for deletion here, Donaldson feels, is that the deleted passages would make us too fond of Henry. Properly understood, Henry is a man who has contemplated desertion for some time, is a failure as a military man, seeks solace in food, drink and sex and generally tries to forget the war and later, after her death, Catherine.

Frederick Henry is a man burdened by guilt. As Hemingway had written on a page of deleted manuscript, "the position of the survivor of a great calamity is seldom admirable." Henry has survived both the war and his love affair and in telling his version of the story strives to make himself appear more passive than active, more sinned against (by the cosmos) than sinning. Hemingway, Donaldson reminds us, did *not* wish readers to identify him too closely with this writhing hero.

In another close reading of a published text, Alan Josephs has some unsettling remarks to make about *For Whom the Bell Tolls,* a novel which rarely comes in for anything but praise. His subject is Hemingway's Spanish, nearly a sacred topic.

Josephs takes a revisionist approach to this problem, demonstrating that Hemingway was far from bilingual and that *Bell* is filled with dozens of errors in Spanish, from the most harmless to some that are egregious, if amusing.

On the factual level, Josephs shows that Hemingway makes a great many errors in usage, spelling and accent marks. Further, he discusses the connotations of Robert Jordan's nickname for Maria, "rabbit," and the implication of using that in Spain. He tells us, amusingly, what the English equivalent of this Spanish slang word would be. Also Josephs suggests, this nickname seriously undermines the presentation of Maria as pristine in spite of everything, a virgin in spirit, and so on. It changes things.

More troublesome, however, are what Josephs sees as the possible implications of these errors. First, they call into question Hemingway's much-vaunted knowledge of Spain and Spanish and also his scrupulous attention to detail: getting it right. Have we been giving Hemingway too much credit in these areas? Is he the serious student and the meticulous craftsman we have long credited him with being? On the other hand, if Hemingway *knew* better, if his Spanish was in fact excellent, is he careless about it? Is he a kind of chauvinist, paying scrupulous attention to his own tongue but granting little of that attention to a foreign tongue?

Josephs is pretty tough on Hemingway, calling into question the status accorded him by Carlos Baker: "citizen of the world." Josephs concludes strongly that, for those who know Spanish well, Hemingway's errors, whether they stem from ignorance or carelessness or chauvinism, ruin *For Whom the Bell Tolls*.

W. Craig Turner takes as his subject the "problem" novel *Across the River and Into the Trees*. This novel and *To Have and Have Not* seem to cause the same kinds of difficulties in the Hemingway canon as the dark comedies like *Measure for Measure* cause Shakespearean scholars. Turner feels *Across the River and Into the Trees* has been unjustly maligned over the years, that it is, in fact, something of an experimental work and in it Hemingway pushes out the boundaries of his craft, takes chances. Not all of these chances pay off.

The most important area of experimentation is in the narrative mode: the story is told from several points of view other than Colonel Cantwell's, including third person omniscient and first person interior monologue. This subtlety and variety of narration, Turner argues, is matched by subtlety of theme and the theme here again is death. In this case, however, it is death by disease, not death by violence and, as Hemingway himself remarked, this is a much more complicated matter. So it requires a more sophisticated narrative technique.

Cantwell is dying. He rebels against death, like many another Hemingway hero, by taking upon himself one of the prerogatives of God: delivering death. In this case it is delivered to some ducks, but he also seeks to expand his circle of existence through his relationship with Renata, "the reborn one."

Turner discusses a number of the flaws we had previously recognized: Cantwell's honorific-laden speech, the excessive military jargon, Cantwell's now famous defecation at the scene of his wounding. Of more value, however, is Turner's study of the ways in which certain words, reappearing in the story, take on symbolic value here just as the Hoffmanns demonstrate they do in *In Our Time*. The wind, bridges, scars and journeys all serve in this novel to carry the theme of the inevitability of death.

This is, as Philip Young termed it, a "revealing" novel. It tells us a good deal about Hemingway's own attitudes concerning the plight of the sensitive man and his relationship to the life of action. Cantwell is the man Hemingway liked to think he would have been had he been a professional soldier. But we can move forward from this biographical reading, Turner argues. This is a novel of which Joyce or Faulkner should have approved. Hemingway experimented, took chances in technique when his voice and his style were already established and successful. Hemingway here, like Santiago later, went out farther than he had ever gone before and the sharks got him.

Philip Young, who begins by very good-naturedly assuring the reader that this is his last farewell appearance in the theater of Hemingway studies, undertakes to explain the causes of Hemingway's decline in power in the last decade or so of his life.

Young, who is, along with Carlos Baker, the dean of Hemingway studies, is best known for his thesis that there is a suicidal, a self-destructive obsession with death in the Hemingway Hero. Young did not mean to psychoanalyze Hemingway himself in his critical study and he does not mean to do that in this paper either. Yet certain relationships between Hemingway and his highly autobiographical fiction must be acknowledged.

Young's thesis here is, put simply, that the early Hemingway had a "confident self-absorption"; he wrote out of his own feelings and experiences but with confidence that they were significant, not out of ego. The later Hemingway, Young argues, developed an "insecure obsession with self," and this "self" found its way into the fiction in a raw state. The life was not subjected, to use Henry James' phrase, to the "alchemy of art."

In the course of examining the Hemingway collection at the Kennedy library, Young came across a number of letters by Hemingway, addressed to him, but never mailed. In these letters he finds a good deal of corroborating evidence for his thesis. Hemingway objected to biographical criticism not merely because some of the implications were unflattering or unsettling, but because having his own life story widely discussed deprived him of material he would use in his fiction. His life was his subject; he needed it for his work! He romanticized it, shaped it, used it to suit his purposes, but it was still his life. This is especially true, Young feels, for *A Farewell to Arms* and *The Sun Also Rises*.

But, starting with *Across the River and Into the Trees*, there is a turn for the worse. Cantwell is a kind of idealized self-portrait which turns out to be caricature. Santiago is much more successful in this respect, but is still overdone. *A Moveable Feast*, Young feels, is a minor masterpiece, but can be explained in two ways. First, it is nonfiction. Second, the forty years which had passed lent enchantment as well as distance. It is in *Islands in the Stream* that this problem is most fully apparent.

Young feels that Thomas Hudson, like Jake, is Hemingway, but in a most unhealthy and, in terms of the novel, unsuccessful, way. There is too much ego here. Hudson is not a tragic hero to anyone but his creator, for Hemingway identifies all-too-much with his protagonist. And worse, rather than self-admiration, we have self-pity. The central fact about Thomas Hudson is his despair, and Hemingway's own loss of confidence and his own despair show through clearly.

This debate over the meaning and merits of *Islands in the Stream* is continued in the last two essays in this collection.

Richard Hovey has not much good to say about this book, and I suspect that many Hemingway afficionadoes will object strongly to his argument, but it is not far out of line with Philip Young's. Hovey begins by admitting that *Islands* is a book of considerable power and locates the source of that power in Hudson's malaise which is, all too obviously, Hemingway's malaise. Hudson has lived by the code, is a successful artist but is, nevertheless, a miserable man, suffering from chronic and severe depression and melancholia. For Hovey, as for Young, Hudson *is* Hemingway, and the identification is too close for comfort, to say the least. Hudson is Hemingway's vehicle for self-pity in this novel, and whereas Hudson's alter-ego, Roger Davis, is accorded a second chance at life, Hemingway will not grant that second chance to Thomas Hudson. For Hudson, destruction must be complete.

In the novel, it is. Hudson's sons are killed, all three of them, and for no good reason except that their creator wants them dead. Hudson himself then turns to submarine-chasing to try to deal out a little death himself, again to take that God-like prerogative to himself. In a phrase which may offend some, Hovey terms this "pleasure" in killing, "criminal pathology" and the Hemingway hero a sadistic, twisted and perhaps dangerous person.

Hovey goes on to say that this need for bloodshed and violence comes out of Hemingway's insecurity about the manhood inherent in an artistic career. Are artists manly enough? After all, homosexuals can be artists too. Therefore, is Hemingway fascinated by death and does he place himself and his heroes in dangerous situations time after time, does he have Hudson reject his first wife's overtures and does he have his sons killed *all* to reaffirm his and Thomas Hudson's manhood? Hovey thinks so and supports his thesis with detailed and closely reasoned argument.

Gregory Sojka closes the debate over *Islands* on a more positive note. He urges, as many in this volume have, that we dismiss the autobiographical issue and concentrate on the work. He agrees with Edmund Wilson that the book is really about hanging on in the face of madness, defeat and death and that Hudson is struggling to maintain self-respect and not give in to self-pity. Sojka maintains that Hudson is successful, remaining faithful to his art and then to his duty, as he sees it. It is Roger Davis who has been unfaithful to his art, forsaking serious writing for commercial success, and it is Hudson who urges him to go straight and write truly.

In an earlier manuscript version, Sojka tells us, Davis (then called Hancock) had been the protagonist. His ruminations concerning returning to serious writing are too clearly Hemingway's own and Hemingway was wise to change his focus and cut his material.

Sojka also has high praise for the sequence in which Hudson's son David fights the broadbill. This is, he argues, a rehearsal for Santiago's long struggle with the marlin, written three years later. Sojka notes that Hudson handles the boat and lets Davis coach young David. This is wise since the father is too involved emotionally and it also gives Davis the opportunity of encouraging himself by hearing the advice and encouragement he is giving the boy. We can have some confidence that Davis will redeem his own talent and, through what John Barth in *The End of the Road* called scriptotherapy, "write out" his personal problems in the bargain.

For Hudson, however, the end is not so promising. Overcome by despair and self-pity in the "Cuba" section, Hudson is close to the breaking point. He redeems himself in his duty to his country. Although other commentators have criticized his submarine-chasing as melodrama, Sojka agrees with Hudson: when everything else is gone, one still does his duty. Through his commitment to his duty, to the last, Thomas Hudson gains back a modicum of self-respect, a modicum of peace.

Hemingway Criticism:
Getting at the Hard Questions

by Jackson J. Benson

Few scholars nowadays become lifelong students of one particular author, especially if they are involved in modern literature. So it is that yesterday's expert becomes today's opening footnote, tomorrow's "mistaken early critic," and the day after tomorrow is inadvertently plagiarized without any footnote at all. All of which is to say that this address is by way of a minor farewell by a minor Hemingway commentator. Since I am not in as much demand as Philip Young, I plan to make my farewell but once and passionately.

Having had something to do with the running of two conferences similar to this one, I know that many of the experts asked to speak at such affairs feel that they have already "done" the author or topic in question and wonder, in coming back to a topic no longer at the center of their attention, if there is anything more they can say that they haven't already said. So this is my farewell topic—has Hemingway been done? What is the condition of Hemingway scholarship and criticism in the mid-Seventies? And what is left to be said? While I may propose a few tentative ideas here and there, my primary tactic will be to make some harsh judgments, ask some hard questions, and then get the hell out before the questions have to be answered and the judgments come back to haunt me.

Another good reason for a quick getaway is that writing about Hemingway, or at least about his critics, is becoming expensive and dangerous. A. E. Hotchner, as you may have read in the newspaper, just collected $125,000 from Doubleday and Co. and the author of *Hemingway in Spain*, Jose Luis Costillo-Puche, for saying unkind things about Hotchner's expertise. Now since I have made at least one remark questioning Hotchner's accuracy,

I am holding my breath. I am praying he will not sue, for at $125,000, he is liable to put Duke University Press out of business. At $125,000 he is liable to put Duke University out of business.

Hotchner and his law suit seem to me to be symptomatic of our times—everything, even disputes among critics, must be settled in court—as well as typical of the worst tendencies of Hemingway scholarship. It has always been a bit tainted with showmanship and greed. Both sides of the law suit might even serve as a text for the sermon which follows later in my presentation: the dreariness of scandal and the importance of getting things right. While I don't like to think of my own work on Hemingway as being rather quickly outdated and forgotten, I do look forward to a Hemingway scholarship that will be harder, tougher, and in general, more responsible.

I

I'd like to begin my look at the criticism by reviewing what we have by way of books. It is not easy to be exact in accounting for all the books written about Hemingway and his work, first, because there are several pamphlets and extremely short books, and second, because there are several books that are so poor that they are seldom included in scholarly listings. But according to my judgment, leaving out the shortest and the worst, I have counted a total of sixty-seven books.

As for Hemingway's own publication, for purposes of comparison, leaving out pamphlets, editions, repeating anthologies, and anthologies put together by others, I count nineteen book publications. So we are already to a ratio of more than three to one, books about the man and his work as versus the work itself, and we have begun the process of writing books about the single Hemingway books. This latter trend is always unsettling when it occurs, even when the quality of criticism is good. In our library there are only two authors who appear to have larger shelf space than Hemingway—Faulkner and Shake-speare. This may reflect the strange character of our university, but it is still somewhat disturbing.

Even more disturbing is the realization, after looking back over the titles and thumbing through some of the volumes in order to refresh my memory, of how many really terrible books there are about Hemingway. I can't think of another author that has drawn forth so many bad books, except perhaps Byron. And perhaps there is a moral in that, somewhere. As we are all only too well aware, the basic problem, from the beginning, has been Hemingway's popular appeal as generated through the media, an appeal that does not seem to have abated even fifteen years after his death. The name still makes the news magazines regularly, and the weakest, most tenuous books purporting to expose some aspect of his life call forth a rash of reviews from coast to coast by reviewers anxious to add their two cents to the evaluation of the Hemingway personality. Hemingway may have achieved a level of popularity in this country higher than that achieved by any writer in any country in modern times. This popularity has caused a number of problems for Hemingway criticism: it has allowed a number of things to be published that shouldn't have been published; it has created prejudice against Hemingway's work as a result of a negative backlash among literary scholars generally; and it has made it very difficult for us to see the work itself clearly. In time, works like *Green Hills of Africa* may be seen to be far better than we perceive them now, and works like *The Sun Also Rises*, far less impressive. The great interpretive book on Hemingway's work has not yet been writ-ten, and I doubt that it can be for several more decades.

Under the circumstances, we shouldn't be surprised that we have a rather large number of bogus biographies, picture books, and scrapbooks, as well as fourteen, more-or-less legitimate books of memoir or reporting. Listing these by the last name of the author, I have included Ross, L. Hemingway, G. Hemingway, Sanford, Hotchner, Arnold, McClendon, Miller, Kilmo and Oursler, Castillo-Puche, Farrington, Sokoloff, Sarason, and M. Hemingway.[1] (Included, you might notice, are two sisters, a brother, two wives, and a son.)

Of these fourteen (one I have not yet read, Mary Hemingway's book, which saves me the embarrassment of having to judge it while standing next to her), only four seem to have much value for the scholar. The most valuable is Marcelline Hemingway Sanford's *At the Hemingways*. It is entertaining and informative, even though much of the insight that sister Marcelline gives us into the Hemingway household is given inadvertently. The second book of some value to the scholar is Bertram Sarason's collection of memoirs as background to *The Sun Also Rises*, although it is poisonous, as I'll explain later. The third is brother Leicester's book which provides a number of good insights into the man. And the fourth is the publication of Lillian Ross's *Portrait*, which, taken in the context of a fuller knowledge of the biography, has a certain marginal value. With one or two possible exceptions, the other memoirs tend to be either so shallow that they are not even entertaining or so filled with prejudice or error as to be misleading and even destructive.

The Alice Hunt Sokoloff book based on interviews with Hadley Mowrer, Hemingway's first wife, is not a bad book. But as Jackson R. Bryer has noted in his annual review of Hemingway materials, the contents justify an article or two, but not, without further research and development, an entire volume.[2]. The sad truth, again, is that Hemingway's popularity seems to justify the publication of books which in other circumstances wouldn't be published. As per the recent flap over "grade inflation" in the colleges, we might call this the "Hemingway inflation." Items that should have been notes have been padded to articles; items that should have been articles are padded to books. And a number of unrevised Hemingway dissertations have been published, some by university presses that wouldn't normally touch any kind of dissertation with a ten foot pole.

Of the scholarly books, there are fifty-three, which I have divided into seven groups: (1) bibliography and collecting, (2) biography, (3) critical biography, (4) criticism, (5) foreign reputation and criticism, (6) anthologies of criticism, and (7) linguistic studies. (I will not comment on categories five and seven which contain two and one items respectively.) We have been extremely fortunate in the first two groups. The reliability of those working in bibliography and biography has offset the unreliability of other Hemingway publications. I have listed under "bibliography and collecting" books by Cohn, Samuels,

Hanneman (2), Young and Mann, and Bruccoli and Clark. Of chief importance here, of course, is the work of Audre Hanneman on the *Comprehensive Bibliography* and the *Supplement*. If you have used other single-author bibliographies, then you must appreciate the clarity of organization, the exhaustive detail, the excellent cross-referencing and indexing, and the overall accuracy of Hanneman's volumes. In the course of working on my short story checklist, I physically checked hundreds of her entries and found only one small error.

I have listed only one book, Baker's *Life*, under biography. As with the Hanneman volumes, Baker's biography has been subjected to some unfair criticism. That he has chosen to present as much useful information as possible, rather than indulging in psychological speculation, seems to me to be a great virtue. The product of a stupendous amount of hard work over a long period of time, the book is clear, detailed, comprehensive and as accurate as any such book which depends in part on witnesses can be. I found it remarkable, again while working on the short stories, to find that every one of the fifty-five published stories was referred to in Baker's text, in most instances with reference to both the time and circumstances of composition.[3] Such completeness can be appreciated by anyone who has struggled to write a full-length biography and has been driven close to madness by the overwhelming number of details.

For the category of "critical biography," I have listed Montgomery, Fenton, and Joost. Although any number of critical books have employed some measure of biography in approaching the study of the work, only these three include a substantial amount of fresh biographical material. (Michael Reynolds'book on the background and writing of *A Farewell to Arms* could be included here, although its major thrust seems to me to be critical.) All three of these critical biographies have demonstrated their value over the years. Each is well-focused on a relatively narrow range of material. Although time has eroded some of the usefulness of Fenton's *Apprenticeship* (1954), the book remains instructive, particularly in regard to early attitudes and techniques. Unfortunately, it is too often overlooked by current scholars.

But my main nominations for good books too often overlooked go to Joost's *Ernest Hemingway and the Little Magazines: The Paris Years* and Robert O. Stephens' *Hemingway's Nonfiction: The Public Voice*. I suspect the titles of these books have worked against them—when there are so many books whose titles promise so much, these books sound very narrow. They aren't. Joost provides an excellent discussion of Hemingway's beginnings as a writer, and Stephens tells, directly and indirectly, as much about the fiction as the non-fiction. The larger point here is that one offshoot of the Hemingway inflation has been a competition among Hemingway books for an audience, a competition which has sometimes resulted in good books being shuffled aside for such superficial reasons as title, paperback publication, or distribution to booksellers.

Under "criticism" I have listed twenty-six books, books by C. Baker, Young, Atkins, Rovit, Lewis, S. Baker, Gurko, Hovey, Stephens, Benson, Peterson, Nahal, Watts, Waldhorn, Grebstein, Wagner, Reynolds, Wylder, J. Bakker, De Falco, Sutherland, Sanderson, Broer, Shaw, Pearsall, and Killinger. Of these, the books by Peterson, Nahal, J. Bakker, Sanderson, Shaw, Sutherland, and Pearsall probably should not have been published, and there are four or five others I have grave doubts about. I don't mean to be imperious in my judgments nor insensitive to the hard work and grief that may have been attached to the writing and publication of some of these books. I simply feel I didn't learn anything from them, nor can I see that they fulfill any special function or address any special audience that would justify their existence.

The Killinger book is a special case. It takes a marvelous title, *Hemingway and the Dead Gods*, and an important topic, Hemingway's implicitly expressed philosophical stance, particularly as related to existentialism, and pre-empts both title and topic without really exploring the material very fully. The tragedy is that because of Killinger's book, we are unlikely to get the penetrating book we need on this topic. The Watts discussion of Hemingway and art is also a special case. The book is well-researched and interesting. Furthermore, it puts Hemingway convincingly into a context where we can perceive him to be, as he was, a serious artist and highly skilled craftsman. Yet, the opportunities to illuminate the fiction, as in the Killinger book, are too often neglected in favor of exploring the special material itself, in this case the graphic arts.

If one sets aside these and other special cases, such as volumes on individual Hemingway works, as well as those books that clearly never should have been published, the remaining books tend to look, at least on superficial examination, pretty much alike. They all tend to be general, interpretive books which deal with Hemingway's major works, chapter by chapter. This superficial similarity may be one good reason why many recent critics seem so ill-prepared. There are so many such books, and who wants to spend months reading all of them, often reading some of the same things over and over, just to write a short article or two?

Yet, in almost every case, each of these books, while duplicating other publications to some extent, has made notable contributions to Hemingway studies. Too many research efforts and interpretive perceptions have been lost in the welter of good and bad material, and any number of articles by newcomers seem to reflect a complete innocence of what has been said before. There isn't much of a critical dialogue going on; instead, there is simply one shot after another in the dark. As an example, Robert W. Lewis, Jr.,'s book *Hemingway on Love* includes several excellent readings, including one of *A Farewell to Arms* which has become definitive as one of several valid, major approaches to the novel. Three substantial articles on *A Farewell to Arms* in the last few years have made many of the same points as Lewis has made, without even a nod in his direction.

But I don't think that plagiarism is involved. The case is even worse than that. I would be willing to bet that these writers didn't even read Lewis. What we have, to put it bluntly, is professionals exhibiting some of the same weaknesses that we used to think were characteristic of college sophomores. To stop this reductive drift—aside from what could be done by editors and editorial readers to tighten standards—it seems to me that we need someone, someone like Jackson R. Bryer, to take up the difficult task of writing a detailed and objective history of Hemingway criticism, a book which would describe both chronologically and thematically the evolution of the criticism and the scholarship and the interrelationships between critical ideas. Because of the hugh quantity and uneven quality of Hemingway criticism, one of the hard questions is, what has already been done? It is not a question easily answered even by those who have tried to keep up with their homework.

The interpretive books can be roughly divided into two categories: those which tend to be rather general, employing several different critical approaches in their analysis, and those which are more closely bound to a strong central thesis or a particular analytical direction. Since most books claim to have a strong central thesis, this division is somewhat arbitrary on my part. Of the first kind of critical book, the strongest—that is, the book from which I have learned the most—is Earl Rovit's, although Baker's *Artist*, especially in the fourth edition, is quite good. Since I have mentioned Rovit, let me say a word more about his work in passing. Although his book has been cited in footnotes over the years almost as much as it has been stolen from, it has not received the high ranking, particularly from non-Hemingway experts, that it should have received. This lack of recognition seems to have been the result of a snobbish reaction (if not snobbery, at least an assumption of guilt by association), to the Twayne's United States Authors Series. A case in point is a paperback bibliography for students called *A Reader's Guide to English and American Literature* by Andrew Wright.[4] Wright lists Carlos Baker's *Life* and his *Critics* collection, the Weeks collection, books by Sheridan Baker and Philip Young, and, of all things, Lillian Ross's *Portrait*. The reason I suspect Wright of snobbery is that he also omits the fine book by Warren French, also in the Twayne series, on John Steinbeck. I have been pleased to see that Hemingway specialists, at least, have recently in their own work and in reviews given Rovit the credit he deserves.

The best of the rest of the general critical books are Arthur Waldhorn's *A Reader's Guide*, Leo Gurko's *The Pursuit of Heroism*, Sheridan Baker's *An Introduction and Interpretation*, and Delbert E. Wylder's *Hemingway's Heroes*. All of these are well-written and perceptive. While they offer something to the specialist in each case, they might find their best use as introductions to undergraduates (although the Wylder book does not deal with the short stories).

As for the second kind of interpretive book, those bound to a strong central thesis, no one yet has matched the drama and power of Philip Young's *Hemingway* (and its second edition, *Ernest Hemingway: A Reconsideration*). Having said that and in spite of the fact that Philip Young is sitting right in front of me, I must add that I have always viewed the book with mixed feelings. Part of the mixture is no doubt envy. But I also wonder, because of the author's talent, if the book hasn't done almost as much harm as good. It is a brilliant exposition of partial truths that has so heavily influenced nearly everyone that has ever written seriously about Hemingway's work, that I wonder if Hemingway's own misgivings about the book have not, in a way, proved true after all. But that fault, if it is one, is not Young's so much as it is ours, the rest of us that have written thematic interpretations, that we have not written boldly enough and well enough to act, even all of us together, as a counter-weight to the force of Young's arguments.

The best of the thematic critical books beyond Young's are Richard B. Hovey's *The Inward Terrain* and Lewis's *Hemingway on Love*, and the best of those employing a particular analytical direction are Sheldon Norman Grebstein's *Hemingway's Craft* and Emily Stipes Watts's *Ernest Hemingway and the Arts*. These books, it seems to me, find their best use with advanced students.[5]

The last major category of critical books is that of critical anthologies. A Hemingway critic wrote to me not long ago to congratulate me on my short story book, although, as he said, he disapproved of such books as acting to spoon-feed students what they should be able to manage on their own. And I suppose he's right, except that there are times when I would use anything to encourage student ingestion. But I have always looked upon the critical collection not so much as a study aid, as a focusing device and as a source of critical energy. Teachers refer to them as quick reviews of the critical literature before teaching undergraduates and as stimuli to their own thought as they search for new approaches and new questions. Scholars, both student and professional, tend to start with critical collections as they prepare for their own projects. As the Hemingway critical literature becomes larger and more unwieldy, the role of the critical anthology becomes more and more important, whether we like it or not. Quality of selection, representativeness (in various ways) of selection, and quality of documentation and of bibliography all have a crucial impact on the quality and direction of Hemingway studies as a whole. So it appears that in general we do not have the anthologies we need. Such books in the future should be directed at a wider academic audience, since, in fact, it is not just students who use them.

The earliest anthology, the McCaffery, has long ago lost its usefulness except as a reference work on the shelf of specialists. The Baker *Hemingway and His Critics*, which was not a very good anthology to begin with, seems to have lost what value it may have had. Two other relatively early critical collections, the Baker *Critiques of Four Major Novels* and the Weeks Twentieth Century Views anthology have held their value fairly well. I would like to see an update of both, if nothing more, an updating of the bibliographical sections. I would prefer to see Baker's *Critiques* completely redone, but since he is probably no longer interested, perhaps someone else could come out with a *Critiques of Three Major Novels*, omitting coverage of *The Old Man and the Sea* and reprinting about twelve to fifteen substantial articles for each novel, rather than the current five or six. Why can't anthologies be updated just as critical books often are?

Two more recent general anthologies don't really replace either the Weeks or the Baker *Critiques*. Both the Waldhorn *Collection* and the Wagner *Five Decades* serve better as resources for the advanced student than as general introductions for beginners. I agree with Bernard Oldsey who in his review of the Wagner collection mourned the fact that the book was not able to be the five decades review the title promises (no doubt because of publisher's requirements), combining the best of the old with the best of the new on a large scale.[6] The other general anthology is the Astro and Benson *Hemingway in Our Time* which is a collection of original essays directed primarily toward scholars and teachers.

The remaining seven of the fourteen available collections are all specialized, dealing with individual novels or groups of stories. Six of them, published either in the Merrill Studies series or in the Twentieth Century Interpretations series, are relatively short and intended as study guides for undergraduate students. This group includes books on *A Farewell to Arms* by Graham and by Gellens, on *For Whom the Bell Tolls* by Grebstein, on

The Sun Also Rises by White, on *The Old Man and the Sea* by Jobes, and on the two African stories by Howell. The best of these seems to me to be the Grebstein and Howell volumes, although all of them are about as good as the limitations of their size and intended audience will allow them to be. My own book, the seventh of these specialized anthologies, tries to deal comprehensively with the short stories as a whole.[7]

II

You may rejoice that it would be impossible for me to attempt any kind of comprehensive commentary on the periodical literature. But I have made a survey of the literature for the first four years of the Seventies, 1971-1974. The main surprise that came to me in accounting for the articles during this period was that the number of Hemingway articles, rather than gradually increasing, as most of us had assumed, has dropped rather dramatically. In my count I have left out dissertation abstracts, reviews and review essays, foreign language articles, and articles in books, except for those appearing in the *Fitzgerald/Hemingway Annual*. I count sixty-nine articles for 1971, sixty-eight for 1972, and then a drop to fifty-nine for the next year, and a further drop to forty-three for 1974.[8] So if we accept the count as accurate, it suggests that after a gradual increase in scholarly activity on Hemingway during the Sixties, to a high point at the end of the decade, this activity is declining rather rapidly to a little more than half of what it was before. Nevertheless, the total number of articles for the period of 1971-1974 is still an overwhelming two hundred and thirty-four.

For these years taken all together, the category with the most items, as one might expect, is that of the "general article" with fifty-seven. This is followed in turn by the short stories with fifty-four items; memoir and biography with forty-seven; *The Sun Also Rises* with twenty-one; bibliography, text, and collecting with fifteen; *A Farewell to Arms* also fifteen; *For Whom the Bell Tolls*, ten; *The Old Man and the Sea*, eight; *Islands in the Stream*, four; and a sprinkling of one or two items for each of the other Hemingway works. This distribution is again what one might expect, although I was a bit surprised by the large number of articles on the short stories and the small number of articles on *Islands in the Stream*. The largest total for a single year, by the way, was twenty-three on the short stories in 1971, followed by eighteen memoir or biographical items in 1972.

As with the books, the overall impression I received in reviewing and rereading the articles of this period tended to be negative (by comparison, the Faulkner articles for the same period seemed, as a whole, more scholarly and convincing). The test for me is whether the article tells me anything useful—did I learn something I didn't know before? or have I been led to see something differently from the way I perceived it before? And my feeling was that there was a lot of useless articles during these years. The Hemingway inflation can be observed year after year in the number of articles that would seem to grasp at any nearby premise, no matter how tenuous, for launching a discussion. Too many items appear to be based on a single and rather limited interpretive inspiration, which although perhaps interesting, and of possible value in the classroom, seems hardly substantial enough for anything more than a note. But before going on with this self-righteous tirade, let me turn first to the good material.

Of the "general" articles, only two impressed me enough at the time that I took notes on them, and both of them were published in books rather than periodicals: Alfred Kazin's chapter, "A Dream of Order: Hemingway" in *Bright Book of Life*, and Ihab Hassan's chapter "The Silence of Ernest Hemingway" in *Shaken Realist*. The latter article struck me as particularly perceptive. The largest number of good articles attached to particular documents had to do with the short stories, as one might guess from the total number of articles published in each category. Best among these I thought were Carl Ficken's "Point of View in the Nick Adams Stories," an article which involves a lot of hard work with the story texts; Sheldon Norman Grebstein's "The Structure of Hemingway's Short Stories," which displays perceptive close reading of several stories in order to determine their patterns of development; Scott MacDonald's "Implications of Narrative Perspective in Hemingway's 'The Undefeated,' " a fine article on a popular story that has needed careful analysis;

and John M. Howell and Charles W. Lawler's "From Abercrombie & Fitch to *The First Forty-Nine Stories*: The Text of Ernest Hemingway's 'Francis Macomber,' " which, aside from getting the prize for the longest title, does an excellent job of research, compilation of texts, and close reading. I was also moved to take notes on Kenneth G. Johnston's "Hemingway's 'Wine of Wyoming': Disappointment in America," another excellent essay on, this time, an almost totally neglected story, and on Paul P. Somers, Jr.'s article, which I will refer to later, "The Mark of Sherwood Anderson on Hemingway: A Look at the Texts."[9]

Two articles about *The Sun Also Rises* attracted my admiration: Scott MacDonald's "Hemingway and the Morality of Compensation" and Carole Gottlieb Vopat's "The End of *The Sun Also Rises*: A New Beginning." (MacDonald seems to have a Hemingway factory somewhere—perhaps a dimly lit room in a warehouse filled with graduate students in Women Studies Programs—but factory or no, his quality control is very good.) Two articles on *A Farewell to Arms* impressed me, despite the fact that both of them are source studies and I have become very suspicious of (other people's) discussions of sources and influences: Bernard Oldsey's "Of Hemingway's *Arms* and the Man" and Robert O. Stephens' "Hemingway and Stendahl: A Matrix of a Farewell to Arms." Other good articles for the period include Linda W. Wagner's "The Marinating of *For Whom the Bell Tolls*," Joseph DeFalco's article on *Islands in the Stream* (although because it was published in a book, it was not included in my count), John Bowen Hamilton's on *The Old Man and the Sea*, and Kenneth E. Bidle's on *Across the River and into the Trees*.

So I can point to thirteen periodical articles (and three more articles in books) that struck me at the time I read them as being particularly useful. There were, of course, other good articles during this period that for one reason or another didn't attract my attention. But allowing for my eccentric taste and even if we were to double or triple my number of articles, the ratio, compared to the overall total of two hundred thirty-four, is disappointing. It can be depressing to have to read that much to get that little.

What's wrong? Several areas of weakness seemed to announce themselves as I was going back over this material, looking at it for the first time in one lump. One such problem area is that involved in the frequent attempts by writers to trace a source or influence, or failing that, to show parallelism or some other vague relationship between a work by Hemingway and some other work of literature. This is a problem that goes beyond Hemingway studies into recent criticism generally, a problem caused by the revolt against the New Criticism and the decades of "readings" spawned by the new criticism. In the competition for prestige, journal editors in the last few years have increasingly insisted that articles submitted have some "hard" basis for interpretation, preferably research that has uncovered new information about the document itself or its circumstances of composition. Such insistence may be laudable in theory, but in practice it has led to a desperate search to legitimatize articles by such devices as the discovery of "possible" sources. Such articles often turn out, paradoxically, to be flabbier than the straightforward interpretations which they have replaced.

The list of "other works" brought in some fashion to bear on Hemingway's writing during the period of my focus is a long one: Emerson, Thoreau, Wordsworth, Wister, Dreiser, Donne, Pound, Anderson, T. S. Eliot, Twain, Baroja, Dante, Bierce, Henry Adams, Villiers, Stendahl, Peele, Shakespeare, Proust, St. John of the Cross, and anonymous (the York Play of the Crucifixion)—and there are several others that I dimly remember from my reading, but forgot to jot down in my notes at the time.

Among these articles, there are several sound ones, including detailed studies of already proven influence, such as Paul Somers, Jr.'s article on Sherwood Anderson's impact on Hemingway's early writing. And there are good, detailed examinations of texts in order to establish influences that had not yet been firmly established, such as Robert O. Stephens' article on Stendahl and *A Farewell to Arms*. But there are some approaches to Hemingway that clearly say more about the critic, his ideas and tastes, than about Hemingway. As Mary Hemingway has said, "A number of people are beginning to attribute to Ernest interests and activities in which they themselves are interested and I find it shameful."[11] When a writer talks about the relationship of "Tintern Abbey," *Cymbeline*, or the York Play of the Crucifixion to Hemingway's work, I would think that he is talking about his own perception of a similarity which may be of more value to him than to the reader. When that writer goes on to talk about how different *Cymbeline* is from Hemingway's work, he would appear to be trying to create an article out of an absurdity.

Another area of weakness is one that I referred to earlier, that is, the failure of some recent critics to do their homework. The impression given by a number of articles written during the 1971-1974 period is of the same things being said over and over again, things that have been said before, often going back decades. The solemn pronouncement of such critical judgments as if for the first time is almost laughable, except that it does harm to the original thought that lies behind the cliché. Thus, we have a writer in one article telling us, as if it had never been mentioned before, that T. S. Eliot must have been an influence on Hemingway's early writing.

And we have another critic, in the mid-1970's writing this:

> But the Hemingway hero is not, as many people have thought, a tough, insensitive brute obsessed by an appetite for blood-sports, drink, and women. He is, on the contrary, deeply sensitive and suffers profoundly from the shocks of experience. Hemingway, himself, was not the hard-boiled tough guy that many would have us believe.

What I can't believe, at this stage of the game, is that anyone could write that with a straight face or that anyone would print it. Suddenly, it is as if Philip Young and Earl Rovit had never lived. I think we would have to call this "born-again" criticism. Later in the same article, the writer says, "Some critics have said that Hemingway wrote out his experience of being wounded as a kind of therapy which would help him get rid of emotional scars." "Some critics," indeed. Poor Phil. And then the writer goes on to really put poor Phil in his place: "But if this theory is true, why were those memories not gone after he had written about them?" Answer that, if you can. "Take, for example, his wounding. He did not rid himself of that memory by writing about it; on the contrary, he wrote about it again and again and over a long period of years. I do not think he really wanted to lose such a memory—he valued it and it was an important part of his writing." In all of this, there is not a single reference to Young, nor is Young even cited anywhere in the article. When the writer tells us that Hemingway himself really was sensitive, he cites as his authority Michael F. Maloney.

Although I will not give the name of this writer nor the title of his article, I am being a little unfair to him by singling him out, when I could have taken my example from a half-dozen other articles. The sad thing for Hemingway criticism itself is that the topic of this essay is a good one which with proper preparation and further thought could have led to a very valuable article. Now don't mistake me—I have said things in my own writing which I regret, things almost as naive as that which I have quoted above. So I am not trying to trumpet my own superiority, but to make several larger points: many current writers about Hemingway aren't reading; they have little knowledge of previous criticism; they don't document very well; and they are repetitious, telling us things we already know.

A third problem raised by the articles of the Seventies has to do with the contagious spread of the biographical fallacy and the destructiveness of much recent biographical publication. This is not just a problem which concerns articles, of course, but books as well, although I believe that the overall weakness of article publication on Hemingway can be traced in part to the prediliction to publish biographical junk. Let me make myself clear from the beginning—the burning search to describe in graphic detail and catalogue each one of Hemingway's sins and excesses has got to have its limits somewhere. And the limits can only be drawn by the editors. As long as people will print it, there seems an inexhaustible supply of "friends" to write it or give it to an interviewer. It would be different if Hemingway really needed debunking. But he has been standing before us, warts and all, for nearly a decade. For God's sake, let's let him pull up his shorts and then we can get on with the difficult enough problems of the writing itself.

A good deal of Hemingway criticism over the years has been in part biographical, and many of us in Hemingway studies have trod very close to the line of biographical fallacy. It is a temptation that comes out of the nature of the material itself: if a writer choses to use his own name as the name of the central character in the early drafts of his fiction, if he models his characters very closely after his own family and friends, and if he appears to be using his writing, often in very direct ways, as a tool to expiate the ghosts and goblins of his own psyche, then the critic is almost inevitably involved in some very sticky critical problems.

Yet, whatever flirting with the fallacy that may have gone on in the past, it seems very tame in terms of the compounding of that fallacy in recent years. Rather than becoming more cautious in response to a trap already clearly marked, much recent criticism seems determined to ignore the trap completely, as if once discovered, it is no longer worth worrying about. Castillo-Puche, for example, in writing of the novel *For Whom the Bell Tolls*, criticizes it severely as if it were history and to be judged as history, rather than fiction, pointing indignantly and at some length to the novel's "errors."

Bertram D. Sarason in his book *Hemingway and "The Sun" Set* goes about as far as one can go in this direction. He states that he met some resistance to his investigations of the background to Hemingway's novel because "the *characters* of *The Sun Also Rises* had been *subjects of loose talk* and, some people thought, even *looser fictionalizing* at the hands of Hemingway." (My emphasis.) I find that an extraordinary statement. What is even more extraordinary is how many reviewers of Sarason's book read that statement and didn't even blink. What Sarason means, presumably, is "the people who were models for the characters"—although one begins to wonder as his introductory essay continues.

"Loose fictionalizing"? How in the world does one "loosely" fictionalize? By the end of his essay, Hemingway becomes a really first-class-son-of-a-bitch, largely as a result of his unfair treatment of his models for the novel. The novel's characters don't accurately reflect what the models were in life—he doesn't show their artistic accomplishments, for example, or properly display the better sides of their personalities. One doesn't know from page to page whether Hemingway has been cruel, sadistic, or treacherous (to use Sarason's terminology) by "fictionalizing" any given character too much or too little. This kind of discussion is sheer madness.

But Sarason goes even further in the current issue of the *Fitzgerald/Hemingway Annual* (1975) by suggesting in an article, with very flimsy evidence, that Hemingway may have been a thief. This kind of thing, which has crept into material printed earlier in the *Connecticut Review* (for example, Leo Schneiderman's rather nasty psychoanalysis of Hemingway as based on the fiction) is now creeping into the *Fitzgerald/Hemingway Annual*. Such articles lack proportion, verification, scholarly objectivity, and have little or no connection to the literature. I can see no justification for any periodical, except perhaps the *National Enquirer*, to print them.

A word in passing about the *Fitzgerald/Hemingway Annual*. In general, I am grateful for its existence and grateful to the editors for their hard work. But while the *Annual* has published some of the best Hemingway criticism, it has also published some of the worst. I don't want to sound like a purist, because I do enjoy the relaxed format of the *Annual*. I enjoy the facsimiles, the illustrations, the catalogs, and even some of the interviews. The checklists and the bibliographical work are usually excellent. But having said all that, I still hope for higher standards in regard to both biographical material and articles. No matter how sincere the author may have been, a note on "how I touched Hemingway's hand" seems to me a good prescription for an emetic.

III

Ten years ago, I would have given a figurative arm and leg just to have one hour with the first draft of *The Sun Also Rises*. It's hard for me to believe that today, in just a few minutes, Michael S. Reynolds is going to get up here and talk about that first draft. I have the terrible feeling that somehow in my own work on Hemingway I have managed to be both too late and too early at the same time.

Yesterday, Jo August described the treasure room at the Kennedy and its mouth-watering abundance: eight hundred manuscript items, twenty linear feet of correspondence, nine thousand still photographs, piles of memorabilia, and to top it all off, a station wagon full of material from Carlos Baker. Such riches stir up fantasies of getting together an over-the-hill gang of disreputable Hemingway scholars to raid the place—an academic *Topkapi*. We could fill *American Literature* with anonymous articles for two hundred years and never even get to the really good material.

Such riches do not automatically guarantee, of course, that the general level of Hemingway criticism will improve, but they may well raise the level of expectation on the part of both editors and readers. With so much hard information available, critics may have to be a bit more careful about knowing what has already been discovered and discussed. And if there has been a weakness in the overall direction of Hemingway criticism over the years, it has been that the Hemingway personality has tended to generate a deductive rather than inductive approach to his work, a dwelling on thesis often at the expense of careful work with the language and language patterns. One of the strange, and very telling, peculiarities of Hemingway criticism is that its subject has been called by many the greatest prose stylist in English of the twentieth century, and yet we have fewer than a half-dozen substantial articles, in books or periodicals, which carefully examine that style. If we can hope for anything, we might hope that our new riches will lead us closer to the words rather than farther away.

Good criticism begins, as most of us would probably agree, with the attempt to see the work itself clearly. While it is ultimately the search for truth, it starts by looking closely at the words. The hard questions of Hemingway criticism begin here; what did Hemingway actually write? And they go on to related questions, such as what are the differences between one manuscript and another, one edition and another? What kinds of revisions did Hemingway make? And, did the amount and kind of revision change during the course of his career? What makes these questions about text hard is that a great deal of hard work is involved in trying to answer them, work that many scholars are reluctant to take on, since the glory is often small and the chance for error great. In the criticism of modern literature very often reputation has been gained by the gunfighters who shoot from the hip, rather than the miners and homesteaders who do

the dirty work. In short, now that the new territories have been
opened up, we need fewer people comparing "A Day's Wait" to
Doctor Zhivago, and more people willing to get their hands dirty
doing the necessary digging and plowing.[12]

Beyond the foundation of the text is the analysis of language meaning. I am not talking here about style, although, as I
noted a moment ago, there is much to be done yet with style.
(Recent discussions by Richard Bridgman and by Floyd C. Watkins, while interesting and helpful, have by no means given us a
definitive account of these matters.[13] Indeed, an adequate analysis of style as meaning may well have to wait for an adequate
analysis of Hemingway's philosophy of composition—a matter
I'll take up in a moment.) What I am talking about is close reading based on research, first textual study and then biographical,
historical, and social research. Close reading has been, naturally
enough, rather spotty up to now, as various readers have been
attracted to this passage or that and as analysis has gone forward
without the possibility of referring to the relevant background
materials. What we need at this point is a coordinated and con-
certed effort by someone who would be willing to take all we
know now about the words, their dimensions of meaning, pattern, and reference, and put that together with a sustained attack, in depth, for each of the works where such a sustained
attack seems justified. The hard question here is, what did
Hemingway actually say? If we have learned anything in thirty
years, it should be that Hemingway almost always is saying more
than we, at first, think that he is. He does not include things or
leave them out by whim. Nearly everything included is there for
a reason, from objects, landscape features, and events, to colors,
shapes, and physical positions, arrangements, and movements.
The *precise* words used by a character are important. The lack of
response by a character is important. In addition to the careful
and sustained analysis of these things, we need a more consistent
attack on image, image patterning, and metaphor; on pun and
allusion; on tone and ambiguity.

Connected to this effort are genuine source study and the
discovery and analysis of larger patterns of motif and structure.
By "genuine" source study, I mean study similar to that recently
done by Michael Reynolds in a book that is surely one of the
best written and researched efforts we have seen in a long time.

We can hope that as more books on single Hemingway works appear, that they will roughly follow this pattern of research as applied to the meaning of the words on the page (I wish Reynolds had pressed even harder), rather than just summarizing and repossessing interpretations which have already been offered.

By "larger patterns" I mean pretty much what Sheldon Norman Grebstein means by "Hemingway's craft." While Grebstein has produced a fine book, my feeling is that his hard, detailed work over so many years may do more to open the door, than to describe in any final way the contents of the room. Surely there is more involved here than—so to speak—inside and outside, mountains and plains, tyros and tutors. There is a root difficulty in dealing with both sources and patterns in Hemingway that, in my view, may make him ultimately a "harder" author to analyze than James Joyce. Joyce was an intellectual and a scholar; therefore what he wrote was accessible to intellectuals and scholars. Hemingway was neither, but he was an artist, an artist in the old sense as magician. He is the master of illusion and misdirection. Scholars trained in the Joycean tradition stand confused in the face of an author who spends much of his time either absorbing, transmuting, or hiding his germinal emotion and his mechanisms for communicating that emotion. His theory of composition, I suspect, was that meaning must come intuitively, even subliminally, out of a fabric of suggestive stimuli, stimuli that on the surface may have little to do with the recreated experience. The fabric is both coded and incomplete, so that we may never be able to understand Hemingway the way we do Joyce. To put my point another way, Hemingway took art seriously, whereas Joyce, ultimately and finally, did not.

A good symbol for this difficulty in Hemingway's work might be the incomplete circle. The pattern must never close, for if it closes, that is sufficient evidence in itself that it is there. Like the magician with his magic rings, he tosses them into the air where they dissolve and reappear, magically connecting and disconnecting from each other. He is totally devoted to effect (rather than, as the cliché holds, to technique), to the quality of illusion. As the magician must never reveal his secrets, Hemingway can never talk directly about his methods and hates the critic for trying to discover them. As per Gertrude Stein, for Hemingway experience is in the mind of the experiencer. Art

takes place in the mind: all the circles are completed or dis-
connected to be joined again in the mind. This is, as Earl Rovit
has discovered (perhaps the most important discovery thus far),
the real "secret" of the Hemingway hero-persona tangle—the
story is almost always the story of the observer observing and almost never the story of whom or what is observed. But the
process is more complicated than that. The story ultimately lies
in the observer of him who is observing—rings within rings.
Which ones close, at what level, and by whom? Can we ever look
at the open ring and not think of it as flawed? Joyce is to what,
as Hemingway is to Cézanne?

Somewhere, I think in a recent review, Sheldon Grebstein
complains about the constant writing of critics about the Hemingway hero and the Hemingway persona. I, too, am tired of
hearing the same things, usually uninformed clichés (often in
recent years from feminists, who I support in nearly everything
except their misuse of Hemingway and advocacy of Lesbianism).
But the problem is still there. Since Rovit, there has been little
progress in straightening out the roles, functions, and inter-
relationships of implied author, narrator, observer, and observed,
except in the work of Wylder and in Grebstein himself. The
tricky disguises and complex forms of the Hemingway persona
still baffle us. Perhaps we will find some help in the now available manuscripts and letters.

As you can see from my outburst on the matter, above, I
also think that a very crucial question yet to be satisfactorily
answered has to do with Hemingway's philosophy of composition. So many other things, such as style and structure, may be
approached with more success once we can determine this
philosophy with more certainty. Throughout his career, Hemingway dropped a number of hints that suggest that he was consciously applying certain techniques to produce several dimensions in his work. While these hints may have been just another
part of the misdirection, they seem to me more like notes from
the hunger artist who needs someone to believe that indeed art
is in progress. All attempts thus far to determine what these
techniques are and to explain the rationale which may be behind
them have been less than successful.

One such hint given to us several times concerns what he

may have learned about writing from the paintings of Cézanne. We hear about it in a letter to Gertrude Stein, in the original ending to "Big Two-Hearted River," in the Nick Adams fragment "On Writing," in the Lillian Ross interview, and in *A Moveable Feast*, where he says, "I was learning very much from him [Cézanne] but I was not articulate enough to explain it to anyone. Besides it was a secret." Earlier articles by James Thrall Soby and Robert L. Lair and more recent discussions by Edward T. Jones and Emily Stipes Watts don't really satisfy my curiosity as to what this secret was or how it worked in the writing itself.[14]

Could it be the flatness of Cézanne's work or the equal weight that he often gives to details in his pictures? This seems to match the character of writing in *In Our Time* and *The Sun Also Rises*. Was it the order and balance of his composition, the repetition of geometrical forms, or the emphasis on the essential character of things observed? I don't know, but I do think that the secret derived from Cézanne is but one indication among many that there may be a good many things, among them very basic things, that we do not yet know about Hemingway's techniques. Indeed, going back to what I said earlier, to even talk about "techniques" tends to trivialize what I feel certain has been a literary revolution that we have only barely sensed, a revolution as profound as Cézanne's and somewhat more difficult to locate. These are very hard questions—what were Hemingway's theories of composition? Did they change? If so, why and in what ways? If Hemingway's art has been as "complete" as I think it has, such questions may be almost impossible to answer.

In order to have some chance of answering them, we are going to have to take Hemingway far more seriously that we have in the past. We are going to have to consider the possibility that he was not just an innovator, but a genius. Not just a disciple of others, such as Stein, but an artist who emerged with his own intensity. If the post-modernists have often chosen to follow Joyce, it may be that Hemingway's act has been simply too difficult to follow. Ihab Hassan, the most talented of the observers of the contemporary literary scene, has talked about the "problematic of fiction" as "a crucial element of the postmodern sensibility" and suggests that "unlike their predecessors, postmodern writers pretend not to 'create a world' (of course they do); they pretend to plagiarize or play."[15]   What we have now is the decadence of cleverness (what Gore Vidal has called the "university novel") which inevitably follows the real thing—Hemingway's art of despair and Joyce's play in despair of art. Unlike Bellow and Malamud who have striven to transcend despair *in* their art the Pynchons, Barths, and Berthelemes seem trapped in the act of playing *at* playing. Perhaps they are saying that Hemingway and Joyce in their greatness, and each in his own way, have destroyed fiction, at least for the time being, just as Cézanne and Picasso in their greatness destroyed painting.

How was Hemingway's philosophy (or perhaps, philosophies) of composition formulated? is a question that might precede or follow the previous questions.   It seems certain, in line with what I've just been saying, that this is far more than a matter of early influences and tutoring.   And I am primarily concerned with that "more" and that it not be forgotten or neglected, whether it can be specifically traced and identified or must be left up in the air as "X."   Yet, we don't even know much about that famous early tutoring.   Too much emphasis on this is dangerous, in that, again, it tends to lead us down the path of thinking about Hemingway as derived, dependent, and secondary.   Nevertheless, an in-depth study of what Hemingway learned from Sherwood Anderson, Ezra Pound, and Gertrude Stein is possible and probably desirable.

Either Nicholas Joost, who has already written well of these things, or Paul Somers, Jr., who did such a good dissertation on Hemingway and Sherwood Anderson, could do a fine job with such a project were he willing.   Although Somers seems to have covered Anderson's influence fairly well, the contributions of Pound and Stein have yet fully to be explored.[16]   The names of these two literary giants have come up so often in Hemingway studies that many may have the false impression that the subject has been covered.   The problem has been that those really expert in Pound and Stein have had little interest in or knowledge of Hemingway and vice-versa.   And the work of these two writers is so obscure and complex that it has been impossible for the casual article writer to dash off quickly a series of parallels and relationships.   The hard research involved here is what makes this one of the hard questions, particularly as applied to what Hemingway may have learned from Stein, a subject little more than gingerly passed over in the critical literature.

One clue always mentioned but seldom followed is Hemingway's debt to Stein in regard to language rhythm. In *A Moveable Feast* he says, "She had also discovered many truths about rhythms and the uses of words in repetition that were valid and valuable and she talked well about them."[17] Stein's theories regarding this are complex and abstract. Precisely what did Hemingway learn about this from her, or did he simply imitate, as Stein has vindictively suggested, without understanding? Another clue comes in an early letter from Hemingway to Edmund Wilson when he said about Stein, "Her method is invaluable for analyzing anything or making notes on a person or place." What was this method?

I have looked through Stein's writings on writing and Stein's critics on her methodology, but I have been unable to find anything as yet that I'd want to put a two dollar bet on. I suspect that this question may bring us back to Cézanne, since Stein introduced Hemingway to Cézanne's philosophy and paintings (although Hemingway has suggested otherwise) and the painter was one of the major things that they shared an admiration for. The "deepest and most immediate sources" for Stein's own theories "lay in painting."[18] All three—Stein, Cézanne, and Hemingway—have shown concern for two-dimensional surfaces that produce psychological depth; all three were concerned with the art object expressing the emotion of the viewer. If I were to guess what is involved here, I would guess that one part of the method would be to determine what needs to be cut away in order to suggest the essential character, in *effect*, of person or scene. Another part might be the association of shapes and colors, or other basic characteristics, in order to establish a fundamental pattern expressing the truth of what is viewed.

The connection between Hemingway and Stein seems to have been far deeper than most Hemingway biographers have indicated. He apparently dropped by nearly every day for months (or at least that is the impression I get from both Stein's *Autobiography* and Hemingway's *A Moveable Feast*) and talked to Stein, or perhaps more accurately, listened to Stein hour after hour. (No one, by the way, seems to have thought that one of the main things Hemingway may have learned from Stein is how to behave as a writer. He may have learned from Stein—and others of the Paris group—that you do not allow yourself to be linked to competitors or suffer them to gain any advantage over you. When Sylvia Beach published Joyce's *Ulysses*, Gertrude resigned from Sylvia's book club and cut her off.[19] Pound seems to have been cut off, not because he fell out of her chair in the heat of argument, but that he would argue at all, "village explainer!" What Hemingway may have learned, more specifically, is that one could be kind to those too young to count yet or those whose talents were clearly inferior, or one could flatter [as Stein flattered Anderson] those who can give you some advantage. (Who says that Hemingway was overcompetitive?) Once when Hemingway was away from Paris, he hit a dry spell and wrote Stein an anguished letter asking for help. This gesture alone suggests a closer and more dependent relationship than Hemingway was ever able to acknowledge. What *did* they talk about all this time? Stein seems to have discussed her own work, painting and painters (their lives, ideas, and eccentricities), and certain general principles of art related to both.

In the *Autobiography* in connection with her tutoring of Hemingway she says, "Gertrude Stein never corrects any detail of anybody's writing, she sticks strictly to general principles, the way of seeing what the writer chooses to see, and the relation between that vision and the way it gets down."[20] Does that sound familiar? In "On Writing," Nick thinks, "He . . . wanted to write about country so it would be there like Cézanne had done it in painting. You had to do it from inside yourself. . . . You could do it if you would fight it out. If you'd lived right with your eyes."[21] Then in *Narration*, as Donald Southerland tells us, "Gertrude Stein analyzed the difficulty of newspaper writing for example as the suicidal attempt to make the events of yesterday real tomorrow, so that the event is never real in the present writing."[22] Does that sound familiar?

Stein's thoughts about seeing and about time lead us to yet another difficult question regarding Hemingway, and that has to do with the various aspects of his larger philosophy—epistemology, metaphysics, ethics, as well as the already mentioned question of his aesthetic theories. In the past, generalist critics have laughed at the very notion of Hemingway's having a philosophy. The fact, is, of course, that everything Hemingway wrote questioned the nature of reality and the possibility of existence. In reading him, we find ourselves constantly involved in the problems of knowing and the problems of determining right action. More directly than any other modern American writer of fiction, Hemingway confronts the central questions of a scientific, industrial, bureaucratic age wherein man's sense of cosmic and domestic order has broken apart, his connection with ultimate purpose has been lost, and he finds himself cast adrift alone in an open boat to find his own course as best he can.

If someone were to write a book about these things, assuming that the Killinger book has not blocked such a project, he would not only have to deal with the manifestations and interrelationships of Protestantism, Catholicism, Paganism, and Existentialism, but also, more thoroughly than before, such other systems as myth and tragedy. But beyond these, there are philosophical concepts that require careful consideration. One certainly is time. Time has been discussed in regard to the vignettes of *In Our Time*, and there have been cursory considerations of time problems in some of the novels, particularly *The Sun Also Rises* and *For Whom the Bell Tolls*.

But we seldom think of Hemingway as an innovator in respect to the uses of narrative time in the same sense we think of Joyce and Faulkner as innovators. Yet, I suspect there may be here a whole dimension of Hemingway's work that has yet to be thoroughly plumbed which might produce some surprising discoveries. Again, Gertrude Stein may provide some of the clues. Southerland points out that "the idea that present thinking is the final reality was to be the axis or pole of Gertrude Stein's universe, and her work from the beginning was oriented and reoriented upon that idea."[23] And Allegra Stewart states that "her theory of the moment of discontinuity between being and existence is crucial. For at any level 'being-existing' unites past and future—but at its highest level it is the product of this moment, not of causal forces."[24] These ideas, so fundamental to Stein's philosophy, seem to me to have profoundly influenced Hemingway's own thinking about time, existence, event, sequence of event, and causality.

As you can tell by the way I have been carried away now and again by the implications of my own questions, I am sorely tempted to pursue many of them. Yet I cannot and must leave them all to others. Looking at my topic, you may have thought that I would spend my time uncovering a series of exotic research possibilities. And I may have disappointed some of you, since I haven't done that at all. For as it turns out, the hard questions are the basic questions of text, close reading, technique, structure, sources, and philosophy. They are the same questions that have been there from the beginning. At this point in Hemingway studies, the cream has been taken off the top. The easy things have been done. It's time to start at the beginning once again.

NOTES

[1] So that the footnotes for this printed version of my speech do not run longer than the speech itself, I will not footnote the books mentioned in this section. Full title and publications information for these books can be obtained from Audre Hanneman's *Ernest Hemingway: A Comprehensive Bibliography* (Princeton, New Jersey: Princeton University Press, 1967) and the *Supplement* (1975). For books published after 1973 (the cut off date for the *Supplement*), consult the *PMLA* annual bibliographies or the checklists in the *Fitzgerald/Hemingway Annual*. The most recent books, not yet listed in bibliographies, are Gregory H. Hemingway, M. D., *Papa: A Personal Memoir* (Boston: Houghton Mifflin Co., 1976) and Mary Welsh Hemingway, *How It Was* (New York: Alfred A. Knopf, 1976). I learned at the symposium that two books are in production and will be published shortly, a critical book by Scott MacDonald and a study of critical reputation by Robert O. Stephens.

[2] "Fitzgerald and Hemingway," *American Literary Scholarship: An Annual* (Durham, North Carolina: Duke University Press, 1974), pp. 144-145. I have used Bryer's articles (for the volumes 1971-1974) extensively as an aide to my memory and to supplement my meagre notes. Bryer performs a valuable service, producing excellent reviews of the scholarship year after year. He has the great virtue of being able to apply strict standards to

the material he reviews without being nasty.

[3]Without the help of Baker's *Life*, I would never have been able to sort out the short stories and the circumstances of their composition and publication for my collection of critical essays on the stories.

[4]Glenview, Illinois: Scott, Foresman and Company, 1970.

[5]I have not placed my own book, *The Writer's Art of Self-Defense*, in these listings of critical books.

[6]The Oldsey review appears in *College Literature* I (Spring 1974), p. 147.

[7]If I were going to recommend a book to an undergraduate beginning Hemingway study, I would choose Waldhorn's *Reader's Guide*; for a more advanced undergraduate, I would recommend Rovit and the Weeks collection. As introductory readings for a proseminar or graduate seminar, I would recommend an early reading of the Baker biography and assign the books by Rovit and Young (possibly adding either Baker's *Critiques* or Wagner's *Five Decades* as base from which to assign further individual reading of critical articles).

[8]It is possible that not all the articles for 1974 have yet been accounted for, but I checked all available listings against each other, as well as adding in items like the *Annual* which come out later than their date.

[9]Kazin, *Bright Book of Life: American Novelists and Storytellers from Hemingway to Mailer* (Boston: Little, Brown, 1973), pp. 3-20; Hassan's essay in Melvin J. Friedman and John B. Bickery, eds., *The Shaken Realist: Essays in Modern Literature in Honor of Frederick J. Hoffman* (Baton Rouge: Louisiana State University Press, 1970), pp. 5-20. Ficken's article is in the *Fitzgerald/Hemingway Annual: 1971*, pp. 212-235; Grebstein in the *Annual: 1972*, pp. 173-193; MacDonald in *Journal of Narrative Technique*, II (January 1972), pp. 1-15; Howell and Lawler in *Proof: The Yearbook of American Bibliographical and Textual Studies*, II (1972), pp. 213-281. Johnston in *Western American Literature*, IX (November 1974), pp. 159-167; and Somers in *South Atlantic Quarterly*, 'XXIII (Autumn 1974), pp. 487-503.

[10]MacDonald in *American Literature*, XLIII (November 1971), pp. 399-410; Vopat in *Fitzgerald/Hemingway Annual: 1972*, pp. 245-255;

Oldsey in *College Literature* I (Fall 1974), pp. 174-189; Stephens in *PMLA*, LXXXVIII (March 1973), pp. 271-280; Wagner in *Journal of Modern Literature*, II (November 1972), pp. 533-546; DeFalco in Richard Astro and Jackson J. Bensen, eds., *Hemingway in Our Time* (Corvallis: Oregon State University Press, 1974), pp. 39-51; Hamilton in *Renascence*, XXIV (Spring 1972), pp. 141-154; and Bidle in *Fitzgerald/Hemingway Annual: 1973*, pp. 259-270.

[11] In a letter to Emily Stipes Watts as quoted in the preface to her book, *Ernest Hemingway and the Arts* (Urbana: University of Illinois Press, 1971), p. xi.

[12] I should mention that a number of scholars have done good work in the area of Hemingway textual study, including Matthew J. Bruccoli, Charles W. Mann, John Howell, Robert W. Lewis, Sheldon Norman Grebstein, James B. Meriwether, and Michael S. Reynolds.

[13] Bridgman, *The Colloquial Style in America* (New York: Oxford University Press, 1966), pp. 195-230; Watkins, *The Flesh and the Word: Eliot, Hemingway, Faulkner* (Nashville: Vanderbilt University Press, 1971), pp. 95-166.

[14] Soby, "Hemingway and Painting," *Saturday Review*, XXXVII (December 4, 1954), pp. 60-61; Lair, "Hemingway and Cézanne: An Indebtedness," *Modern Fiction Studies*, VI (Summer 1960), pp. 165-168; Jones, "Hemingway and Cézanne: A Speculative Affinity," *Unisa English Studies*, VIII (1970), pp. 26-28; Watts cited above.

[15] From a manuscript, "Bernard Malamud: 1976—Fictions within Our Fictions" to be published in *The Fiction of Bernard Malamud*, edited by me and Richard Astro, Oregon State University Press, 1977.

[16] Recent discussions of Pound's influence on Hemingway include an article by Harold M. Hurwitz, "Hemingway's Tutor, Ezra Pound," *Modern Fiction Studies*, XVII (Winter 1971-1972), pp. 469-482; the first two chapters of Linda Welshimer Wagner's book ("Beginnings" and "Hemingway as Imagist"), *Hemingway and Faulkner: Inventors/Masters* (Metuchen, New Jersey: The Scarecrow Press, Inc., 1975); and the last section of my own essay, "Ernest Hemingway as Short Story Writer," in *The Short Stories of Ernest Hemingway: Critical Essays* (Durham, North Carolina: Duke University Press, 1975).

[17]New York: Charles Scribner's Sons, 1964, p. 17.

[18]Allegra Stewart, *Gertrude Stein and the Present* (Cambridge: Harvard University Press, 1967), pp. 21-22.

[19]James R. Mellow, *Charmed Circle: Gertrude Stein & Company* (New York: Praeger Publishers, 1974), p. 249. Mellow says, "Gertrude clearly viewed Joyce as her principal rival as a literary innovator, and she was fond of quoting Picasso's remark: 'Yes, Braque and James Joyce, they are the incomprehensibles whom anybody can understand.' Sylvia Beach's sponsorship of a major work by Joyce was evidently regarded as a form of disloyalty" (p. 249).

[20]"The Autobiography of Alice B. Toklas" as included in *Selected Writings of Gertrude Stein*, Carl Van Vechten, ed., (New York: Random House, Inc., 1962), p. 202.

[21]*The Nick Adams Stories* (New York: Charles Scribner's Sons, 1972), p. 239.

[22]*Gertrude Stein: A Biography of Her Work* (New Haven: Yale University Press, 1951), p. 151.

[23]*Ibid.*, p. 7.

[24]Cited above, p. 30.

Hemingway, Painting, and the Search for Serenity

by Alfred Kazin

The eye sees more than the heart knows.

William Blake

*The more your painters paint apples, and even lines which do
not represent objects, the more they talk about themselves. For
me it is the world that counts.*

Kama the painter in Andre Malraux, *Man's Fate*

Fifteen years after his death, I still feel saturated with
Hemingway the man, the influence, the style. My greatest tribute to him is that I can reread his best work with the same feeling
of being recharged that I had thirty and forty years ago. His
most fervent conviction—d'abord, c'est faut durer, the first
thing is to last—has turned out to be truer of his work than of the
man. He reiterated this as his usual appeal to magic when the
bottom began to fall out of things in the 1930s. I used to think
that this formula was just Hemingway swagger hiding all-too-
understandable fear and was the late Hemingway blather directed
to bartenders and gossip columnists, the more tiresome troops in
his world-covering entourage, collecting around our hero to tell
him how great he was.

Blather it was, at the end. But as with so many of his say-
ings, he lived it. He may have been as complicated a man as ever
was, but for the best part of his career the artist, as he liked to
say, was simple and true. Hemingway fulfilled his deepest instincts as a writer. His personality, even for an American writer,
was chaotic to an extreme. He frightened many people. He
could seem the most far-out expression of the acquisitive bluster-
ing American ego. No American writer of his gifts so narcissis-
tically exploited his celebrity. Most of his hangers-on, several of
his friends and certainly some of his women, did not know the

difference between his celebrity and his talent. Yet what remains is in a sense everything. One can read him, one must read him, with the feeling of being turned on to life. The best of Hemingway brings you back to the keenest sensations of being alive.

Great novelists have given us other things and many more things. Hemingway made real and concrete the first essential in the act of writing: to put life back on the page, to make us see and feel and taste the gift of life in its unalloyed and irreducible reality. Since all we really know is the vivid possession of our own consciousness, since the alternative to life is something we know nothing about, the livingness of being alive is the inescapable drama of our existance. We naturally respond to the best writers because they make us feel even more alive. When I read Hemingway, my spontaneous reaction is pleasure. My pleasure has been formed by the cunning way the sentences fall, by the bright echoing separateness of the words, by the picture a passage immediately brings to mind. My lasting impression is of being personally revivified. I have been brought closer to an exceptional vividness, closer to the picture in Hemingway's mind, closer to the insatiable grasp of life that is a writer's first quality.

Closeness to something nebulous and fleeting in the writer's mind is what writing does for us. The impressions fleeting through our heads all day and night are insubstantial and fugitive. They can feel so far away to the writer himself! But when realized, they bring us close to a world so dense and thick, each detail oddly magnified, that the unexpected stimulus to our consciousness can be a sense of excess. Like many esthetic achievements, this may be felt first as pain. The greatest single moment for me in *A Farewell to Arms* is the confrontation on the bank of the river between the Italian battle police and the officers separated from their troops in the retreat at Caporetto. I never turn back to this scene without a quiver of terror as the questioning of the hapless officers is followed by their immediate "execution." It is night. The lights being flashed by the battle police into face after face reminds us of the unnaturally bright faces of the condemned men being shot by the light of torches in Goya's *Disasters of War*.

> They took me down behind the line of officers below the road toward a group of people in a field by the river bank. As we

walked toward them shots were fired. I saw flashes of the rifles and heard the reports. We came up to the group. There were four officers standing together, with a man in front of them with a carabiniere on each side of him. A group of men were standing guarded by carabinieri. Four other carabinieri stood near the questioning officers, leaning on their carbines. They were wide-hatted carabinieri. The two who had me shoved me in with the group.

. . . . . . I looked at the man the officers were questioning. He was the fat gray-haired little lieutenant-colonel they had taken out of the column. The questioners had all the efficiency, coldness and command of themselves of Italians who are firing and are not being fired on . . .

"Your brigade?"

He told them.

"Why are you not with your regiment?"

He told them.

"Do you not know that an officer should be with his troops?"

He did.

That was all.

"It is you and such as you that have let the barbarians onto the sacred soil of the fatherland."

"I beg your pardon," said the lieutenant-Colonel.

"It is because of treachery such as yours that we have lost the fruits of victory."

"Have you ever been in a retreat?" the lieutenant-colonel asked.

"Italy should never retreat."

> We stood there in the rain and listened to this. We were facing the officers and the prisoner stood in front and a little to one side of us.

> "If you are going to shoot me," the lieutenant-colonel said, "please shoot me without further questioning. The questioning is stupid." He made the sign of the cross. The officers spoke together. One wrote something on a pad of paper.

> "Abandoned his troops, ordered to be shot," he said.

The "picture" is certainly very distinct—and so is the paragraphing. The "fat gray little lieutenant-colonel" is on that page forever, especially when he says with perfect contempt, "Please shoot me at once without further questioning. The questioning is stupid." *Stupido* itself is a word of total contempt. Generations of students have by now learned *reduction, foreshortening, irony* by which to describe how Hemingway makes us see, bring us close to, that scene by the river. The *seeing* is all-important; Hemingway learned many things from painters, and from extraordinarily visual scenes by other novelists, that enabled him to get Caporetto just right. But a key to the scene is Hemingway's need to show that while the questioning and the shooting are mistaken, totally unjust, as hideously *wrong* as anything can be, this is what stoical men "in our time" like the fat little lieutenant-colonel have to accept.

Hemingway had many gifts. His greatest gift, the foundation of all his marvelous pictorial effects, was his sense of some enduring injustice, of some fundamental wrongness at the heart of things. "There is a great disorder under Heaven," the Chinese say. Today they draw political cheer from this. Hemingway, brought up on the old American religion of the self-sufficient individual, felt that the public world was pushing him and everyone else toward an abyss. His great teacher in Paris, Gertrude Stein, who was as resentful of him when he became famous as he was of her for condescending to him—and he was a frighteningly, a violently insecure man whom it was dangerous to slight—nevertheless put the forthcoming theme with her usual aphoristic brilliance when she said that in the 20th century nothing is in agreement with anything else.

Hemingway was born in the last year of the old century and fated to become one of the great expressions of enduring disorder in this century. His sense of incongruity came out as an uncanny intuition of stress, of the danger point, the intolerable pressure level in life personal and political. Women have their body fears and men have theirs: both related to the sexual organs, to sexual vulnerability and sexual fears. I do not know just where and how this famously rugged, fearless, sometimes madly aggressive sportsman developed that special fear of violation and of mutilation—it is hinted at in *Up In Michigan*—that he was able to project back on the world with a burning intuition of the *world's* inherent cruelty, danger, injustice. No good artist is explained by sexual vulnerability. If that were so, the world would be crowded with Hemingways. But in the mysterious inner transaction between Hemingway's gifts and his easily bruised psyche something resulted—a form of self disapproval at being so vulnerable that had to be hidden, a profoundly shrewd premonition that the 20th century would be a chain of wars, of violent revolutions and holocausts. More phlegmatic types would not have suffered *and* understood. Gertrude Stein was so vain that living under the Nazi occupation in France, she felt mysteriously protected—and was.

Hemingway was brought up to be a proper young Christian gentleman in the most suffocatingly proper suburb of Chicago, Oak Park, "where the saloons end and the churches begin." He was a natural rebel and at eighteen ran off to serve as an ambulance driver with the Red Cross in Italy. He certainly convinced his family that he was just another hell-raiser, like many other young men of good families bursting with sexual energy and general lust for action. But while he assumed this role to the end of his life, he had the intuition of something terribly wrong in his immediate moral environment, of something wrong with his family's pious professions and with the surrounding Midwest optimism. He was to make presentation of the "real thing," as he liked to call the necessary truth, vital to his sense of life. As professors of English do not tell the young—but leave their students to discover for themselves—society, the body politic, the "world" that makes continually for war and social disorder, works as fiercely on people's unconscious as sex, becomes their true intuitions. This often unhinges them without their recognizing it as politics, common fate.

Hemingway's attraction to violence, to hunting and fishing, to war—he saw a lot of war, but was never a soldier—was not just a form of adventure and roaming and self-testing in the usual flamboyant masculine way. It was a way of coming close to certain fundamental ordeals. From the beginning, despite or because of his upbringing, these fascinated him as a clue to what he graphically called "In our time." Like so many great modern writers, he was of solid bourgeois background and therefore knew that morally, the bourgeois world was bankrupt.

Confronting danger, seeking everywhere what I call the pressure points, he made himself one with his time by running full tilt into everything that would bring a fresh emergency into his life. And everything certainly did. Gertrude Stein laughed in *The Autobiography of Alice B. Toklas* that for a man so professionally virile and athletic, Hemingway was certainly fragile. John Dos Passos was to say in *The Best Years* that Hemingway was always having to go to bed to recuperate from his many injuries. When he did not seek damage, it sought him. From boyhood on he had suffered accidents that were grotesque in their violence to this body they did not kill. As a boy he fell and had a stick driven into the back of his throat, gouging out part of both tonsils. In 1918 when he was a Red Cross worker in Italy distributing supplies to soldiers, a mortar shell exploded more than twenty fragments into his legs: he was then hit twice by machine gun bullets while carrying a more seriously injured man to the rear; as a young writer in Paris during the 20s, he was clipped on the forehead by pieces of a skylight that fell just as he was standing under it. In Wyoming in 1930 his car turned over and his right arm was pinned back by the top of the windshield and badly fractured, the bone sticking through the muscle. Another time, his brother Leicester reports, Hemingway shot a shark with a rifle, but the bullets split into several small pieces of hot lead that ricocheted into the calves of both legs. In 1949, while duck shooting in the marshes near Venice, he got a bit of shell wadding blown into his eye, and a serious infection developed; in 1953 he crash-landed in Africa; the rescue plane that picked him up crashed and burned; when he reached medical aid at Nairobi, just in time to read his obituaries, his internal organs had been wrenched out of place, his spine was injured, and he was bleeding from every orifice.

It is absurd to separate Hemingway from his work. He pushed his life at the reader, made this fascination with death and danger the central theme in his many pages about bull-fighting, sports, war, brought the reader closer to his own fascination with violence and terror as a central political drama. His great gift was to locate these repeated episodes of violence (so linked by some profound compulsion that we anticipated the shotgun suicide) in the Turks expelling the Greeks in the lacerating inner chapters of *In Our Time*, in the horns perforating the bullfighter in *Death In The Afternoon* so that all the internal organs were sliced through at once, in the very impotence of Jake Barnes in *The Sun Also Rises*, Colonel Cantwell in *Across the River And Into the Trees*.

One could go on, as Hemingway certainly did, from the early story "Indian Camp" where the Indian husband in the upper bunk cuts his throat as the doctor in the bunk below performs a caesarian on his wife with a jack-knife and sews her up with nine-foot, tapered gut leaders, to the ridiculously inflated episodes in the posthumous *Islands In The Stream* which tell us that Hemingway talked of going after German submarines all by himself. But the point is that Hemingway was a soul at war. He wins our assent perhaps now more than ever, because it is the "outside" world that is increasingly violent. Hemingway may have been as big a braggart and egotist as ever lived, but he had the stamp of the true artist. His emotions were prophetic, his antennae were out to the truth. He knew that destruction is a god over our lives, that fear of death shapes us, that without any belief in immortality there can be no expectation of justice, so that the whole ghastly century is beginning to look like one unending chain of murder and retribution.

Hemingway's greatest gift was to identify his own capacity for pain with the destructiveness at large in our time. The artist works by locating the world in himself. Hemingway did something more: he located in himself his century's infatuation with technology, technique, instruments of every kind. Hemingway was recognized as an original, he fascinated and magnetized, because his theme was the greatest possible disturbance. His own sense of this was cold, proud know-how professionally detached and above all concerned with applying a systematic consistent *method* to everything he described. Obviously, one attraction of

sport, war, bullfighting was that each called for the maximum
concentration of technique. Hemingway was clever and informed and quick to tell you what he knew. He always made a
point of giving you in the midst of a story the exact name of a
wine, the exact horsepower of a machine, even the exact moment
in Paris—remember Lady Brett's entrance in *The Sun Also Rises*—
when a woman appeared in a tight sweater and skirt so that she
looked like the sides of a yacht. "She started all that."

Hemingway liked to write, as Nick Adams liked to make
camp in "Big Two-Hearted River," from technical detail to detail. He had grown up in a world where men still travelled by
horse, took care of their horses, still repaired things themselves,
walked everywhere, often grew or shot their own food. He believed in the work of your own hands even to the point of usually writing by hand. It was this that led him to his great discovery
of what painting could do for writers. Newspaper work for the
Kansas City Star and the *Toronto Star* had taught him the first
basic: to write professionally is to write *to* somebody else's
mind and you have to lay out all the facts in an assured, flat,
knowing manner without the slightest suggestion or indecision or
demonstrative emotion about what you know. You have to
"reach the reader," said managing editors, to write for a newspaper so that said reader will distinguish Ernest M. Hemingway
from a dozen other newsvendors.

The paintings young Hemingway saw in France, most intimately at Gertrude Stein's flat, 27 Rue de Fleurus, were spell-
bindingly the work of an artist's own hand, of new theories of
perception, of common physical materials. Nothing could have
been more instantly pleasing to his imagination and his native
sense of things. Painting was the decisive experience for an
American abroad; "Europe" could seem one great painting.
Painting stimulated a young reporter, already shrewdly aware of
war and sport as the stuff of literature, to think of writing as a
method. Painting was to do more for Hemingway than it was to
do for Stein, who in the end cared for painters more than for
painting. "Genius" and "personality" were to become her
topics. Stein could not draw at all and in fact had to leave Johns
Hopkins Medical School because of this and other failures in
observation. Her famous Cézannes had been discovered and
bought by her erratic brother Leo, her Matisses by Michael and

Sally Stein. She kept the family collection when Leo was in-
furiated by cubism and stopped buying paintings. She depended
on painting for the mental impressions that were her specialty.
Unlike Hemingway, she had little feeling for the sensuous world.
Her great interest was psychology, the "bottom truth" about
anybody she met. Proceeding from psychology to composition,
she became fascinated by what she felt to be the human mind as
its own self-sufficient subject. "The human mind writes what it
is. . . . The human mind consists only in writing down what is
written and therefore it has no relation to human nature."

Stein was a profoundly clever theoretician, a great aphorist
and wit, and a true inventor of composition based on what she
called "the continuous present." Without seeing her paintings,
without listening to the infatuated conversation about painting
at 27 Rue de Fleurus, Hemingway might not have become Hemingway at all. As *she* was jealously to charge in *The Autobiography of Alice B. Toklas*, Hemingway was a sedulous ape, an
all-too-adept pupil of other people's ideas and methods. But her
comparative indifference to the subject matter of painting and
the way she took off *from* painting to emphasize for psychological purposes the authority of the eye gave Hemingway the
advantage over her.

Stein was fascinated by the small particular difference that
distinguished identically made objects, like her Ford car, from
each other. Sentences were all sentences, but each sentence was
itself. She believed that the single sentence is the key to writing,
and she certainly practiced what she preached: "in composition
one thing is as important as another thing." As Kenneth Burke
was to say, we have been sentenced to the sentence. It was
sentences she heard from her family's black retainers. As a very
bright student in William James's psychology courses, she was on
the track of the individual self-contained statement as disclosure.
She was to see the sentence as orphic revelation: Hers! So a
sentence could become the glowing unit of a page, the building
block of literature. But she was arrogant, she saw herself as a
sybil without fear of reproach, and writing through the night
(in the morning Toklas would worshipfully pick up and type the
scattered scrawled sheets) she heedlessly wrote straight from the
ear to the paper. Her last books, like Hemingway's last books,
showed the expansion and disintegration of a style founded on

concentration.

Stein's genius was for conversation and especially for listening to other people's conversation. What fascinated her in the "new" painting by Cézanne and Matisse was the fact that something, anything, could be done by a temperament sufficiently self-willed. The slashing lines and thickly encrusted colors, Matisse in particular with his use of color *as* line, the thick joyously rhythmical color building up an impression totally sufficient to the design that would satisfy the eye! Every image is made up of minute particulars. Every particular is realized by the maximum concentration and toil. The *world* is built up from such particulars. As the cubists soon proved, an object is a form made up of inherent forms. We go from cube to cube, atom to atom, as nature did in the long creation of every living thing that makes up the whole.

Hemingway's approach to painting was more diffident but actually closer to sensuous content and to his own delight in method. The difference between the two can be seen even in their handwritings. Her letters were tall, sprawling, intensely mental with the large tell-tale spaces between words that were so characteristic of her reflective mind. His letters were close, carefully and slowly shaped. They remind me of Nick Adams making camp in "Big Two Hearted River," another demonstration of Hemingway's own planned, anxiously careful tidy assemblage of words as objects.

> He started a fire with some chunks of pine he got with the ax from a stump. Over the fire he stuck a wire grill, pushing the four legs down into the ground with the boot. Nick put the frying pan on the grill over the flames. He was hungrier. The beans and spaghetti warmed. Nick stirred them and mixed them together. They began to bubble, making little bubbles that rose with difficulty to the surface. There was a good smell. Nick got out a bottle of tomato catchup and cut four slices of bread. The little bubbles were coming faster now. Nick sat down beside the fire and lifted the frying pan off.

Of course the great precedent to all this, Hemingway acknowledged, was *Huckleberry Finn*. There is a passage in "Big Two Hearted River" in which Nick Adams packs his captured trout between layers of fern. It reminds me of Huck planning to escape his father. He methodically lists the things he has, the things he has gained, the things he is sure of. "The old man made me go to the skiff and fetch the things he had got. There was a fifty-pound sack of corn meal and a side of bacon, ammunition, and a four-gallon jug of whiskey and an old book and two newspapers for wadding besides some tow. I toted up a load, and went back and sat down on the bow of the skiff to rest. I thought it all over and I reckoned I would walk off with the gun and some lines and take to the woods, when I run away. I guessed I wouldn't stay in one place but just tramp right across the country, mostly night-times, and hunt and fish to keep alive and so get so far away that the old man nor the widow wouldn't ever find me any more."

Hemingway was naturally drawn to painging in France because it celebrated homely natural materials—like the world he knew and wanted to write about. Although he knew the pioneer collections of the Art Institute in Chicago, it was the double experience of writing English in France and of being daily stimulated by the streets, the bridges, the museums, by meeting Gertrude Stein, Ezra Pound, James Joyce, Ford Madox Ford, that helped to form this cunningly obedient listener into the powerfully undercutting stylist that he became. Stein said: "One of the things I have liked all these years to be surrounded by people who know no English. It has left me more intensely alone with my eyes and my English." That is what Hemingway felt; it is his marvellous representation of this vital early experience that makes his Paris in *A Moveable Feast* so beautiful, though the book is wicked in its attempt to destroy Stein, Ford, Fitzgerald and a downright lie in his underhanded description of the collapse of his marriage to Hadley. He does not say that when he became famous he became insupportably arrogant. He was unknown, "poor and happy" in *A Moveable Feast*, but he became ferocious in the days of fame. Fame inflamed him more than liquor and turned Stein's obedient little "ape" into an inferno of unrelenting ego. It did not make him happy. Painting at least took him out of himself.

French painting did more for Hemingway than reinforce his American passion for technique, for method, for instruments, utensils. It gave him, as it did a whole generation of foreign artists in Paris, a sense of what Baudelaire called *luxe, calme et volupte*. Marc Chagall, another foreigner in Paris, said: "These colors and these forms must show, in the end, our dreams of human happiness." Hemingway lived a life of danger, near-catastrophe, was inwardly ravaged by his attraction to danger and the boozy life he led in the company of sycophants all over the world; he became a victim of his own celebrity. He was attracted to the harmony in painting as he was influenced by the direction it gave his imagination.

One of the recurrent themes in his work is the rallying from discomfort to comfort, from danger to safety, from death to life, from ordeal to escape. He was as much a romantic about himself as he was a cold-eyed observer of the world at large. In fact, he was so savagely competitive and such a brutal antagonist to other people that the pastoral, harmonious, cuddly sensations he described were as vital to his existence as the seeking of danger. Painting, even the most violent-looking painting by those whom the French once called *les fauves*, wild beasts, usually subsides into a source of peace. You can look at a Cézanne in 1906 and walk away from it, but in 1926 you will not remember what once jarred you. When Leo Stein first went to the picture dealer Ambrose Vollard to look at the Cézannes that Bernard Berenson told him about, he had to turn them over, one after another, from a dusty pile. Leo and Gertrude Stein, usually Leo, had to talk night and day to their friends to make them see these paintings. When the great Stein collection was exhibited at the Museum of Modern Art in New York, the room seemed to blaze with sunlight. In 1959 I saw at the Hermitage in Leningrad post-impressionist paintings bought up by Russian merchants in Paris in the early 1900s. After fifty years, they were just being brought up from the cellars. Looking at them propped up against sofas, I thought of Bergotte in Proust's *La Prisonniere* seeing his first Vermeer and saying to himself, "That is how I ought to have written."

Painting far more than writing suggests the actual texture of human happiness. Hemingway understood that; what excited him as a writer about painting was a promise of relief from civilization, a touch of the promised land. The Hemingway hero is usually alone in nature, and the landscape he sees (and will bring back in words) is in minute particulars unseen by anyone but him. Again and again in his work this often cruel writer shows himself to be an unabashed American romantic positively melting in the presence of BEAUTY. The opening lines of *A Farewell to Arms* cast a spell. They don't altogether make sense except as pure visual impressionism, repeated and echoing Hemingway's own effort to get these "impressions" down.

> In the late summer of that year we lived in a house in a village that looked across the river and the plain to the mountains. In the bed of the river there were pebbles and boulders, dry and white in the sun, and the water was clear and swiftly moving and blue in the channels. Troops went by the house and down the road and the dust they raised powdered the leaves of the trees. The trunks of the trees too were dusty and the leaves fell early that year and we saw the troops marching along the road and the dust rising and leaves, stirred by the breeze, falling and the soldiers marching and afterward the road bare and white except for the leaves.

If Cézanne's greatness lay in the removal of his subjects from the contingent world, this opening paragraph is an imitation of that removal. It is exclusively an impression from the outside, rests within the eye of the beholder. As an impression it is static, for it calls attention to the beholder's effort to capture one detail after another rather than to the scene of war. As so often happens in Hemingway's prose forays into war, bullfighting, marlin fishing, hunting, there is an unnatural pause in the last sentence—"leaves stirred by the breeze"—a forced transition made necessary by "painting" the scene in words. We positively see the writer at his easel.

What Stein caught from painting—it was a literary idea—was the ability of the writer to call attention to each stroke. Hemingway said that writing is architecture, not interior decoration. When he turned from the obedient pupil into the world-famous Ernest Hemingway, he made a great point, in talking about his own writing through his contempt for many other people's writing, of saying that they were "unreadable." *Readable* meant the reduction of the world to a line of glitteringly clear sentences. Ironically, Stein criticized his first writings as being *inaccroachable*, not hangable on a wall, not ready to be looked at. It was she, with her thousand page soliloquies and meanderings, who turned out to be *inaccroachable*. She longed to have a great public like Hemingway. When she and the G.I.'s discovered each other in 1944, she wouldn't let a single Brewsie and Willie go.

Hemingway had the magnetic gift of fame, of arousing attention with every word, that Stein bitterly missed. He had learned his lesson from her all too well. He had in fact learned to lasso the reader, to become his eyes and ears exactly as a Cézanne or a Matisse rivets our attention, obliterates everything around it. This works better in Hemingway's marvellous short stories, which are short and consistent, all "composition," every inch of the canvas filled, than in his novels. There he often stops the action to do some scene painting and is often swaggeringly self-indulgent, both in self-portraiture and as a maker of beautiful effects.

A picture is an action that must fill up its available space. Stein was fascinated by the concentration that is behind all true painting. She was always telling Hemingway: "concentrate." He certainly learned to concentrate. The inter-chapters of *In Our Time*, condemned men being carried to the gallows in a chair because they lost control of their sphincter muscles and German soldiers climbing right over a wall and being potted one, two, three—"We shot them just like that"—showed that Hemingway was concentrating all right, right on the reader. Hemingway influenced a whole generation of journalists to become pseudo-artists, especially around Time, Inc., where every little article was called a "story," and was rewritten and rewritten as if it were a paragraph by Flaubert instead of the usual Lucite over-emphasizing the personal characteristics behind some big shot who had made this week's cover story.

Eventually, Hemingway's influence began to influence *him* too much. The famous brushwork became bloated and sometimes suggested the relaxed inattention that all good American writers seek *after* writing. But Hemingway at his best understood that a short story by its very compressiveness comes nearest a lyric poem or haiku in its total intactness. A novel is by tradition too discursive, epic and widespread. Of all Hemingway's novels, *The Sun Also Rises* has the best chance of surviving, for it is more consistent in its tone, its scene and even Hemingway's scorn than *A Farewell To Arms*, which veers between the sheerest personal romanticism and Hemingway's desire to give an essentially lyric cast to his observations of the Italian-Austrian front in the first World War.

More and more in his big books Hemingway, for all his
genius at intuiting the trouble spots and danger points in human
existence, used his well-developed style as a lyric diversion from
his increasing sense of being closed in. The old rugged individu-
alist had somehow known from the beginning that the coming
century was going to be war on the individual. That was the dark
and even ominous climate of feeling—and in the fewest, somehow
punitive words—he got so unforgettably into his great stories and
especially into "Big Two Hearted River" a story that sums up the
Hemingway hero's courage and despair, his farthest need and
his deepest fear, in a way that also sums up the Western American's virtually sexual encounter with Nature, his adoration and
awe, his sense of being too small for it, his abrupt unfulfilled
confrontation of what once seemed the greatest gift to man, but
somehow always threw him off.

Hemingway was a deeply personal writer. The immediacy,
sometimes the deliberate brutality, but above all his vulnerability
to anxiety, rage, frustration and despair, gave him a masterful
closeness to his kaleidoscope emotions. He was by turns so
proud yet so often stricken a human creature that the reader
again and again surrenders to him. For Hemingway makes you
feel in painfully distinct human detail how much "the world"
merely echoes the endless turmoil in the human heart.

> Ahead the river narrowed and went into a swamp. The river
> became smooth and deep and the swamp looked solid with cedar
> trees, their trunks close together, their branches solid. It would
> not be possible to walk through a swamp like that. The branches
> grew so low.
>
> . . . He did not feel like going into the swamp. He looked down
> the river. A big cedar slanted all the way across the stream. Be-
> yond that the river went into the swamp.
>
> Nick did not want to go in there now. He felt a reaction against
> deep wading with the water deepening up under his armpits, to
> hook big trout in places impossible to land them. In the swamp
> banks were bare, the big cedars came together overhead, the sun
> did not come through, except in patches; in the fast deep water, in

the half light, the fishing would be tragic. In the swamp fishing was a tragic adventure. Nick did not want it. He did not want to go down the stream any further today.

Hemingway was a painfully complex man who was indeed as gifted and yes, as "brave" as he claimed to be. He did his work. He hauntingly intimated on paper some fundamental conflicts that like all of us he did not resolve in the flesh. Especially not in the flesh. Nor did he realize these conflicts in his novels as the great novelists have done. He was too immature and self-absorbed, in the fashion of so many gifted Americans maddened by the gap between their talent and their vulnerability. What made Hemingway important, what will keep his best work forever fresh, was his ability to express a certain feeling of hazard that men in particular do not suffer any less just because they go out of their way to meet it. Who is to say how much this sense of hazard, peril, danger, with its constant rehearsal of the final and perhaps only real battle, with death as the embodiment of a universe that is simply not ours alone, that may not be ours at all, who is to say how much Hemingway sought it out for his natural subject matter as much as it constantly whipped *him* to prove himself again and again? In Gregory Hemingway's memoir, he says that he felt "relief when they lowered my father's body into the ground and I realized that he was really dead, that I couldn't disappoint him, couldn't hurt him anymore. . .

"I hope it's peaceful, finally. But oh God, I knew there was no peace after death. If only it were different, because nobody ever dreamed of, or longed for, or experienced, less peace than he."

This is the truth about Hemingway that all the carousing and boasting could not conceal. Yet it is one that every reader recognizes with gratitude as the heart of the darkness that Hemingway unforgettably described: the sense of something irremediably wrong. Against this, Hemingway furiously put forth his dream of serenity, of nature as the promised land, for which composition—the painter's word that he picked up as his ideal— suggested the right order of words in their right places. As Ford Madox Ford put it so beautifully in his introduction to *A Farewell to Arms*, "Hemingway's words strike you, each one, as if they were pebbles fetched fresh from a brook. They live and shine, each in its place. So one of his pages has the effect of a brook-bottom into which you look down through the floating water."

Nature as a non-human ideal has always been an American romantic dream. Thoreau said that he found in Emerson "a world where truth existed with the same perfection as the objects he studied in external nature, his ideals real and exact." All the great American landscape painters have always portrayed Mother Nature as too big for the solitary man on the cliff looking down. By contrast, as Malraux wrote in *Man's Fate*, painting to Orientals has been the practice of "charity." Charity is hardly what Hemingway found in the world or for which he went to painting. There is no charity in his writing at all. Serenity on occasion, a rally, a promise of peace. He was a tough sharp realist about other people, for in portraying himself so exhaustively, he portrayed us and the pitiless century into which he was born.

Hemingway and the Magical Journey

by Leo Gurke

Travel was conspicuously one of Hemingway's well-known obsessions, and from an early age he moved about incessantly. If a log were kept of his numerous journeys to Europe and Africa, to upper Michigan, Canada, Cuba, and back and forth across the United States, it would probably reveal that he racked up more mileage than any writer in the English language with the possible exception of Byron.

These journeys did more than cover space; and they were initiated by something stronger than the familiar desire for a change of scenery. They seem in Hemingway's case to have been motivated by a persistent if not always immediately definable quest for experience. It wasn't a change of scenery he was after but a change of life. And in almost every instance he succeeded. His first trip from Chicago to Kansas City at seventeen introduced him not only to the life of a newspaperman—itself a striking change—but to the crushing realism of the police and hospital beat where even the routine task of hauling reporters and rewrite men out of drunk tanks and getting them back to their desks exposed him to areas of experience not available to him under the middle-class canopy of Oak Park.

At eighteen, magnetized by the war, he journeyed almost five thousand miles to Italy where he promptly suffered the terrible—and fruitful—wound that was to transform him utterly. At twenty-two, and married, he transplanted himself to Paris, a move that did more than inaugurate his expatriate years; it rid him of the parochialism that, at the time, could not have been shed by simply moving elsewhere in his own country. His later travels through Europe and Asia Minor as a foreign correspondent, his immersion in Spain, Italy, and Africa, his safaris to Idaho and Montana, his soundings of the Caribbean carried with them,

in each instance, objectives and responses far below the immediate physical surface. Even his first involuntary summer journeys
as a boy to Walloon Lake stirred in him something fundamental
by introducing him to the Ojibway Indians and supplying him
with the scene of his early stories.

Hemingway was not only an energetic traveler. He was a
supreme traveler, and the act of travel became essential to his art.
Among the four or five universal experiences available to us—
love, friendship, parenthood, the controlled pleasures of eating
and drinking—experiences that Hemingway deals with in varying
degrees—it was the process of voyaging from one terrain to
another that he turned into one of his tenacious illuminations.

Journeys in pursuit of some significant goal or releasing
emotion appear everywhere in Hemingway's work. There are of
course the celebrated voyages: Jake's from Paris to Pamplona,
the flight across Lake Maggiore in *A Farewell to Arms*, Santiago
pulled along the Gulf Stream by the mysterious action of an
invisible fish, Harry Street "reaching" the summit of Mt. Kilimanjaro, Robert Jordan's journey from Montana to the remote
Spanish countryside of the guerrilla band, Nick Adams crossing
the burnt landscape on his way to the trout stream, Hemingway
himself, in *Green Hills of Africa*, chasing the small-horned kudu
over large stretches of what was then Tanganyika.

But there are many other journeys, less publicized and
pored over perhaps, but no less consequential. One remembers
Harry Morgan commuting back and forth between Cuba and Key
West, the train ride from Marseilles to Paris in "A Canary For
One," the Macombers trailing their shattered emotions through
the African bush, Colonel Cantwell retracing his steps years after
the event to the precise spot where he had been wounded and
there exorcizing the trauma, the grim travelogue on Fascist Italy
in "Che Ti Dice La Patria." Even journeys that are emotionally
or morally sterile and lead nowhere—like those of the unhappy
lovers in "Hills Like White Elephants" or the circuiting from race
track to race track of the crooked jockey in "My Old Man"—have
their significance albeit negative. And every kind of transport in
almost every mode of movement is on display: plane ("The
Snows of Kilimanjaro"), train, bus and car (*The Sun Also Rises*),
boat (*A Farewell to Arms*, *The Old Man and the Sea*), on foot

("Big Two-Hearted River," *For Whom The Bell Tolls*), on skis ("Cross-Country Snow"), even underwater ("After the Storm"). Whatever its meaning or context, the act of voyaging is complexly and pervasively there.

If the journeys taken leap to the eye, those *not* taken are equally revealing. At the urging of the priest, Lt. Henry wants to visit the Abruzzi but never does, a failure that lights up his undernourished spiritual state. The same is even more vividly true of Harry Street: he longs to climb to the top of Mt. Kilimanjaro, yet in the end, reaching as it were his final stage of self-betrayal, can do so only in fantasy. Very early in the novel which they dominate, Robert Cohn and Jake Barnes exchange travel proposals; each rejects the other's. Robert wants them to go to South America where he hopes, naively, to start writing again. Jake, who knows better, makes a counter-proposal: he'll go with Robert to British East Africa where they'll hunt big game. Cohn turns that down. He is a boxer who doesn't like to box and a writer who doesn't really like to write, and shooting animals is too concrete and immediately productive an activity. It leaves no room for those flights of sentimental fancy where everything is possible, the very Mecca of Robert's romantic ego. The two journeys are thus aborted, yet their non-existence says something pivotal about the two men who do not take them.

The journeys in Hemingway share certain characteristics. To begin with, their destination is generally some ideal place. Every summer Jake leaves Paris—that "pestilential city," as Lady Brett calls it—to spend a week in Pamplona attending the bullfights during the festival of San Fermin. His anticipation is quickened by the train ride through the south of France where weather and landscape embody his mood:

> It was a lovely day, not too hot, and the country was beautiful from the start. . . . The grain was just beginning to ripen and the fields were full of poppies. The pastureland was green, and there were fine trees, and sometimes big rivers and chateaux off in the trees.

Jake and Bill, who accompanies Jake on this occasion, pick up Cohn in Bayonne and hire a chauffeured car to drive them over the mountains to Pamplona. The country changes, becomes more dramatic; the light is clearer and more intense, pressing down upon the senses. Bill and Jake nod to one another in appreciation, but Cohn, who is nearsighted anyway, sleeps through it all. His presence, blindly insentient and unresponsive, mars the journey, and it is with a certain relief to the others that he remains behind in Pamplona while they travel on to the hills beyond Burguete.

There they reach the unspoiled earth, suggested by the wine-drinking peasants in the bus, the secluded country inn, the sun-filled woods dotted with wild strawberries, and the Irati River teeming with fish. After packing his trout between layers of fern and putting them carefully in the bag, Jake, alone, sits under a pair of joined trees, and is refreshed. He has gone back to the beginning of things. Sun, woods, earth, heat, river—unspoiled and all but untouched—release him from the tensions and complexities of civilized life, the life of Paris and presently of Pamplona. Here even human ties are simple and unclouded. They make friends with Harris[1] easily and without strain, a friendship symbolized by the small yet moving totem of the flies he gives them as they part. The journey to this ideal final stage takes place at the exact center of the novel, a position that deliberately expresses its importance in the overall scheme of *The Sun Also Rises*.

The movement toward some ideal place marks the other journeys in Hemingway with equal clarity. The lovers in *A Farewell to Arms* flee across the great lake toward Switzerland, a country that may solve all their difficulties. It is neutral, and will provide them with a splendid natural setting for their deepening love. It is scientifically advanced, and will provide them with the medical technique and hospital facilities needed for the birth of their child.

Ideal elements are visibly, almost self-evidently present in the forest floor covered with pine needles where Robert Jordan comes to rest at the end of his long hegira from America. Lying with his body stretched out at full length on the Spanish earth, his existence comes to its consummation. It does so twice: at the beginning of the novel when he arrives to carry out the crucial deed he has been assigned; and at the end when, the deed done, he covers the retreat of his comrades at the expense of his own life.

In some mysterious way—a mysteriousness which contains the ultimate appeal of "Big Two-Hearted River"—the trout stream toward which Nick is headed appears as a kind of Nirvana. If he can reach it, he will somehow be "saved." The same ideal note is struck in *The Old Man and the Sea*. Pulled out to the farther reaches of the Caribbean, the old fisherman finds himself in a universe of supreme beauty and splendor—the stars, the flying fish, the currents of wind and water held together in a single blazing orbit by the giant marlin exerting and exuding its titanic energy from the depths of the sea.

A second characteristic of the journey is that is brings with it an intensification of consciousness. Far out on the Gulf Stream, Santiago feels closer than ever to the circumambient universe, and this heightening of the present is accompanied by a heightened evocation of the past: his recollection of the young lions sporting on the African beaches appears to him with an extraordinarily vivid immediacy. The feelings of Frederic and Catherine for one another escalate with each stage of their difficult journey to the mountains of Switzerland, where they spend their last months together moving toward a state of absolute emotional harmony. Freed at last from his gangrenous leg, his dying body, and the febrile paranoia of his life, Harry Street flies toward the pinnacle of Mt. Kilimanjaro in a growing ecstasy so real that we are for the moment convinced it is happening in actuality: in Hemingway's numerous sallies against death, he records here one of his singular triumphs. And the final intention of "Big Two-Hearted River" is reached when Nick, on the second morning of the story, looks over at the swamp and resolves that he will fish there one day. This is the first time in which he has not been locked into the immediate act and gesture, in which it has been possible for him to lift his head from the tyrannizing present and contemplate some future release. The journey to the trout stream is at last successfully consummated only when it produces this significant broadening of consciousness.

The journey in Hemingway is marked also by some kind of psychic restoration or rebirth. Nick's transformation is plain enough. What happens to Jake is less overtly visible but no less potent.   His sojurn in the Spanish countryside produces more than a relaxation of strained nerves.   It provides a resurgence of the spiritual energy he needs to cope with the harsh facts of his own situation and with the tangled emotions of his unhappy friends.   Since coping is his supreme objective in life, any help he can get is indispensable to him.   So he makes his annual journey back to the heart of nature for the necessary renewal of his energies.

Harry Street's passage from one stage of existence to another, from life to death, is embodied in his soul journey over the peak of the great African mountain during the course of his final dream.   In the case of his aged fisherman, Hemingway deliberately calls our attention to the metamorphosis of Santiago in his fateful sea voyage by the obtrusive references to him as a Christ figure as he returns home.   Elsewhere in his work the motif or rebirth is not always so plainly spelled out, but it is pervasively there and invests the voyage with a transcendent purpose crucial to Hemingway's art.

At the climax of their journeys, the travelers find themselves absolutely alone, as though maneuvered toward this state by some secret intention.   The movement away from society and social connections has been one of the deep American drives, manifested by the original flight—itself one of the great magical journeys of history—from crowded Europe to a new, seemingly untouched, relatively empty continent.   Hemingway is never more emphatically an American writer than in his embodiment of aloneness as an underlying condition.   His admiration for Ishmael and Huckleberry Finn, those characteristic escapers from the connected life, suggests his linkage with the strain in American history once symbolized by the frontiersman or the pioneer alone in the wilderness.   Yet they are not more solitary than Nick by the trout stream, Santiago on the primal sea, the lovers rootless and isolated in Switzerland (the one country in Europe standing absolutely by itself), Robert Jordan alone on the floor of the forest, Jake alone by the far-off Spanish river reading with sublimely pleasurable detachment an absurd romance by A. E. W. Mason.

This solitariness often expressed only subliminally, this release into another frame of existence, carries with it the sense of slipping back or fitting back into a universal harmony. It is our unavoidable fate to be involved with others, but our souls yearn for disengagement. The impulse toward disengagement animates the figures in Hemingway profoundly and incessantly. Jake longs to disengage himself from his troublesome friends; Frederic and Catherine struggle to disengage themselves from the war. Harry Street wants to rip loose from the irksome ties that bind him to his wife, his past, and even his talent. The distance they put between themselves and the social order is usually the exact span of the journeys they take—and often must take—to do so. Hemingway's fiction is crowded with "loners"—one remembers *inter alia* Wilson, Krebs, Morgan, Jack Brennan, the unnamed older waiter in "A Clean Well-Lighted Place"—all en route toward that miraculous moment when they can separate themselves from the human scene altogether.

Yet the moment, no matter how integrative or even sublime it may be, comes to an end. Implicit in the journey *to* is the journey *back*. The travelers in Hemingway not only make their odysseys but return from them; indeed in some ways the coming back is weightier than the going and, at the very least, essential to their dramatic completion.

The psychic restoration does not necessarily imply an obvious alteration of character or new approach to life. In the three early novels[2] the characters return to their respective starting-points visibly unchanged. Jake gets back to Pamplona and eventually to Paris exactly the same man he is at the beginning. Like the sun that rises every morning, makes its journey across the heavens, sets, only to rise again the next day, Jake's annual excursion from France to Spain and back to France leaves him precisely as he was. Recharged, he resumes his struggle for survival on the same terms. The Frederic Henry we see at the end of *A Farewell to Arms* is the very man who appears at the start, unconnected and unillusioned. He has made his journey, both emotional and geographic, to the only paradise available to him, and is now reverting to the usual low-key state of things. Harry Morgan shuttles back and forth between Cuba and Key West, those twin poles of his existence. He earns his living in one and makes spectacular love to his wife in the other. Plying his dangerous trade, he loses first an arm and eventually his life, but his psychic stance—gloomy, tough-minded, uninflectedly blunt—

remains intact. The early protagonists make their tremendous voyages not with any real hope of gaining ground but in order not to lose any. In this they succeed brilliantly. Their spiritual state is preserved unimpaired.

There is a remarkable change in the last three novels. The characters move out of their defensive redoubts and advance toward new ground. The last thing Robert Jordan wants to do is stay put in his quiet Montana backwater. He travels halfway around the earth to fight for and eventually give up his life for a cuase that he believes—at the beginning anyway—will make the world a better place. His journey is triumphant in every way: his love affair with Spain, and with Maria (a microcosm of the country), is supremely consummated. The bridge, which is the farthest point of the journey and its ultimate objective, is successfully blown up, and the return home begun. The accident which leads to Jordan's death only heightens the state of exaltation in which he finds himself at the end.

Colonel Cantwell is caught up in a similar exaltation. He is the most posturing and narcissistic of Hemingway's creations, and perhaps the most repulsive. But his journey to Venice yields him the same psychic dividends as does Jordan's to Spain. To be sure, he has no desire to improve the world but only to intensify himself. In this he succeeds, despite his middle years and beat-up condition, beyond his most fervent expectations. The three great loves of his life—Italy, Renata, and himself in rising order—fuse in a final ecstasy, so that when the time comes to leave, he is filled with a sense of potent completeness. He begins the return journey only, like Jordan, to die, replete, almost at once. Their novels are paeans not just to the two men but to the two countries they have come to love, and it is this that strengthens the credibility of their expanding emotions.

The hero of the last of the novels[3] performs greater deeds defending the marlin on the way back than he does capturing it on the way out. With the skeleton of the epic fish tied to his skiff like a figurehead of mythic power, Santiago returns to his native village spent and bleeding. Yet the contrast with his departure could not be more extreme. Then he had been a pariah, cursed with bad luck, deserted by Manolin, avoided as an eccentric, senile figure. Now his return arouses wonder, awe, and admiration. His exploit is regarded by the villagers, and even by the tourists, as a feat of unparalleled valor, and the link between himself and the boy is reestablished more firmly than ever. This fusion of man and community at the end of *The Old Man and the Sea* brings the journey in Hemingway to a spectacular climax.

The changing ages of Hemingway's protagonists reveal the change in Hemingway himself. In the opening three novels they are all more or less the same age, somewhere in their thirties. In the closing three there is a radical shift. Robert Jordan is no older than Jake or Frederic Henry but Cantwell is in his fifties and distinctly middle-aged while Santiago is in his eighties and distinctly old. In now ranging over the whole span of life Hemingway suggests his own shift in viewpoint from static to expansive.

The journeys in Hemingway derive from similar enterprises in Joseph Conrad. We begin to perceive Conrad more forcefully than ever as a supreme influence on the American novelists of our century, specifically on Fitzgerald, Faulkner, and Hemingway, the three major ones. *The Great Gatsby* is an updated rewrite of *Lord Jim*, with Jim as Gatsby, Marlow as Nick Carraway, and the theme of the adolescent hero *manque* who arouses our sympathy central throughout. Without too much strain one can see certain lineaments of *An Outcast of the Islands* refracted in *Tender Is The Night*: like Willems, Dick Diver is transplanted to another culture, exposed to a temptation he cannot resist, betrays first his profession (as Willems does his race) and then himself, and in the end is left drained of all energy and will. Faulkner's enthusiasm for Conrad goes back to his youth. When he came to write his novels of conjecture, as Albert Guerard shrewdly noted twenty years ago, they owed a heavy debt to Conrad's own enigmatic novels of conjecture, of which *Chance* stands to this day as the purest, most austere example.

On Hemingway, Conrad's impact is visible in every area. Hemingway embraces Conrad's metaphysics, his ethics, and what one might call his psychogeography. Both men share a vision of the universe as empty, and define life as essentially a manichean struggle between the forces of light (Marlow's last view of Him as a blob of white in a darkening world; Hemingway's well-lighted place) and the forces of darkness (the cosmic *nada*). In ethics both believe in moral choices but in moral choices whose distinctiveness has become blurred ("There was not the thickness of a sheet of paper between the right and wrong of this affair" [*Lord Jim*, chapter eleven]). As to the psychological uses of nature, Hemingway learned a good deal about this from Turgenev and D. H. Lawrence but from Conrad most of all. Landscape is a perpetual and absolutely reliable guide to the emotional state of Hemingway's characters as it is a profound metaphor of illumination in the lives of the figures in Conrad.

But perhaps Conrad's influence on Hemingway is seen most plainly in the motif of the voyage. The voyages in Conrad—from the very long one taken by the crew of the *Narcissus* to the very short one when Decoud and Nostromo ferry the silver ingots across the Golfo Placido to the island of Santa Isabella—are journeys across an emotional as well as a physical space, and it was Conrad's particular genius to keep the geographic and psychological journeys of his characters moving along the same track and reinforcing each other without either losing its individual identity. This interpenetration of space and mind enriches each immeasurably, lending Conrad's voyages their special character, making him in modern literature the master, perhaps even the creator of psycho-geography.

The inherent danger in this kind of writing is the pathetic fallacy, in John Ruskin's view a sure sign of a second-rate mind. If nature is that useful as an analogue to human emotion, the temptation to manipulate it to suit the fictional scheme can become irresistible. It is to the credit of Conrad—and Hemingway after him—that they resist this temptation almost from the start, and in Ruskin's terms establish their authority as first-class writing minds. The rivers, whether in Malaya or Africa, along whose tortuous winding courses Lingard, Marlow, and Jim make their astonishing ventures remain themselves, unaltered and intact, free of the novelist's contriving hand. There were overt signs of both animism and anthropomorphism in Conrad's first two novels, recounting the melancholy adventures of Almayer and Willems, but beginning with *The Nigger of the Narcissus* these double pitfalls were avoided. From that point on Conrad's oceans, jungles, estuaries, gulfs, and mountains remain inflexibly and austerely integral to themselves.

As in Hemingway the Conradian journey is almost literally a matter of life and death. The *Narcissus* is threatened by the Atlantic gale, yet no more so than by the internal upheaval generated by Wait and Donkin. The disintegration of the crew's morale, the incipient mutiny, exercise exactly the same pressure from within as the hurricane winds do from without, making the voyage from Bombay to London a test of endurance that is as much moral as physical. Marlow's journeys in *Youth* and *Heart of Darkness* trigger profound traumas of identity, in which the voyager passes from one stage of life and self-knowledge to another under the severest difficulties. The journeys in the later works—whether treated in a comic vein as with Captain Mac-Whirr's in *Typhoon* or in a sombre one, as with the unnamed young captains of "The Secret Sharer" and *The Shadow Line*—always bring the journeyers to the brink of dissolution.

The most fabulous of these adventures, and probably the best known, occurs in *Heart of Darkness*. Here, as much depends on what Marlow feels and does on his return to Europe as on his experiences in Africa. The story, couched in the form of an oral report that Marlow delivers to his European friends, emphasizes the idea of the voyager's return as the climax, perhaps even the catharsis of his enterprise. The human record is not complete until the report is filed, and it cannot be filed until Marlow gets back. Kurtz, Marlow's predecessor on the journey, sought to file *his* report while still in Africa and broke down in the middle of it. Marlow, profiting from Kirtz's errors and profoundly indebted to him for having paved the way and having, however inadvertently, mapped out the dangers, returns in good order. He is deeply shaken by the experience and greatly sobered, but he has brought back some hard-earned insights. He has learned, for example, that choosing among nightmares is a necessary moral act; that a lie can be a complex form of truth; that men *au fond,* whether black or white, African or European, primitive or civilized, are locked into the same nature and share the same fate; that every human being has a pressure point beyond which he cannot venture without disintegration. He has come to realize that in our perpetual self-exploration the identification of that point is the most vital discovery we can make about ourselves.

But the particular conclusions are less important than the fact of their delivery to others, to that highly skeptical yet highly receptive audience Conrad evokes perpetually. No such formal reports are present in Hemingway except by implication, but the return of the traveler to the starting-point, a point sometimes bleakly the same, sometimes subtly altered, is as decisive in Hemingway as in Conrad.

Their journeys have little in common with the traditional voyages of mythology and literature. They do not have the supernatural machinery that spurred Jason and the Argonauts in pursuit of the Golden Fleece or the supernatural overtones that gave the fateful journey of the Ancient Mariner its special ambience. Nor do they carry the weighty representative-of-all-humanity burdens present in *Moby Dick* and, dropping a few notches, *Ship of Fools*. Instead they derive their meaning and certainly draw their sustenance from ordinary, even commonplace reality. A highlight of *Heart of Darkness* is Marlow driving fresh nails into a water-logged boat he is trying to salvage. Among the decisive acts in *The Old Man and the Sea* are Santiago's careful fishing arrangements: preparing the bait, gauging the wind currents, assaying the flight of the birds.

The minutiae, the physical routine of the journey contain its overall meaning; they are therefore attended to with utmost fidelity. Nick's tiniest motions—strapping his pack on right, brewing the coffee well, catching the grasshoppers at the correct moment, even putting one step after another—are not only crucial but decisive. If he succeeds in them, he will succeed in everything. Working the ship, getting through the voyage, living through the everyday tedium of familiar duties are the supreme motions and tests of the human spirit for Conrad, arousing in him a sense of the sublime so that the "lowest" acts become, finally, the "highest." This exaltation of the physical universe, this infusion of craftsmanship and technique with the finest strain of spiritual energy are what distinguish the journeys in Conrad and Hemingway, and mark them off from their literary and certainly their mythological predecessors.

In this respect Hemingway's debt to Conrad is monumental. It was a debt that Hemingway himself formally acknowledged. A characteristic comment appeared in the *Transatlantic Review* shortly after Conrad's death:

From nothing else that I have ever read have I gotten what every book of Conrad has given me. I saved up four that I would not read until I needed them badly. Two months in Toronto used up the four books. . . . In Sudbury, Ontario, I bought three back-numbers of the Pictorial Review and read *The Rover*, sitting up in bed in the Nickle Range Hotel. When morning came I had used up all my Conrad like a drunkard. I had hoped it would last me the trip, and felt like a young man who has blown his patrimony (October, 1924).

But Hemingway brings to the voyage an element peculiar to himself, a note of nervous excitement, of subtle almost fateful tension that he manages with singular skill and that in the end makes his journeys special in themselves. When Santiago, after eighty-four days of bad luck, ventures beyond the traditional fishing limits on the eighty-fifth day, we know that something extraordinary is about to occur, so that his smallest gestures involving such normally undramatic objects as hooks, bait, lines, his smallest reactions to ripples of wind and water, seem suddenly invested with tremendous meaning. Similarly with Nick's trek across the burned landscape; our hackles rise with every move he makes however small. So that even before we really know what is happening we already experience that slight quiver of agitation, that particular Hemingway *frisson* which rises from the deepest level of his work. The quiver has its physical reflection in the first vibration of the fishing line when the as yet unidentified marlin nudges the bait a mile below the surface. And it is present regardless of the direction of the journey: it is as much there in Jake's journey away from tension and toward serenity as in Robert Jordan's away from the relative quiet of Montana toward the Spanish entanglement that will in the end prove fatal.

Yet the journeys in Hemingway deliberately eschew the spectacular and cling tenaciously to the mundane. Conrad's by contrast are filled with gales, typhoons, mysterious doldrums, and a kind of perpetual, surcharged hovering between one mesmeric psycho-physical state and another. No such thrilling dramatics are to be found in Hemingway. On the contrary, it is precisely this psychological and verbal inflation that he is in revolt against and wants to get away from. When Jake leaves for Spain, it is the routine aspect, the fact that he has been there before, that is emphasized. On the way down we are regaled with nothing more exotic than Bill's slightly mordant jokes about Catholics and tourists, by a cockroach in the hotel room at Bayonne, by Robert Cohn falling asleep, by the constant reminder that for the most part the Spanish countryside looks about like North Dakota. It is the ordinary that is highlighted, and the usual expectations of novelty and excitement present at the beginning of a journey are deliberately tamped down. When the overt excitement does come, when the full-scale emotion does emerge, it is all the more powerful for having been withheld. Hemingway's discovery of climax in anti-climax distinguishes his individual journeys just as it sets off his art as a whole.

In the end his journeys appear to us not only as dramatic vehicles but as human necessities, somehow imperative to the proper functioning of spirit and soul. The incurable lesion in Jake can be made endurable only by his pilgrimages south: to the bullring in Pamplona where, as an *afficionado*, he can be released into emotions not his own; and to the remote seclusion of unspoiled nature in the Spanish hills where, drinking wine and catching fish, he can return in spirit—if only momentarily—to what he was before the terrible burden of his wound was thrust upon him.

The brief yet painfully chracteristic journey underwater taken by the narrator in "After the Storm" sums up his life situation. He is a scavenger and beachcomber who feeds off the disasters of others. The pickings are slim and existence hazardous. What keeps him going is the prospect of a great coup, the wreck of a luxury liner, say, which he will be the first to reach. After a storm his chance comes; he swims out to the sunken ship, sees through a porthole the naked body of a woman with long hair floating inside, and knows that just inches away the treasure is there for the seizing. But in his eagerness he has forgotten to bring tools heavy enough to break through the glass, and is forced to return to shore in livid frustration. By the time he gets back it is too late. Others have already been there: first the Greeks, then the birds, have picked the wreck clean. His amphibious little journey is a shattering disappointment; nevertheless, by bringing him so tantalizingly close to the promised land, it revives the hope and supplies the energy that make it possible for him to keep going.

The particular human necessity of each voyage varies, of course, with each voyager. Harry Street must scale the summit of his unconsummated talent; since he cannot do it in fact, the flight that carries him over the top of Mt. Kilimanjaro can take place only in dream. Yet the content of the dream is so necessary to him that it becomes clearer, intenser, and more real than the longed-for reality itself. Santiago is also on the edge of death and must come to some final terms with life. Since his life was a skein of heroic impulses successfully realized, the ultimate journey that he takes on the bosom of his beloved Caribbean Sea leads him to an ecstatic melding with the universe that surrounds him and stretches out to the distant stars. With Nick Adams and his shattered nerves, the journey serves still another purpose but one no less intimately related to his deepest need; it is nothing less than the instrument that will save his sanity, the singular process that will restore him to himself.

The journeys in Hemingway wind their way through a tangle of complex functions. They supply a requisite change of place and thus advance the plot. By shifting the physical scene they make it possible for psychological positions to be altered and even radically rearranged. But whether triggering the story or releasing the concealed emotion, they remain unalterably faithful to the characters who make them. By exposing the hidden seams, rifts, and qualities of the journeyers, by providing them with the opportunity—often unique, always charged with tension hovering delicately beneath the surface—to work their way through themselves, these journeys can be described as truly magical.

The purpose they serve envelops the familiar world in which Hemingway deliberately encases them. By journeying to the limits of that world, his figures acquire the energy needed in their continuous struggle to endure in it. For the great drama in Hemingway, as in Conrad before him, is the endurance of the everyday. In that struggle—against boredom, against meaninglessness, against defeat—the journey plays its vital and determining role.[4]

NOTES

[1] His name is really Wilson-Harris. A point is made of the friends "simplifying" the name to just plain Harris (*Sun*, chapter thirteen).

[2] Not counting *The Torrents of Spring*, a wonderfully well-wrought parody but a mutation among Hemingway's fictions.

[3] The last in the strict technical sense is *Islands in the Stream*, published posthumously and without the author's imprimatur. This narrative is low-grade Hemingway, lots of pitchblende and very little radium, yet even here the ecstatic note of the later books—as contrasted with the severely restrained tone of the earlier—is clearly audible.

[4] It is surely significant that the one novel by Conrad in which everyone is defeated and life, including the life of London, is a universal disaster is his one work in which everyone is locked into a fixed position and cannot move, in which no journey is possible. I refer, of course, to *The Secret Agent*.

Hemingway's British and American Reception: A Study in Values

by Robert O. Stephens

When Ernest Hemingway wrote his "Situation Report" for *Look* magazine in 1956, he turned to the British critic Cyril Connolly for his text. Connolly's advice was to put aside the temporary distractions of literary fame and get back to work on the masterpiece.[1] It was fitting in several ways then that Connolly also provided one of the key statements on the difference between British and American responses to Hemingway. Reviewing *Men Without Women* in 1927, Connolly observed that "Mr. Hemingway remains easily the ablest of the wild band of Americans in Europe and is obviously capable of a great deal of development before his work reaches maturity. . . . Mr. Hemingway is considered, falsely, a second Joyce in America; at present he is more of a dark horse than a white hope, but his book makes a good test of one's own capacity to appreciate modernity."[2] The implications of such terms as "wild band of Americans," "dark horse" and "white hope," and "appreciate modernity" are clues to the differences in values brought to the initial reception of Hemingway by British and American reviewers over the middle fifty years of the twentieth century.

We are all of course indebted to D. S. R. Welland for his perceptive summary of the British response to Hemingway, and his acute observations on British peculiarities in reviewing suggest the need for still more incisive probes into the ways British critics responded to Hemingway as a chief representative of literary modernity.[3] But it is also useful to go beyond summary treatments to determine the basic preoccupations of both British and American reviewers and to see what contexts they invoked as they judged the validity and relevance of Hemingway's contributions to literary thought in the twentieth century. Initial responses are especially useful in this sort of investigation, as they tell, without chance to second guess, what literary values govern the reception of works into that body of thought we call literature. They obviously reflect changing views as to what constitutes literature, and these changing views are observable not only within the context of passing time but also within the differing expectations of two literary traditions.

The problem was, however, that some British critics did not fully recognize at first that two different literary traditions were involved. In his essay on "Contemporary American Letters" in June 1927 Hugh Walpole reflected this misconception. Writing soon after his return from four years' travel and lecturing in the United States, Walpole reported on literary trends in America as if they were the American branch of that larger empire of English letters. In particular, he reported that the publishing industry was burgeoning in America, that quick and large fortunes were being made by publishers, authors, and book clubs, that American literary taste was a "mixed bag"—a taste unguided by influential critics, and that American writers were endangered by early monetary success and by declining careers of self-imitation. Contrasting English and American practices, he doubted whether book clubs would be successful in England, "where readers are neither so docile nor so eager," noted that American critics tended to emphasize American talent over British, and noted further that with English fiction no longer ruling in America, it was harder for an English novelist to gain a hearing in America than it had been before the war. Within that context he saw Ernest Hemingway as "the most interesting figure in American letters in the last ten years" and recommended his new novel *The Sun Also Rises* to the attention of "anyone who cares for the discovery of new talent" when it was published in England.[4]

This view of Hemingway as the interesting Young Man from America dominated British comment on him throughout most of the twenties. He was to the British a brilliant young stylist, an innovator found in the Paris outpost of English letters, a writer of short stories who produced in "The Killers," Walpole thought, "one of the best stories in the American language." D. H. Lawrence characterized him as a young rebel, an educated trapper or cowboy, whose fragmentary but unsentimental stories were like striking a match or lighting "a brief sensational cigarette."[5] He was courageous, thought Lawrence, in making his narrative fragments no more than moments only and in having no illusions that they led to anything larger. But by that same judgment, British critics doubted that the Hemingway style was adequate for novels, particularly as the novel was known in the great tradition of British fiction. When *The Sun Also Rises* was published as *Fiesta* in England, the *Times Literary Supplement* thought the dialogue brilliant for the first hundred pages but "frankly tedious" afterward and that the plotless episodes provided little in story or character development as one had a right to expect in a novel.[6]   Edwin Muir also thought the dialogue brilliant and the descriptions precisely rendered with the economy of Maupassant, but though the lives of American expatriates were laid bare, nothing of importance about human life was told through them.[7] Put beside Virginia Woolf's *To the Lighthouse* or Thomas Mann's *The Magic Mountain*, then also being currently published, Hemingway's work was original but severely limited. Still, said Muir, his novel "raises hopes of remarkable achievement." Ford Madox Ford thought Hemingway wrote "extremely delicate prose" but that his first novel, though "finely alcoholic and irregular," did not provide a balanced record of life even for the Paris expatriates.[8]

By contrast, Hemingway was indeed the white hope in American eyes. Appearing first as a product of the Paris school of avant garde writing, Hemingway's work was characterized by Edmund Wilson as "strikingly original." The vignettes of *in our time*, said Wilson, constituted an "almost newly invented form," and his stories were records of the "harrowing barbarities" in the modern world.[9]   Robert Wolf in the *New York Herald Tribune Books* saw Hemingway as "something new under the sun in American letters," a young author who "produced in his own right some of the most sensitive and subtle short stories that have come from any young American."[10] "Here is a writer," proclaimed *Time* magazine when the New York edition of *In Our Time* was published: "Make no mistake. Ernest Hemingway is somebody; a new, honest, un-literary transcriber of life—a Writer."[11] And like several other reviewers, the man from *Time* pondered how Hemingway could know things so clearly and write so naturally. He must have had a long, austere preparation to write that purest, sweetest prose, said Ernest Walsh in *This Quarter*.

Generally the American view was that Hemingway was a product of Gertrude Stein and the Paris School with Ring Lardner and Sherwood Anderson as earlier antecedents. But the attribution of sources was not so much a genealogical inquest as an attempt to characterize the new style. It was compared to machine-age art, to cubist painting, to Stravinsky's music, to Goya's lithographs, to Kipling, to Katherine Mansfield, and by Allen Tate, to the work of Fielding, Defoe, Swift, and Sterne, when they were discovering the power of expression in English prose. Hemingway's use of colloquial language in a distinctively modern idiom was clearly the central feature of that style in American eyes. Herschel Brickell, for example, pointed out how Hemingway used the vernacular to do remarkable things with a handful of words in his short stories.[12] And when the test of that vernacular style came in the bigger leagues of the novel, the *New York Times Book Review* thought that *The Sun Also Rises* put "more literary English to shame"; its effect was beyond analysis, the words were specific but "betray[ed] a great deal more than is to be found in the individual parts" and the novel was "unquestionably one of the events of an unusually rich year in literature."[13] In his more general appreciative essay in *Bookman*, F. Scott Fitzgerald argued that style was the secret of the modern vision. American writers, he said, had been obsessed since Irving's time with the need to cultivate American materials, and in their studies of farms, cities, and other American scenes had succeeded only in wasting material. *In Our Time*, Fitzgerald thought, was tempermentally new and emotionally real because Hemingway proceeded according to the demands of style.[14]

While the English were content to describe Hemingway as a young writer of promising talent throughout the twenties, Americans identified his promise with the publication of *In Our Time* and declared that promise fulfilled with *The Sun Also Rises*. By mid-1927 the English critic Edwin Muir was still hoping for "remarkable achievement" from Hemingway, and in late 1927 Cyril Connolly, reviewing *Men Without Women*, saw Hemingway still expressing postwar dissatisfaction when "the postwar period is nearly over." Hemingway, he thought, was one of "those talented authors who substituted impatience for ambition and struggled bravely on without the great driving power of tradition." But, said Connolly, "the literature of the future will be in the hands of a bland and orderly generation about which

absolutely nothing is known."[15]   In America, however, Allen
Tate began his review of the expatriate novel by saying that *The
Sun Also Rises* supports the promise of *In Our Time* that Hemingway will be "the big man in American letters." Cleveland
B. Chase began his review in *Saturday Review of Literature* by
saying that the new novel fulfilled the promise of the short
stories and, in echo of the old bardolatry question of the nine-
teenth century, that Hemingway wrote with "Shakespearian
absoluteness." Herbert S. Gorman opened his review of the
novel with the declaration that Hemingway had kept his promise
but saw the novel promising still more: it placed Hemingway "in
the front rank of the younger group from whom we expect so
much."[16]

   Although *Time* magazine and the Chicago *Tribune* thought
the expatriate novel disappointing after the promise of *In Our
Time*, their disappointment centered on the subject matter, "the
soggy cafe life" and the "gestury" theme, rather than on the
style itself. By the time *A Farewell to Arms* appeared in 1929,
Henry Hazlitt observed in the *New York Sun* that it was the
fashion to compare new writers with those already established,
like Conrad, Hardy, Hamsun, Proust, and Joyce. In 1929 Hemingway was the standard by which the new was measured.[17]
Malcolm Cowley observed that in five years Hemingway had
"won an extraordinary place in American letters," had been
imitated by writers older as well as younger than himself, and
had achieved the status of a virtual tradition.[18]

   The British reception of *A Farewell to Arms* likewise acknowledged, at least tacitly, that Hemingway had achieved full
literary stature. The difference between the British and American responses, however, was one so fundamental that it dominated responses to Hemingway's work for the remainder of his
life. Once British critics accepted Hemingway as a writer of full
stature, his work became part of a mature literary tradition, and
the emphasis in reviews of his new works was on the subject
matter as a contribution to literary knowledge. *A Farewell to
Arms* was reviewed as an addition to the growing list of novels
on the great war. Its distinction was that it exploited the war on
the Italian front and presented a fresh view of the war experienced by avoiding the overexploited interest in the western
front. *Death in the Afternoon* was, to the British, really a book

on bullfighting, and *Green Hills of Africa* was a report on African life and landscapes, seen within the context of other reports from the empire by colonial officials. Reviewing the book for *New Yorker*, Clifton Fadiman saw the tendency: it was, he said, in the genre of books written by retired Indian Army colonels.[19]

The American emphasis, however, was to concentrate on the writer rather than the subject. Most American reviewers seemed obsessed with the predictions of Van Wyck Brooks that American authors were subject to the law of early flourishing and mid-career decline because they had no sustaining literary tradition. After the success of *A Farewell to Arms*, most American reviewers thought the prime question was whether Hemingway could maintain that high level of performance. The later American reception of Hemingway's works was a series of disappointments, calls to wait for the big novel in preparation, declarations of recovery, and other disappointments and calls to wait for the masterpiece. Indeed, Hemingway's success or failure became almost a personal concern for American critics, and they imposed on him, in many cases, the critical fortune of American writing. Further, American critics wrote as though the novel were the only legitimate test of Hemingway's powers as artist and man, and such books as *Death in the Afternoon* and *Green Hills of Africa* and even the collections of short stories were, in their eyes, only temporary, personal indulgences of the author, no more than holding actions while he prepared a new novel, the only genre that really counted in the world of reviewing.

Thus, while the London *Times* declared that Hemingway was the man and *Death in the Afternoon* was the book to consult if one wanted to understand bullfighting, and while the *Times Literary Supplement* review was written by a critic more concerned with correcting Hemingway's bullfight terminology and his evaluations of toreros than the literary qualities of the book, American critics were concerned with a kind of book they had not expected from Hemingway. Although most recognized it as a logical extension of interest in bullfighting central to *The Sun Also Rises* and "The Undefeated," many also puzzled over the genre of the book, some deciding it was a kind of anatomy like Burton's or Browne's. In short, they had to consider Hemingway as a man of letters as well as a novelist. But mostly American reviewers saw *Death in the Afternoon* as a personal statement, part autobiography, part explanation of his artistic credo, part self-indulgence in the use of gratuitiously bawdy situations and bawdy talk, as in the Old Lady passages. Although H. L. Mencken thought it the best treatise on bullfighting in English and an extraordinarily fine piece of exposition, he also thought it marred by gross, irritating cheapness in its attempt to shock by the use of four-letter words such imagined readers as the Ladies Temperance Society of Oak Park.[20] In *The Nation* Clifton Fadiman emphasized the personal dimension, calling Hemingway an American Byron. Hemingway, he said, had triumphed more as a hero than as an artist and would have gained a legendary place in the popular mind even without good writing.[21] Max Eastman carried the personal element of criticism to its extreme in his review "Bull in the Afternoon," where he accused Hemingway of truculent he-mannishness and of wearing false hair on his chest.[22] That Hemingway responded to the review personally we know from accounts of the shoving match between the two when they next met in Maxwell Perkins' office at Scribner's. More moderate reviewers concluded with Seward Collins in *Bookman* that the writing in *Death in the Afternoon* was as good as that done previously but showed no advance, or with R. L. Duffus in the *New York Times Book Review* that it was minor Hemingway and would gain no new admirers. *Time* magazine similarly said that the book was genuine Hemingway but might alienate new disciples. Malcolm Cowley noted that all of Hemingway's books had been elegies and that *Death in the Afternoon* was in effect a farewell to Spain. But when, he asked, would Hemingway give a farewell to farewells? In a similar vein, Clifton Fadiman reviewed *Winner Take Nothing* by noting that Hemingway's previously good stories had made admirers more demanding in wanting better than good stories and the stories of 1933 were too much like those of the twenties. "Why not go on to something else?" he urged.[24]

When we turn to Wyndham Lewis' classic British review of the thirties, however, the concern though intense, is for the world of Hemingway's fictional people rather than for the writer. Although he calls Hemingway "the Noble Savage of Rousseau, but a white version, the simple American man," it is clear that Lewis sees the Noble Savage as a pose Hemingway chose in order to write for the modern world. Like Aldous Huxley, who thought Hemingway one of those modern intellectuals posing as

primitive toughs, Lewis wrote of Hemingway's hero, not Hemingway himself, as "the Dumb Ox." When he says "Hemingway" in
the following passage, it is clear by the context that he speaks
synecdochally, that "Hemingway" is short hand for the characters created by him:

> He lives, or affects to live, *submerged*. He is in the multitudinous
> ranks of *those to whom things happen*—terrible things of course,
> and of course stoically borne. . . . Hemingway has really taken up
> his quarters in the stupid *bêtise* of the herd, and has mastered the
> medium entirely, so that he is of it, and yet not of it, in a very
> satisfactory way.[25]

Not only were Hemingway's characters will-less and politically
unaware victims of the world, the books and stories in which
they were presented were unacceptable to Lewis and his long
line of adherents in two other ways: they were modern and
proletarian, and in a secondary way, they were American. Thus,
in Hemingway's style,

> The rhythm is the anonymous folk-rhythm of the urban prole-
> tariat. . . . But what is curious about this is that the *Beach-la-mar*
> in which he writes is, more or less, the speech that is proposed for
> everybody in the future—it is a Volapuk which probably will be
> ours tomorrow. . . . And the Anglo-Saxon *Beach-la-mar* of the
> future will not be quite the same thing as Chaucer or Dante, con-
> trasted with the learned tongue. For the latter was the speech of a
> race rather than a class, whereas our "vulgar tongue" will be really
> *vulgar*. . . . Americanization—which is also for England, at least,
> proletarianization—is too far advanced to require underlining, even
> for people who fail usually to recognize anything until it has been
> in existence for a quarter of a century. . . . So the situation is this,
> as far as our common language is concerned: the destiny of
> England and the United States is more than ever one. But it is now
> the American influence that is paramount.[26]

Cyril Connolly had been right. Hemingway tested British readers' "capacity to appreciate modernity," and by 1934—the water-
shed period in Hemingway's British reputation, as Welland has
pointed out—they found it fearful. Hemingway's world was one
of "genuine nihilism," thought William Plomer, despite "that
technical skill, that economy, and that peculiarly American kind

of sophistication which have helped to make his name."[27]

Wyndham Lewis' analysis continued to influence British reviewers even as they read the books for subject matter rather than as indices to Hemingway's artistic health. Cyril Connolly remarked in his review of *To Have and Have Not* in 1937 that Hemingway had showed no profit from Lewis' "Dumb Ox" essay and that Harry Morgan was the dumbest ox of all. V. S. Pritchett thought the Key West book demonstrated a "craving of the educated to be uneducated, to destroy the *bourgeois* in oneself. . . ." W. H. Mellers Saw Philip Rawlings of *The Fifth Column* as a "Hollywooden Hero" and Robert Jordan as "The Ox in Spain."[28] By the time of *For Whom the Bell Tolls*, V. S. Pritchett still endorsed Lewis' view but saw Robert Jordan more active in determining his own destiny, more technically expert if not more politically sophisticated. And by 1950 Henry Reed saw Richard Cantwell still parading an "affected roughness" which evaded difficult problems.[29] But in its review of *Across the River and into the Trees*, the *Times Literary Supplement*, though often out of step with other British reviews of specific works, reminded readers and critics alike that they must see Hemingway's books as authentic works of a major novelist and see them in the context of his whole work.[30]

In America the primary concern remained Hemingway's career. Unlike the British, who assumed that a man of letters might write in many genres, T. S. Matthews complained of *Green Hills of Africa* that Hemingway now thought he could write on anything and call it literature, and Granville Hicks, writing in *New Masses* that the African book was irrelevant to the concerns of a depression-stricken world, thought Hemingway had ignored Melville's dictum that a great book calls for a great theme.[31] When *To Have and Have Not* appeared as Hemingway's first novel in eight years, most American critics thought it a failure and Hemingway finished as a serious writer. In a typical review, Sinclair Lewis said it was time for Hemingway to stop saving Spain and start saving himself.[32] Symptomatic also of the American viewpoint were statements by Louis Kronenberger and Clifton Fadiman that *To Have and Have Not* was only a transitional book; Alfred Kazin thought the Key West book showed Hemingway still capable of writing a great novel, even if the story of Harry Morgan was not that novel. A significant number of reviewers indicated present disappointment but continued their hope for a big novel to come. Indeed, anticipating the big novel had become an American critical habit after 1932.[33] So strong was the personal criticism that in 1939 Lionel Trilling thought American reviewers were responsible for the illegitimate emergence of Hemingway the man over Hemingway the artist. Hemingway, he said, had become the victim of critics' "liberal-radical highmindedness."[34]

When *For Whom the Bell Tolls* was published in 1940, then, the American response was one of outright jubilation at Hemingway's recovery. It is true that the war in Europe, predicted and foreshadowed by Hemingway, gave the novel a special timeliness, but for Americans still on this side of the Atlantic the chief fact was Hemingway's recovery. It was somehow linked in many critics' minds with national recovery after the depression of the thirties, and in his essay entitled "The Return of Ernest Hemingway," Edmund Wilson welcomed back the possibility of credible heroes like Robert Jordan and thought Hemingway's new art was reassuring evidence of the soundness of our intellectual life.[35]   Other welcoming reviews celebrated recovery with phrases like "Hemingway Crosses the Bridge," "Hemingway's Best Book," and "his finest story yet." In 1941 the Limited Edition Book Club voted the Spanish war novel the book published in the previous three years most likely to become a classic.

For Americans the pattern of apparent collapse and recovery was repeated during the next dozen years when *Men at War* and *Across the River and into the Trees* seemed to signal Hemingway's decline and *The Old Man and the Sea* seemed to justify all forlorn hopes. The Pulitzer Prize and then the Nobel Prize made the recovery seem even more remarkable. Meanwhile, the British reviewed *The Old Man and the Sea* as a competent work of the imagination by an established modern writer. Except for doubts about over-solemn simplicity in the opening pages, British reviewers typically praised the sea novel as a sustained act of the imagination. Such phrases as "perfection of a lyric poem" and "biblical simplicity and purity" characterized British views of the work. But in contrast with American tendencies to link *The Old Man and the Sea* with *Moby-Dick* and other sea classics, the British emphasized keeping the novel in perspective. The London *Times* was fairly typical in its comment: "He has often tackled and sometimes achieved more, but rarely has he written less pretentiously or more pleasantly, or within the limits of a small compass shown greater mastery."[36] To the British, it was, in short, a classic performance but a minor one.

After his death, however, British and American critical approaches to Hemingway drew closer together, though they still kept vestiges of their former tendencies. As posthumous works came out of the vault, American reviewers showed a readiness to view Hemingway's performances more dispassionately than before, and British critics emphasized the autobiographical element in the works. Most American reviewers took seriously Hemingway's invitation in the Foreword to *A Moveable Feast* to read the Paris account as a fictional statement, and many preferred to consider it a novelistic performance. British reviewers, used to dealing with autobiographies, letters, and diaries of established persons, accepted the book as a memoir and typically reviewed it jointly with Fitzgerald's letters. Where many American critics lamented the portraits of Hemingway's contemporaries as gratuitously vicious characterizations written within a fictionalized context, British reviewers apparently accepted the idea that memoirists may tell their own version of disputed events and controversial people, even if they preferred Fitzgerald's self-effacement to Hemingway's boasting. In view of Wyndham Lewis' influential "Dumb Ox" essay, they were not surprised to see Lewis characterized as a man with the eyes of an unsuccessful rapist. Similarly, Americans saw *By-line: Ernest Hemingway* as a collection of journalistic pieces valuable for its links with his fiction and of interest primarily to Hemingway cultists. British reviewers typically saw it as a talented writer's report on the world of his time and appraised it for general readers.

When *Islands in the Stream* was published, almost all reviewers, British and American, recognized it as the long-expected big novel Hemingway had referred to since the early fifties. But their answers differed on the question whether the publishers and the estate had been wise to publish the book in its semi-revised condition. The great majority of American critics, still aware of Van Wyck Brooks' warning, thought the novel could only harm Hemingway's declining reputation. Only a few influential critics like Malcolm Cowley and Edmund Wilson thought the novel

would add to Hemingway's stature, and in a relatively late review, obviously written with the knowledge that the book was
taking a beating, Edmund Wilson said that *Islands in the Stream*,
because of its autobiographical resonances, would become more
important than many people presently thought.[37]   British reviewers clearly thought a writer's papers should be published.
Together with the works published during his lifetime, they
would provide the material for a coherent view of the man whose
work represented in a major way the form and matter of modernity. The *Times Literary Supplement* expressed the view of
most British and many American critics in saying that all remaining papers should be published but published as Hemingway had
left them, without the streamlining provided by editors.[38]   Indeed, a bibliographical emphasis began with the reception of
Islands in the Stream and continued when *The Nick Adams
Stories* appeared in 1972. Several reviewers indicated that what
was now needed was Hemingway with footnotes—editorial comments explaining the hiatuses and inconsistencies found in the
manuscripts.   Hemingway's American editors, however, were
slow to admit the necessity of such apparatus, as Professor
Young has explained in his essay on the production of *The Nick
Adams Stories*.[39]

But until definitive editions become available, the personal
dimension in criticism is likely to dominate. British critic Paul
Theroux recognized this governing tendency in his review of
Islands in the Stream: "The reputation is all, and counts for
more than the writing. Asked who is the most popular American
writer in the Soviet Union, the Russian journalist says, 'Papa.'
The note of friendly itimacy is common: it is the man that
matters.   The American writer produces a good book and ac-
quires a reputation. The reputation displaces the idea of literary
quality: the idea of the author is much more important than the
ideas in the work."[40]

That the author and his work finally became inseparable for
both American and British reviewers can perhaps best be seen in
the fact that from the beginning of his career and especially after
1950 Hemingway's books were frequently reviewed by other
novelists. Whether Elliot Paul and Sinclair Lewis were reviewing
To Have and Have Not, John O'Hara, Evelyn Waugh, and William
Faulkner defending *Across the River and into the Trees*, or

William Faulkner praising *The Old Man and the Sea*, those novelists of Hemingway's generation wrote in his behalf as if they were somehow defending their own achievements in new trials. A new generation of novelists like John Updike and Paul Theroux similarly reviewed later works like *Islands in the Stream*, and if they wrote with knowledge of Hemingway's achievements already learned and built upon and judged more austerely than did his contemporaries, they too wrote in the knowledge that for most of them Hemingway embodied literary modernity. To them he was something of a test case, and what happened to him happened to the practice of fiction in the modern world.

NOTES

[1] *Look*, September 4, 1956, p. 24.

[2] *The New Statesman*, 30 (November 26, 1927), p. 208.

[3] "Hemingway's English Reputation," *The Literary Reputation of Hemingway in Europe*, ed. Roger Asselineau (New York: New York University Press, 1965), pp. 8-38.

[4] *The Nation & Athenaeum*, 41 (June 4, 1927), pp. 302-303.

[5] *Calendar of Modern Letters*, 4 (April, 1927), pp. 72-73.

[6] *TLS*, June 30, 1927, p. 454.

[7] *The Nation & Athenaeum*, 41 (July 2, 1927), pp. 450, 452.

[8] "Some American Expatriates," *Vanity Fair*, 28 (April 1, 1927), pp. 64, 98.

[9] "Mr. Hemingway's Dry-Points," *Dial*, 77 (October, 1924), pp. 340-341.

[10]February 14, 1926, p. 3.

[11]January 18, 1926, p. 38.

[12]*New York Evening Post*, October 17, 1925, p. 3.

[13]*New York Times Book Review*, October 31, 1926, p. 7.

[14]"How to Waste Material," *Bookman*, 63 (May, 1926), pp. 262-265.

[15]Muir, *The Nation & Athenaeum*, 41 (July 2, 1927), p. 452; Connolly, *New Statesman*, 30 (November 26, 1927), p. 208.

[16]Tate, *The Nation*, 123 (December 15, 1926), p. 642; Chase, *SRL*, 3 (December 11, 1926), p. 420; Gorman, *New York World*, November 14, 1926, p. 10M.

[17]September 28, 1929, p. 38.

[18]"Not Yet Demobilized," *New York Herald Tribune Books*, 6 (October 6, 1929), pp. 1, 6.

[19]*New Yorker*, 11 (November 2, 1935), p. 80.

[20]*American Mercury*, 27 (December, 1932), pp. 506-507.

[21]"Ernest Hemingway: An American Byron," *The Nation*, 136 (January 18, 1933), pp. 63-64.

[22]*New Republic*, 75 (June 7, 1933), pp. 94-97.

[23]Collins, *Bookman*, 75 (October, 1932), pp. 622-624; Duffus, *NYTBR*, September 25, 1932, pp. 5, 17; *Time*, 20 (September 26, 1932), 47; Cowley, *New Republic*, 73 (November 30, 1932), pp. 76-77.

[24]*New Yorker*, 9 (October 28, 1933), pp. 74-75.

[25]"The Dumb Ox: A Study of Ernest Hemingway," *American Review*, 3 (June, 1934), pp. 289-312, originally published in *Life and Letters*, 10 (April, 1934), pp. 33-45.

[26]Lewis, pp. 296, 297, 306.

[27]*Now and Then*, No. 47 (Spring, 1934), pp. 22-23.

[28]Connolly, *New Statesman and Nation*, 14 (October 16, 1937), p. 606; Pritchett, *Now and Then*, No. 58 (Winter, 1937), p. 30; Mellers, *Scrutiny*, 8 (December, 1939), p. 338; 10 (June, 1941), p. 93.

[29]Pritchett, *New Statesman and Nation*, 21 (March 15, 1941), pp. 275-276; Reed, *The Listener*, 44 (November 9, 1950), p. 515.

[30]*TLS*, October 16, 1950, p. 628.

[31]Matthews, *New Republic*, 85 (November 27, 1935), pp. 79-80; Hicks, *New Masses*, 17 (November 19, 1935), p. 23.

[32]*Newsweek*, 10 (October 18, 1937), p. 34.

[33]Kronenberger, *The Nation*, 145 (October 23, 1937), pp. 439-440; Fadiman, *New Yorker*, 13 (October 16, 1937), pp. 76-77; Kazin, *New York Herald Tribune Books*, 14 (October 17, 1937), p. 3.

[34]*Partisan Review*, 6 (Winter, 1939), pp. 52-60.

[35]*New Republic*, 103 (October 28, 1940), pp. 591-592.

[36]September 13, 1952, p. 8.

[37]*New Yorker*, 46 (January, 1971), pp. 59-62.

[38]*TLS*, October 16, 1970, p. 5.

[39]" 'Big World Out There': *The Nick Adams Stories*," *Novel*, 6 (1972), pp. 5-19.

[40]*Encounter*, 36 (February 1971), p. 62.

"The Truest Sentence": Words as Equivalents of Time
And Place in IN OUR TIME

by Charles G. Hoffman and A. C. Hoffmann

In 1922 Hemingway wrote a series of related declarative statements in his notebook, entitling them "Paris, 1922," with the aim of writing "the truest sentence." These six sentences, quoted in full in Baker's biography, can be viewed simply as an exercise by a young writer seeking to master the craft.[1] However, the significance of the exercise to Hemingway's development lies in his attempt to capture in words the equivalency of what he had observed in Paris without resorting to flowery rhetoric or emotional subjectivity. In this sense the exercise was an important discovery for Hemingway because he found that he could, within a sentence, distill the raw materials of experience into the essence of the event itself as though it were an object to be photographed or a landscape to be painted. It was this ability to condense a feeling or mood into a visual equivalent that provided the breakthrough he needed to write *In Our Time* (1925).

It is true that journalism was Hemingway's apprenticeship, as Charles Fenton has pointed out in his study,[2] but what Hemingway needed beyond a journalist's predilection for condensation was a *literary* understanding of words as equivalencies for events which reverberate spatially and temporally within a thematic and structural pattern. It was Gertrude Stein who taught Hemingway, as he himself paid tribute on her death, "about the abstract relationship of words." This abstract relationship is, as Richard Bridgman suggests in *The Colloquial Style in America*, a "dynamic complex of words in which the various elements were determined quite as much by reference to one another as they were by reference to some observed reality on the printed page."[3] Words become in such a controlled literary context not mere journalistic reportage of events but the objective correlatives of the emotions inherent in related events. Thus, while some of the newspaper articles Hemingway wrote for the *Toronto Star* in 1922 were used directly or indirectly as source materials for *In Our Time*, what is more significant is that Hemingway's mastery of the abstract relationship of words provided him with a means of achieving an objective sense of the times so that personal experiences and observed events could be transformed into a continuum of time and place reverberating back and forth between past and present. Any one time and place—Nick as a boy with his back against a tree innocently reading/ Nick as a wounded soldier with his back against the church wall/ Nick as a post-war veteran with his back against the charred stump of a tree—is a reverberation of all the other inter-related times and places that make up the complex but unified sense of "in our time." Like Stieglitz and Weston who sought with their cameras to create what Stieglitz called "equivalents," a photograph that truly recorded the reality of the object in such a way that it transcended the object itself, Hemingway sought with words to transcend the reported reality of an event so that it becomes a timeless, visual object evoking all the related moments of past, present and future.

In April, 1923, Hemingway published six prose sketches, or "miniatures" as they were called, in *The Little Review*. These sketches evolved out of the basic method of the Paris notebook, a compression of experience into "true sentences" (Baker, 141). A year later he published all the vignettes separately as *in our time* (1924);[4] at the same time he was writing and publishing the stories that were to be integrated with the vignettes in *In Our Time*. While the advance in technique of the sketches over the sentences was a significant development, it is the interrelationship of the vignettes to each other and to the stories that is the ultimate achievement of *In Our Time*.[5] The abstract relationship of words became the key by which the parts could be integrated into a novelistic whole, a unifying technique that goes far beyond the inter-related narrative and thematic structure of Sherwood Anderson's *Winesburg, Ohio* (1919) which to some extent must have served Hemingway as a model. Comprising as they do (in a slightly different order) the first five vignettes of *In Our Time*, plus the ninth, *The Little Review* "miniatures" are a convenient starting point for an analysis of Hemingway's achievement in *In Our Time*, for they show the mastery over craft in less than a year from the entry in the Paris 1922 notebook: "I have *seen* the favourite crash into the Bullfinch and come down in a heap kicking, while the rest of the field swooped over the jump . . . and the crown raced across the pelouze to see the horses come into the stretch" (Baker, 121. Italics ours).[6]

Each sketch is a short paragraph (the longest being a little over 150 words), but there is a qualitative difference between the sentences of the notebook entry and the six sketches that goes beyond the mere quantitative expansion of sentence into paragraph. These carefully wrought paragraphs have a density of meaning that goes beyond length. On the elementary but fundamental level of narrative each sketch tells a story in miniature, in the form of an anecdote or scene: in part the narrative element is a function of the controlling voice narrating the particular sketch. Half of the sketches are in the first person, half in the third person (this pattern holds for the book itself). The controlling narrative voice, whether first or third person, is carefully modulated from sketch to sketch, ranging from a British soldier's breezy, upper-class colloquial account of erecting a barricade across a bridge against the German advance in the first world war to an impersonal and detached journalistic account of Greek refugees jammed along the Karagatch road in the Greco-Turkish war. The first sketch, although in the first person, is nearly as objective as the third-person journalistic reports (the only subjective statement revealing the narrator's emotional state is "It was funny going along that road") because it is told from the perspective of an innocent eye, a kitchen corporal, who like the rest of the battery from officers on down was as yet untried by war. Similarly, the second sketch (Chapter IX of *In Our Time*) although in the third person and mainly objective in its account of a bullfight is, as Bridgman has pointed out, subjectively American in colloquialisms (Bridgman, 204). The effect, then, in these original sketches, which sets the pattern for the later ones, is to suggest a variety of perspectives and narrative voices that make up the over-all ambiance of *in our time*. Even more significant are the inter-relationships in structure, theme and motif, already evident in these six sketches and expanded into the complex reverberations between sketches and stories in *In Our Time*.

The first vignette, by reason of its position, style and

content, is seminal. Its condensed brevity is typical of the sketches: stylistically, the abstract relationship of the words within the vignette binds it together giving unity to the whole and enhancing the thematic content. The device of repetition learned from Gertrude Stein—repetition of the word "drunk" (and its synonym "soused") and the phrase "going along the road" with its echo in the phrase "kept riding"—does more than suggest the unsophisticated naiveness of the narrator whose limited vocabulary and experience sets the tone for the vignette. It gives a rhythmic sense of movement and restless nervousness within the essentially static unity of a narrative that has no beginning and no end, only a middle consisting of a battery of untried soldiers on the road *to* war getting drunk to screw up their courage for the first battle in the Champagne sector (we know only that the kitchen Corporal survived and was probably promoted). The latent fear of the unknown that lies ahead of the men at the end of the road, hidden by their drunkenness, is reflected in the officers, the lieutenant talking to his horse and the adjutant worrying about the fire in the kitchen being seen by the enemy even though they were still fifty kilometers from the front. The fire and the darkness of the night are juxtaposed and inverted to provide contrasting images—the fire which should suggest warmth, companionship and food is seen by the adjutant (however falsely, as a measure of his own nervous fear) as a source of danger whereas the darkness which at first seems to reflect the men's fear of the unknown ahead is revealed as a safe means of protecting their way to the front.[7]

Stylistic and thematic reverberations abound between this first vignette and the others and between it and the stories themselves. The movement of the army battery along the road to war is ironically linked with the next vignette of *In Our Time* (the third in *The Little Review* series and *in our time*): the movement of the war refugees away from war "along the Karagatch road," a thirty mile column of refugees that seemed to have "no end and no beginning." This was at another time and in another war, but using the impressionistic method of time shift developed by Conrad and Ford, Hemingway telescopes and juxtaposes time and place so that they are all "in our time," the same moment in time and place: the movement of the soldiers in the first vignette is the movement of all "innocent" soldiers from "childhood" to initiation into "manhood" on the road to war; the movement of the civilian refugees is the movement of all war refugees chaotically seeking to flee from the war zone, whether it is the first World War or its legacy, the Greco-Turkish war of 1921-1922, described in this second vignette based on Hemingway's own newspaper dispatches published in the *Toronto Star* in October, 1922.

Thematically, the road motif is an important image of *In Our Time*, from the first story to the last. In the first story, "Indian Camp," we find Nick literally starting out in the darkness of innocence as a young boy accompanying his doctor father to the Indian camp. He arrives at daylight into his first initiatory experience which juxtaposes the violence of birth and death, reverberating back and forth in time and place between this early, pre-war experience of Nick in Michigan watching the Indian woman painfully giving birth while her husband commits suicide and the young girl crying and scared sick as she holds a blanket over the woman having a baby in the procession of war refugees along the Karagatch road.

Again, in the story, "The Battler" (Chapter V), Nick is on the road, and although he is an older, more experienced Nick than in the first story, he is still an "innocent" drifting along the road of life (literally, in this case, the railroad tracks which form a seemingly safe causeway through a treacherous swamp on either side). "He must get to somewhere," but he does not yet know his goal. His innocence has already landed him in the middle of this swamp at night because he had innocently trusted the brakeman on the freight train who said he had "something" for him, a sock in the eye which landed Nick on his hands and knees beside the track. Nick had been given something else, a lesson that sheds another layer of his innocence: "They would never suck him in that way again." But there are many ways of being sucked in, and crossing a bridge he sees a fire up the track, the seemingly freindly fire of campers signalling warmth and food as might the kitchen fire to the soldiers in the first vignette. As a result, Nick is nearly knifed by the punch-drunk battler, Ad Francis, the ex-boxer who took too many beatings. Nick's last sight as he goes on along the railway tracks toward his destination, now at least a town with a specific name, Mancelona, is of "the firelight in the clearing," something he must walk away from not only because it represents an immediate danger to him but also because that way lies madness and denigration from taking too many beatings.

There are echoes of the first vignette in other stories—the drunken camaraderie in "Three Day Blow" and the skiing trip in "Cross Country Snow"—but it is in "Big Two-Hearted River" that the road and fire images are major motifs. Nick, having suffered a physical wound along the road of war, has made his "separate peace" with the war but not yet with life. The physical wounds have nearly healed as he tests his control over his body along the ski trail in "Cross Country Snow," but the psychic wounds of life are not so easily healed because the lacerations of memory keep the wounds festering.[8] In "The End of Something" and "Three Day Blow" Nick survives the loss of first love without too much damage. However, in "Cross Country Snow" Helen is pregnant and they are to go back to the States although neither of them wants this. Nothing else is known about their relationship, whether even they are married, and neither Helen nor the baby is mentioned again (the plight of the uncommunicative German waitress who is heard singing German opera and who is also pregnant is contrasted against Nick's need for male camaraderie). However, because of the inter-relationships and reverberations between the stories of *In Our Time*, the relationship between Luz and the wounded American soldier in the earlier story, "A Very Short Story," parallels what might have happened between Nick and Helen, for in "Big Two-Hearted River" Nick is back in the States very much alone and bearing a psychic wound, so much so that it takes all of his control to keep from entering the treacherous swamp of the past.

In "Big Two-Hearted River," the final and climactic story of the book, the mataphor of time and place as the 'good place" draws into its vortex the accumulated motifs and reverberations of the rest of the book so that the story is not only that toward which the whole has been moving but also that in which the whole is contained. The good place is a physical landscape that must be literally possessed as though it were a tangible object before it can become a symbolic landscape. But it is also a place that exists in time, both past and present, so that the *present* moment in *this* place also contains by associational imagery and motifs the separate moments of past times and places that make up the time-place continuum of in our time from Nick's early youth spent in this same area to the present moment of his manhood. Therefore, Nick's journey to the Big Two-Hearted River is a return to the past, a journey into the self even though he deliberately chokes off memory of the past in order to achieve a rebirth of self in the present.

"The train went on up the track out of sight, around one of the hills of burnt timber": thus, the beginning of "Big Two-Hearted River" (Part I) immediately evokes the journey Nick made at another time and place in "The Battler," reinforced by other images (crossing the railroad bridge, the camp fire, the swamp, and even a reference to eating a ham sandwich) so that Nick's earlier encounter and inability to cope with irrational physical violence (the brakeman and the boxer) is juxtaposed against his present battle to control his mind from irrationality by strict discipline, a control of physical movement within the narrow but rational code of outdoor craft and the mystique of sport. The code is reassuring; the rules are known and will not betray if followed. To break the rules is a betrayal of self first and then of others (like the drunken matador, Luis, in the interchapter of Chapter XIII). It is a code of behavior that allows for honor, courage and self-fulfillment without faking when all other codes have broken down whether in love or in war. Its overtones of male sexuality are definite but not primary whether it be the male camaraderie of men without women in the good place as in "Cross Country Snow" or man alone entering the womb-like tent at night to be reborn the next morning as in "Big Two-Hearted River." Danger lends its sexual excitement to the code, and the epitome of the code's mystique is the bullfight, now that war has proved to be an irrational sport of the politicians without rules and love a biological trap set by women who betray their men as Luz did the American soldier and perhaps Helen did Nick. That is why nearly one-third of the interchapters are devoted to bullfighting in all its aspects—honor and dishonor, grace and gracelessness, courage and cowardice, truth and fakery. To Hemingway bullfighting was not a sport but a tragic drama of three acts symbolizing the struggle between man and the beasts in which death is certain for the bull and always a possibility for the matador. Much depends on the skill and grace of the matador in controlling the irrational fury and force of the wounded bull so that at the climactic moment of truth, as described in Chapter XII, the dual nature of man and beast are

united. Man's rationality has triumphed over the beast's irrationality.

Similarly, though of course in a much less dramatic way,
Nick as the psychically wounded Fisher King must depend on his
skill, that is both mental and physical, to control the wounded
fish struggling madly to free itself from death. It is through such
action that is at once real and symbolic that Nick can achieve the
needed balance and control to hold his own steadily in the
stream of life as the trout do in the river and face the more
dangerous, treacherous cross-currents of the swamp. But before
the Fisher King can be reborn he must be saved, and in our time
one man alone can only save himself. Thus, in the modern waste
land Nick must assume the dual role of knight-questor making
the perilous journey to the good place and the Fisher King who
is reborn. Hemingway's debt to Eliot's "The Waste Land" is
evident particularly in "Big Two-Hearted River," but Eliot's
ultimate appeal is to a religion outside the self whereas for Hemingway the way to salvation lies entirely within the self in relation to a code and a ritual of behavior that is essentially self-
imposed and complete within itself.

"There was no town, nothing but the rails and the burned-
over country. . . . Even the surface had been burned off the
ground." The fire's destructiveness is associated on the macro-
cosmic level with the conflagration of the war which destroyed
the symbolic landmarks of an entire pre-war civilization and on
the microcosmic, personal level more directly with the scars and
wounds of Nick's experiences including the war in which he
makes his "separate peace." But the emphasis in "Big Two-
Hearted River," as it is in Eliot's "The Waste Land," is on fire as
purgation: as Nick "walked along the road" through the fire-
scarred countryside, he "felt happy. He felt he had left everything behind, the need for thinking, the need to write, other
needs. It was all back of him." Hemingway's road out of the
waste land is a secular way as Eliot's is religious. As Nick walks
along the road toward the good place, he leaves behind all the
cares and responsibilities of the immediate past (Helen and the
baby), all the wounds of the past (whether physical as in the war
or psychic as in love), all the other still maimed victims of the
war (the American soldier of "A Very Short Story," Krebs of
"Soldier's Home," Mr. and Mrs. Elliot, the American couple of

"Cat in the Rain," the young couple of "Out of Season"). He leaves his youth behind by returning to the good place, to be reborn into a state of grace by following the purgation and baptismal rites of his secular religion. As he emerges from the womb-like tent the next morning (the beginning of Part II), he is reborn not into a new unknown life but into the old life purged of the evils of the past: the hot sun is good, not the hot, sweaty, dirty sun of the war as he sat against the wall of the old religion wounded in the spine; the camp fire is good, not the potentially dangerous kitchen fire of the first vignette nor the deceptive betrayal of irrational violence at the camp fire in "The Battler." The earth smells good; even the grasshoppers are good and not the blackened scarred grasshoppers of the burned-out area, and the simple, ritualistic act of purification, washing his hands in the stream, excites him.

Water like fire, as in Eliot's "The Waste Land," is the paradoxical element of death and rebirth which is the major theme of *In Our Time*: in "Indian Camp" Nick and his father row across the lake to reach the camp where violent birth and death occur simultaneously; in the second and fifth inter-chapters rain is associated with death (foreshadowing *A Farewell to Arms*) as it is with a dead marriage relationship in "Cat in the Rain." It is the death of first love in "The End of Something," and it is the meaningless malaise of post-war lives in "Out of Season" in which the young gentleman not only illegally seeks to fish out of season but also lacks a basic knowledge of the craft and in the end is totally indifferent to whether he fishes or not, unlike Nick's excitement and professional skill and knowledge of the rituals and rules of his religion. "Fear Death by Water" is the ironic double-edged warning in "The Waste Land" for although one must "die" in order to be reborn (baptized) neither death nor birth is easy, as Nick learns in "Indian Camp." At the end of "Indian Camp" Nick felt quite sure that he would never die even though he has been present in the same room with death. The statement is not a young boy's ignorance of the mortality of flesh but a gut reaction that no matter what happens *he* will not die *that* way, the Indian's way, which is an absolute death without salvation, without rebirth. What Nick comes to learn is that there are many ways to die but only one way to live, being true to one's own code. It is *how* one faces death that matters, not the differing masks death wears. Although the Indian, true to his stereotype, had stoically survived cutting his foot badly with an axe three days before, he had not learned how to survive the sufferings of others.

"Is dying hard, Daddy?"

"No, I think it's pretty easy, Nick. It all depends."

The platiduinous assurance by Nick's father is belied by the rest of the book. The fear of death is often more difficult than the fact itself: it all depends on one's attitude towards death. The fear of death leads the untried soldiers and their officers of the first vignette to become drunk in violation of their code. It drives the fear-ridden soldier of the seventh vignette to hysterical prayer for which he is ashamed. It causes Sam Cardinella (Chapter XV) to lose the last vestige of human dignity and manhood with the failure of his sphincter muscles. It causes Luis the matador to violate his code by getting drunk and thus endangering the lives of the other two matadors, Maera and the narrator (Chapter XIII), and a premonition of death leads to Maera's angry outburst at the end of the vignette: "Yes. We kill them. We kill them all right. Yes. Yes. Yes"—until he "lay still, his head on his arms, his face in the sand. . . . Then he was dead" (Chapter XIV).

One antidote to the fear of death is to treat it as a game, as though it were no more than Nick shooting black squirrels in "The Doctor and the Doctor's Wife": "The first German I saw climbed up over the garden wall. We waited till he got one leg over and then potted him. . . . Then three more came over further down the wall. We shot them. They all came just like that" (Chapter III). Just like shooting clay pigeons, "we potted them from forty yards" (Chapter IV), but the game of death takes a serious turn in the larger strategy of the war when the narrator learns "the flank had gone, and we had to fall back"— retreat and death are a closer reality than hunting games. Nick's near-death in the war (Chapter VI) is no longer a game; he is seriously wounded in the spine so that he has made an involuntary peace (in contrast to Frederick Henry). But if Nick is not dying, there is for him the spectre of another kind of death that haunts Jake Barnes in *The Sun Also Rises*, a physical maiming that would be a living death.[9] For the first time in the vignettes the enemy soldiers are seen as human beings shot dead in the war rather than props in a boyhood game of potting squirrels: "Two Austrian dead lay in the rubble in the shade of the house. Up the street were other dead." Whether the other dead were enemy soldiers, civilians or Allied soldiers does not matter now, and Nick can see them clearly in relation to himself, for he too has faced death.

Death in war, though not a certainty like death in the bull-ring, is an ever-present danger, but what Hemingway attempts to show is that war is but one chapter in the twentieth century book of the dead and that the political and social upheavals caused by the war are part of the same pattern of violence and death-wish of in our time. "They shot the six cabinet ministers at half-past six in the morning against the wall of a hospital" (Chapter V): wartime and post-war revolutionary political upheavals whether of the left or right were part of the same general milieu of violence and death, and Hemingway deliberately connects the execution of these six Greek cabinet ministers in the aftermath of the Greco-Turkish war with the other violent sufferings and death. Like Nick ironically propped up against the sanctuary wall of the church, the ministers are stood against the wall of a hospital, one of them so sick with typhoid he could not stand up and so he is shot "sitting down in the water with his head on his knees." The reverberations of the words "against the wall" connects not only with Nick wounded in the war but with the Indian of "Indian Camp" who, bed-ridden in the upper bunk while his wife screams in the agony of childb-birth, "rolled over against the wall" shortly before he commits suicide. Similarly, Hemingway uses repetition to reinforce the reverberations "It rained hard . . . out in the rain . . . in the water"—thus connecting this scene of death with the other scenes of suffering and death in the rain and foreshadowing Nick's symbolic death and rebirth by water in "Big Two-Hearted River."

When death is so prevalent, life is cheap, and the legalized murder of the two Hungarians by two policemen in the eighth vignette is passed off by one of them as a racist joke. It is a kind of anarchistic execution by the forces of law and order and justified by bigotry. The mass execution by hanging of five criminals in Chapter XV is directly linked to the execution of the Greek ministers in that both are ordered by the state; and thus indirectly the execution of the two Hungarians is linked with both of them because the police in whatever country receive their authority from the state, and the state is supreme over the individual whether it be for political reasons or "law and order."

There are other kinds of death in our time: the living death of post-war malaise as in the non-Nick stories "Soldier's Home," "Mr. and Mrs. Elliot," "Cat in the Rain," and "Out of Season." There is Nick's earlier, pre-war experience of the living dead in that he too has nothing to live for; the two sets of living dead are connected with Nick because he too has taken too many beatings from life and seems to have nothing to live for, and thus could end up like them. Although the climax of the Andersonian story, "My Old Man," is about the accidental death of the father, the emphasis in the story is on the close relationship between the boy Joe (the narrator) and his father, an extension of Nick Adams's relationship with his father. The old man dies in disgrace, and Joe is not even left with the illusion that his father "was one swell guy": "Seems like when they get started they don't leave a guy nothing." Nick as a boy worshipped his father although the reader is made aware from the beginning of the father's incompetence as a doctor, his insensitivity to suffering, his platitudinous pronouncements on life and death, his petty cheating and backing down from a challenging insult by turning it around as pettiness on the other person's part. All this Nick did not see then; but whether or not Nick Adams of *In Our Time* literally sees it as the Nick Adams of the later stories does, and whether the reader is to assume the father (like the Indian in "Indian Camp") committed suicide as revealed in the later Nick Adams story, "Fathers and Sons," is not important. What is important is that regardless of the boy Nick's close relationship with his father, the father is "dead" to the man. The father is never mentioned after "The Three Day Blow." Nick has experienced too much to hold on to the illusions of boyhood. In an echo of the Joycean theme, the son displaces the father, and we see Nick in "Cross Country Snow" about to become a father himself. The legacy of the father lives on in Nick's pleasure in hunting and fishing, but beyond that, nada. Nick must first achieve a wholeness of body and soul within himself before he can cope with the swamp of relationships with others present and past.

"In the swamp fishing was a tragic adventure": it is typical of Hemingway that the complications and complexities of human relationships are rendered in terms of the mystique of sport. But unlike Fitzgerald, to Hemingway the death of first love is like a "three day blow," a blustery agony while it lasts but soon over, not a permanent scar saddening all the young men. Nick breaks off with Marjorie because "it isn't fun any more" not because of any romantic idealism, and it doesn't even spoil the "good place" for him. It is the death of mature love, the slow, gradual death of love between Luz and her American soldier, the death of love between Helen and Nick perhaps under similar circumstances, that Hemingway emphasizes. It is all the deaths of the past that must be purged by the fire, burnt out of the mind, before Nick can step into the water and be reborn.

"He stepped into the stream. It was a shock. His trousers clung tight to his legs. His shoes felt the gravel. The water was a rising cold shock": rebirth is not without its difficulties and dangers—the first trout Nick lands is too small and the second, a big one, gets away—and there is always the swamp. But in the end he achieves success and fulfillment; he is reborn and along the road to recovery of himself: "There were plenty of days coming when he could fish the swamp."

We come full circle in the birth-death-rebirth cycle to the water's edge "On the Quai at Smyrna." Not included in the original edition of *In Our Time*, it was first published in the 1930 edition of *In Our Time* under the title "Author's Introduction," but is now published as an integral part of the book.[10] It is both prologue and epilogue, encompassing the movement of the line of refugees toward the harbor at Smyrna (Chapter II) and the king of Greece under house arrest awaiting execution or release in the final vignette, "L'Envoi": for the suffering is endless, the harbor is no refuge, and even death seems no release. The refugees scream every night at midnight, an old woman dies "absolutely rigid," the harbor is filled with "plenty of nice things floating around in it," babies are born in the midst of all this suffering and death, but the worst "were the women with the dead babies. You couldn't get the women to give up their dead babies. They'd have babies dead for six days. Wouldn't give them up." Birth and death merge into one, but there is no hope of dignity intact: birth, suffering, death are all the same animal function in our time:

> The Greeks were nice chaps too. When they evacuated they had
> had all their baggage animals they couldn't take with them so they
> just broke their forelegs and dumped them into the shallow water.
> All those mules with their forelegs broken pushed over into the
> shallow water. It was all a pleasant business. My word yes a most
> pleasant business.

Only one man alone may survive in such a world if he is reborn a
new Adam(s), alone without woman in Paradise, if he finds a
code of behavior to abide with honor, a code which even gives
the trout (mules) a fighting chance. It is only then that the
treacherous swamp can someday be approached and fished.

Thus also, we come full circle to Hemingway's determination in 1922 to write the truest sentence he knew how, a "true
simple declarative sentence": "You remember the harbor. There
were plenty of nice things floating around in it. . . . There were
plenty of days coming when he could fish the swamp." The
harbor and the swamp—the time and place are different, but the
symbolic landscape is the same, the "bad" place where man's
cruelty to man (and to animals) is the tragic reality of our time.
It is a place that can be avoided only temporarily, for it is the
visual equivalent of society itself, the inescapable reality this side
of paradise. "Like all Greeks he wanted to go to America": a
"true" sentence that ends *In Our Time*; the king, waiting possibly
to be executed, dreams of going to "paradise."[11]   But Nick has
learned that although one cannot escape reality one can choose
one's own time to face it, strengthened by an inner sense of
control and a self-imposed code of behavior.

NOTES

[1] Carlos Baker, *Ernest Hemingway: A Life Story*   (London, Collins,

[2] Charles Fenton, *The Apprenticeship of Ernest Hemingway* (New York, Farrar, Straus and Young, 1958).

[3] Richard Bridgman, *The Colloquial Style in America* (New York, Oxford University Press, 1966), pp. 214-215.

[4] "A Very Short Story" and "The Revolutionist" were included as vignettes in *in our time*.

[5] Clinton S. Burhans, Jr. analyzes *In Our Time* from a different perspective in "The Complex Unity of *In Our Time*," *Modern Fiction Studies*. XIV (Autumn, 1968), pp. 313-328.

[6] This sentence is the *donnée* for the story, "My Old Man," written later in 1922.

[7] Bridgman provides a detailed analysis of Hemingway's various stylistic devices, pp. 195-230.

[8] In "Cross Country Snow" Nick can not telemark because of a war wound; when he spills in the snow "he went over and over in a clashing of skis, feeling like a shot rabbit. . . ." His friend George comes down the hill "one leg forward and bent, the other trailing; his sticks hanging like some insect's thin legs. . . ."

[9] The later Nick Adams stories suggest a mental maiming.

[10] Sherwood Anderson's "The Book of the Grotesque" which opens *Winesburg, Ohio* might well have been the model and justification for adding "On the Quai at Smyrna" to *In Our Time*.

[11] It is significant that Hemingway chose to end *In Our Time* with a "true sentence" in the sense that it refers to an actual incident reported by him in a dispatch to the *Toronto Star Weekly* on December 15, 1923.

False Dawn: A Preliminary Analysis of
The Sun Also Rises' Manuscript

by Michael S. Reynolds

Fifty years ago this month, *The Sun Also Rises* was published, metamorphizing Harold Loeb forever into Robert Cohn. And for fifty years we have treated the novel and its characters as if they were our contemporaries, part of that period we still call the Modern Age. In 1926, Hemingway said of Henry James that he was as historical a figure as Byron or Keats and was dead as he would ever be.[1] It is time we took the same attitude toward the Twenties. *The Sun Also Rises* is as historical as *The Ambassadors*, and the Modern Age is as dead as it will ever be. Memories no longer suffice. The text itself is no longer enough. We must become as demanding and as exact in our scholarship as the materials will allow us.

A colleague of mine observed that there was nothing new to be said about *The Sun Also Rises*. The body of critical work seemed definitive. If I had not been to the Hemingway Collection at the Kennedy Library, I would have agreed with my colleague. But having read in the manuscripts, I knew that the entire literary biography of Ernest Hemingway had yet to be written. Now that Mary Hemingway has opened virtually the whole collection, no serious critic can afford to avoid the manuscripts, for if he does, he will sleep uneasy, wondering what he has missed.

This paper is a preliminary analysis of the first draft of *The Sun Also Rises*. It should also be called partial, a beginning. No thesis was brought to the manuscript to be proven. Past critical evaluations were held in abeyance. I was determined to let the manuscript generate its own conclusions. The results are tentative, to be modified, expanded, or rejected as future study warrants.

The physical description of the manuscript, begun by Professors Mann and Young, is still being completed at the Kennedy Library. My analysis is based primarily on the holograph manuscript which contains thirty-seven loose pages and seven stapled notebooks. I also used three typescript fragments and Hemingway's final typescript which lacks the first ten chapters. The last piece of evidence is an eighth notebook, containing a list of titles and an unpublished forward for the novel.[2]

With a work of fiction, we always see the title first, but it is not always the writer's working title, nor did it always preceed the fiction. On the first page of this manuscript is the working title *Cayetano Ordonez*. Beneath it in quotation marks is "Niño de la Palma," the name under which Ordonez fought in the bull ring. Both names are in the same black ink that Hemingway used through most of the first draft. On August 11, with 121 pages written, he shifted briefly to blue ink. About this time he changed the working title to *Fiesta A Novel*, which appears in blue on the covers of all seven notebooks.

On September 27, 1925, six days after he had finished the first draft, he made a list of five alternative titles gathered from Ecclesiastes and Paul's First Epistle to the Corinthians:

The Sun Also Rises—from the familiar quotation

Rivers to the Sea—Eccles. I, 7: "All the rivers run into the sea; yet the sea is not full."

Two Lie Together—Eccles. IV, 11: "Again, if two lie together, then they have heat; but how can one be warm alone."

A quotation from Eccles. I, 18, with no title indicated: "For in much wisdom is much grief and he that increases knowledge increaseth sorrow."

The Old Leaven—I Cor. 1-7: "It is reported commonly that there is fornication among you. . . . Know yet not that a little leaven leaventh the whole lump? Purge out therefore the old leaven, that ye may make a new lump, as ye are unleavened."

Thematically, these titles encompass mutability, permanence, and union, the cost of knowledge, and the wages of fornication. It is misleading to construct an analysis of *The Sun Also Rises* based primarily on the title, for it did not govern the writing of the story. The title came last, just as Hemingway said it did.[3]

There is one other title to which Hemingway gave serious consideration: "The Lost Generation, A Novel." It appears in the eighth notebook immediately following his title list. Beneath it, he wrote what he labeled "Forward," which was never published. This forward begins with the Gertrude Stein anecdote about the "lost generation" that was to appear later in *A Moveable Feast*. The setting, however, is not Paris, but the provinces. The young mechanic is excellent rather than incompetent. The punch line is the same. The garage owner says about the generation of mechanics who came out of the war years, "They are all a generation *perdu*." His mechanics, he explains, have come of age after the war, and are once again competent.

Hemingway comments:

> I did not hear this story until after I had written this book. I thought of calling it Fiesta but did not want to use a foreign word. Perdu loses a little something by being translated into lost. There is something much more final about perdu. There is only this then to say that this generation that is lost has nothing to do with any younger generation about whose outcome much literary speculation occurred in times past. This is not a question of what kind of mothers will flappers make or where is bobbed hair leading us. For whatever is going to happen to this generation of which I am a part has already happened.
>
> There will be more entanglements, there will be more complications, there will be successes and failure. There will be many new salvations brought forward. . . . But none of it will matter particularly to this generation because of them the things that are given to people to happen have already happened.

In a letter to Max Perkins a year later, he said that he had not taken the Stein epigraph seriously. He had meant to contrast her splendid bombast against the simple statement of Ecclesiastes. It was in this letter that he instructed Perkins to cut the "vanity of vanities" part from Ecclesiastes: That, he felt, would make his point clearer, which was that the earth abideth forever. He told Perkins he had not meant the book to be a hollow or bitter satire, but a tragedy with the earth abiding as the hero.[4]

His after-the-fact statement of intention has been taken seriously, for there is evidence in the book to support it. Yet, only six days after finishing the first draft, he had almost used the Stein quotation as his title. It is always dangerous to take an author's statement of intent as the whole truth. Hemingway said that he did not run guided tours through his work, and I suspect his letter to Perkins may have been triggered by the reviews of the novel. There is no indication that he considered the Stein quote as "bombast" when he wrote the forward.

The forward also makes a comment on Hemingway's relationship with Fitzgerald. The "flappers" and "bobbed hair" refer unmistakeably to the then more established writer. In the first draft, Jake, speaking of his wound, says:

> "What happened to me is supposed to be funny. Scott Fitzgerald told me once it couldn't be treated except as a humorous subject."[5]

In his novel, Hemingway accepted the literary challenge.

By referring in the "Forward" to Fitzgerald's fictions as "literary speculation" which "occurred in times past," he put Fitzgerald prematurely into the museum. Consciously competing with Fitzgerald, Hemingway had read *The Great Gatsby* just a few months before he began *The Sun Also Rises*. *Gatsby* was on his mind in April 1926, when he had finished the revised typescript. He wrote a jesting letter to Fitzgerald assuring him that his novel followed the outline of *Gatsby*, but that it had failed because Hemingway had never lived on Long Island. He said Jake Barnes, like Gatsby, was a Lake Superior salmon fisherman (even though there were no salmon in that lake). Set in Newport, R. I., the novel's heroine was Sophie Irene Loeb who was sentenced to die in the electric chair at Sing Sing for killing her mother. That part, he told Fitzgerald, he got from Dreiser, but practically every thing else in the book was his own or Fitzgerald's. The title, he said, came from Sophie's last words as they turned on the current.

In December of 1926, Hemingway wrote Fitzgerald about the reviews. His tone was once again comical but more biting. The reviewers, he said, could not decide whom he had copied most—Fitzgerald or Michael Arlen. He was grateful to Fitzgerald because he liked him. Besides Arlen was an Armenian whom he did not know and it would be a little premature to be grateful to any Armenian. As a token of his gratitude, Hemingway said he would have Scribner's insert a new subtitle in everything after the eighth printing, which would read:

THE SUN ALSO RISES (LIKE YOUR COCK IF YOU HAVE ONE)

A Greater Gatsby

(Written with the friendship of F. Scott Fitzgerald,
Prophet of the Jazz Age)

The Sun and *Gatsby* both deal with unrequited love. Both focus on pandering and fornication. Fitzgerald said that Jake was like a man in a moral chastity belt. If ever there was a man in a moral chastity belt, it is Jay Gatsby.

Having announced the end of his apprenticeship with Sherwood Anderson in *Torrents of Spring*, Hemingway was serving Fitzgerald notice of a challenge to imminence. The vaguely romantic sentimentality of Nick Carraway was no longer visible. There were no more heroes, only survivors. Fitzgerald's recognition of the challenge entered into his critique of both *The Sun Also Rises* and *A Farewell to Arms*.

Still, Fitzgerald contributed to the final shape of the novel. He was responsible for Hemingway's deleting the opening galleys. He was also responsible for a cut in the dedication. Hemingway intended to dedicate the novel to his son as a "collection of instructive anecdotes." Fitzgerald said no. Hemingway explained that the novel was so obviously not a collection of instructive anecdotes and was such a sad story, not one for a child to read, that he had thought it pleasant to dedicate it in this way, but he would take the advice. The reasons for dedicating it to his son, he said, would be obvious.[6] Hemingway's separation and divorce from Hadley, which took place between first draft and publication, is one of the more obvious reasons. The profits from *The Sun* became Hadley's support money. Hemingway made nothing from the novel.

The holograph manuscript is instructive for what it does not contain. The two epigraphs in the published version appeared only after the draft was finished. The manuscript does not divide the action into three books. Nor does the three-book division appear in Hemingway's typescript. Without access to the galleys, conclusions are tentative. In *A Farewell to Arms*, however, Max Perkins made the five book division just before the novel went to press.[7]   More than likely it was Perkins who divided *The Sun*. There is indication that Hemingway used the three-part structure of the bull fight as a model for the novel. While the divisions are structurally sound, they do not represent the author's intention while writing the book.

In the holograph there is a confusion of names. In the opening chapter, they are all real: Ernest, Hadley, Duff, Loeb, Pat, Don, Quintana and Niño de la Palma. Not until the second chapter did Hemingway begin to fictionalize the summer of Twenty-Five. Hadley disappears. Ernest becomes first Rafael, then Jacob. Duff stays Duff to the very end, changing to Brett in revision. Pat Gutherie appears variously as Pat Campbell, Michael Gordon, and finally Mike Campbell. Harold Loeb becomes Gerald Loeb, Gerald Cohn, Robert Cohn. Niño de la Palma changes to Guerrita. He does not become Pedro Romero until the revision stage. So much has been written on the biographical prototypes that I will not rehash it here. Suffice to say that names were a problem. They continued to be a problem through galley revisions where Hemingway acquiesed to Perkins by dropping reference to Henry James and Joseph Hergescheimer.[8] Hemingway told Perkins that it had been a mistake to put real people in a book, one that he hoped he would never make again.[9]

One point the manuscript makes no clearer is the nature of Jake Barnes' wound. Undergoing few revisions, Jake's condition remained ambiguous from first draft to final copy. The deleted portions of the holograph add nothing. In the George Plimpton interview, Hemingway insisted that Jake was not emasculated in the manner of a steer.[10] But Hemingway may have been over-reacting to Philip Young's analysis of the novel. One phrase, added in the typescript, identifies Jake as a WWI pilot who was wounded while "flying on a joke front like the Italian." As I have suggested elsewhere, the source for Jake's problem may have been a Navy pilot Hemingway had known in the Milan hospital, 1918.[11]

Despite substantial revisions in certain passages and the massive deletions from the opening chapters, the holograph manuscript is remarkably smooth. A large portion of it went straight to print with few, if any, revisions. In *Hemingway's First War*, I have proposed an elaborate scheme of daily recopying to account for the smoothness of the *A Farewell to Arms* manuscript. Hemingway would have been amused. After reading *The Sun*'s holograph, I reject my earlier explanation. When the young Hemingway was writing well, much of his draft needed no revision. When it went badly, he tended to take out whole paragraphs and whole pages, sometimes as soon as he had written them.

Some of the deleted material was removed not because it was poorly written, but because it seemed irrelevant to the main story. Hemingway, who saved everything, later used some of the Paris material in *A Moveable Feast*. The anecdote of Ford Madox Ford mistaking Alstaire Crowley for Hillaire Belloc is the most prominent example. Two other Ford anecdotes were cut, never to reappear.

Hemingway also deleted several passages where Jake tries to explain his relationship with Brett Ashley. As narrator, Jake realizes that the reader may find it difficult to believe their hopelessly unrequited love, or that there can be friendship without fornication. One deleted passage gives more background on Jake's recovery in the British hospital where he met Brett. At two other points he insists that he has made a fine life for himself without women. He realizes that his explanations have not made Brett any more understandable. Finally he says:

> As for how Brett Ashley felt and how things that happened to her affected her, I am not a psychologist, I only put down what she did and what she said. You will have to figure that out by yourselves. (VI, 56)

Much of this cut material is laconic, slightly self-pitying, an emotion that Jake, himself, realizes he cannot afford.

In the first draft there is a reference to Turgeniev, vestiges of which appear in the novel. In Pamplona when Jake cannot sleep, he reads from *A Sportsman's Sketches*. This reference has not received much attention from critics, but its presence is not accidental. Between October 1925 and January 1926—the period between the completion of the first draft and the beginning of the revised typescript—Hemingway read Turgeniev's *Lear of the Steppes, A Sportsman's Sketches, Torrents of Spring, House of Gentle Folk* and *Fathers and Children*.[12] On December 15, 1925, he recommended *Fathers and Children* to Fitzgerald. It was not the best of Turgeniev, he said, but it had some swell stuff in it. A writer should learn from everybody who had ever written if they had something to teach. The trouble with most writers was they only learned certain concrete ideas from the classics which were only important as discoveries. If you only got your ideas from other writers, he told Fitzgerald, it was like rediscovering the law of gravity. In a note to himself, he wrote: "Education consists in finding sources obscure enough to imitate so they they will be perfectly safe."[13] Years later he told George Plimpton: "I used to try to write better than certain dead writers of whose value I was certain."[14]

Philip Young has suggested that Hemingway was impressed by Turgeniev's brevity, simplicity and intensity.[15] Further study of *The Sun Also Rises* may show that the Russian's influence goes beyond style. Hemingway's crash reading course may have had a deeper purpose. If he was competing with Turgeniev, he may have been evaluating his opponent. One suspects that the Russian's influences will be found in Hemingway's tone, attitude, and handling of theme. It may be instructive to examine Hemingway's deletions in light of his reading.

Scholars and critics labor under a handicap when they reconstruct an author's purpose, for they are apt to impose their own methods on the author. Hemingway, for example, did not organize his material in the Fitzgerald manner, no matter how much we would like for him to have done so. To suppose that he did in his first two novels is misleading. Hemingway did not plot *The Sun Also Rises* until he was well into the story, and then not carefully.

The opening holograph chapter covers the first day of the Pamplona fiesta. The first nine pages of the second chapter are a false start, giving the background of the principal characters. Crossing out most of it, Hemingway began the revised Chapter Two: "To understand what happened in Pamplona you must understand the quarter in Paris" (I, 10). He intended to begin the novel in Pamplona, flash back to Paris, and cycle the action gradually back to the opening day of the fiesta—a traditional *in media res* structure. His intention held through the entire first draft. When he had finished what is now the Paris section of the novel, he made a brief outline that he generally followed:

Chapter XIII	finishes work. Gerald not going
Chapter XIV	ride to Burgette—fishing, return to Pamplona
Chapter XV	Duff, Gerald, and Mike thru the party at the wine shop. Mike's first outburst.
Chapter XVI	Encieno, first corrida brings back to point where book starts; goes on with that night—the South American—the dancing place. Noel Murphy. Count shows up. Gerald fights with Niño.
Chapter XVII	Duff sleeps with Nino.
Chapter XVIII	Corrida. Duff goes off with Niño. Count refuses Mike a job. Bill goes to Paris. Mike talks, goes Saint Jean de Luz to wait for Duff. Gerald talks, goes to San Sebastian afterwards [to] Paris. I go down into Spain to bring Duff back. Get her letter.

Noel Murphy and Count Mippipopolous did not show up for the fiesta, but the rest is familiar. Like Rinaldi and the priest in *A Farewell to Arms*, the Count is one of Hemingway's fascinating characters who disappears, victim of the unplotted novel.

When Hemingway began his typed revision, he tried three times to open the novel in Pamplona. He tried once in the first person point of view. Twice he tried shifting into a third person, but the attempt was stiff and awkward. Each time he broke off the draft after a few pages. Finally he abandoned his opening chapter, beginning the typed draft: "This is a novel about a lady."[16] For the next fifteen pages, he filled in the biography and relationships of Duff, Mike and Jake. On Fitzgerald's advice, Hemingway cut this from the novel in the galley stage. It is not until page sixteen of the typescript that the familiar words appear: "Robert Cohn was once middle weight boxing champion of Princeton."

These same words appear on page forty-nine of the holograph manuscript. Hemingway solved his difficulties with the opening chapter simply by truncating the novel. He did the same thing at the beginning of "Indian Camp," at the end of "Big Two-Hearted River," and at the end of *A Farewell to Arms*. The structural difficulties that critics have had with the novel reflect the difficulties of the author. Had Hemingway followed his original intention, our exegetical interpretations of structure would never have been devised.

If his opening gave him difficulty, the conclusion was right on the money. The printed version ends exactly as the holograph. Only the final line was revised. It began:

> "It's nice as hell to think so."

to:

> "Isn't it nice to think so."

and finally to:

> "Isn't it pretty to think so."

The ending is tight and understated, but it concludes a story that Hemingway did not intend to tell when he began the manuscript. Early in the first notebook there is a deleted authorial comment on structure:

> In life people are not conscious of these special moments that
> novelists build their whole structures on. That is most people are

not. That surely has nothing to do with the story but you can not tell until you finish it because none of the significant things are going to have any literary signs marking them. You have to figure them out by yourself. (MS. I, 9)

This scaffolding points directly to Henry James. Carlos Baker has already suggested the main similarities of technique and theme between the two dissimilar writers.[17] I suggest that the inception of *The Sun Also Rises* came from just such a Jamesian "special moment."

That moment is found in the first fourteen pages of the holograph. In the hotel on the first day of the fiesta, Ernest and Quintana discuss the need for protecting the promising young bullfighter from predatory women. Immediately afterwards, Ernest introduces Duff to Niño de la Palma, and Pat tells Niño that the bulls have no balls. While they are drinking, Quintana enters the room:

He started to smile at me when he saw Niño with a big glass of cognac in his hand, sitting laughing, between me and two women, one with bare shoulders and a table full of drunks. He did not even nod. All of a sudden I realized how funny it was. (MS. I, 27)

The scene is familiar for it appears in Chapter Sixteen of the novel. Although he cut the first forty-nine pages of manuscript, Hemingway saved this scene for it was the core of his story. When he revised the passage, he understood, as Jake understands, that nothing about the scene was funny, and he cut the last line of the paragraph.

Here, finally, is the exciting force that raises the important questions in the novel: Will the woman corrupt the bullfighter? What role will the narrator play in this possible corruption? Traditionally this moment should have occurred early in the novel. It would have had Hemingway stuck to his original plan. To this point in the novel the sustaining question has been: Who will sleep with Brett? The answer has been *everyone*. All that has taken place has been, in effect, the introduction which traditional novelists dispose of in the first chapter. Hemingway knew what he was doing. In a deleted comment he said:

> Probably any amount of this does not seem to have anything to
> do with the story and perhaps it has not. I am sick of these ones
> with their clear restrained writing and I am going to try to get in
> the whole business and to do that there has to be things that seem
> as though they had nothing to do with it just as in life. (MS. I, 9)

Hemingway is closer to the critical theory of Howells and James
than we have suspected. In *The Sun Also Rises*, he was more
interested in character development than in plot.

The biographical exegetes have underestimated the importance of Cayetano Ordonez, the bullfighter, Niño de la Palma.
His two names were the first words Hemingway set to paper
when he began the draft. The bar scene, which is the germ of the
novel, focuses directly on him. I suggest that Hemingway's initial
impulse was to write a novel about the corruption of Niño de la
Palma, possibly ending with his death or public humiliation.

This hypothesis is supported by substantial internal and external evidence. First, we must realize that Pedro Romero is the
idealized bullfighter whose classic style had been long awaited to
save the bullring from its decadence. Had Hemingway modeled
his matador completely on Niño, he would have told a different
story. In *Death in the Afternoon*, he described Niño's disastrous
career:

> Cayetano Ordonez, Niño de la Palma, could manage the muleta
> perfectly with either hand, was a beautiful performer with a great
> artistic and dramatic sense of a faena, but he was never the same
> after he found the bulls carried terms in hospital, inevitable, and
> death, perhaps, in their horns as well as five thousand peseta notes
> between their withers. . . . Courage comes such a short distance;
> from the heart to the hand; but when it goes no one knows how far
> away it goes; in a hemorrhage, perhaps, or into a woman . . . some-
> times one woman takes away and another gives it back. (DIA,
> p. 87)

Pedro Romero resembles Niño only in his skills, not in Niño's
loss of courage. Pedro loses courage neither to a woman nor to a
wounding, if we are to believe Brett.

One might argue that when Hemingway wrote the book, he

did not know how badly Niño would fail. But the composition of *The Sun Also Rises* took place while Ernest and Hadley were following the bullfights of the post-Pamplona summer. They saw Niño fight more than once. Shortly after revising the novel, Hemingway wrote an unpublished feature story that catalogued Niño's failure as he had observed it during the 1925 season:

> Niño de la Palma who seemed such a beautiful bull fighter decomposed altogether when he had a bad bull . . . if the bull did not want to charge he knew no way to make him. There is one sovereign way to make a bull charge and that is to get close enough to him. But if you approach within a certain distance you will be caught absolutely if you do not know exactly what the bull will do. Niño had not learned . . . his nerve went absolutely to pieces. He went through his seventy-eight corridas, killed one hundred and fifty-seven bulls and was never wounded once. But he did it at the cost of panics, scandals, and being protected by the police from the crowd. . . . Niño de la Palma was last year's hope for a great bull fighter.[18]

What Niño de la Palma proved incapable of doing, Pedro Romero does perfectly. In the last *corrida*, Romero's first bull will not charge the cape.

> Romero had to make the bull consent with his body. He had to get so close that the bull saw his body, and would start for it, and then shift the bull's charge to the flannel and finish out the pass in the classic manner. (SAR, p. 217)

In contrast to the decadent Belmonte, the only name in the book unchanged, Romero is the classic bullfighter. In changing the name from Niño to Pedro Romero, Hemingway changed the character.

A number of curious holograph passages are cut in the typescript. For example, a slightly misquoted couplet from Marvel's "To His Coy Mistress" appears on a loose page preceding the opening chapter and again on the cover of the fourth notebook:

> The grave's a fine and secret place
> But none I think do there embrace.

As no one in the novel goes to his grave, one wonders why Hemingway retained the quote as a possible epigraph almost to the galley stage. If the novel had focused on the corruption and death of the bullfighter, such an epigraph would have been both ironic and appropriate.

In the first version of Chapter Two, there is a long anecdote about death which focuses finally on Niño. The narrator tells how there were certain things his mother would rather see him in his grave than do. As a young boy at his uncle's funeral, he discovered the meaning of "in his grave," and the shock of recognition was permanent:

> It seemed strange that anything I could do would make her wish to see me in that condition and it prejudiced me against all her views and moral values. (MS. I, 8)

He continues, bringing the point of the anecdote home:

> So I will not judge the gang who were at Pamplona and I will not say that it would be better for Niño de la Palma to be in his grave than to train with a crowd like that because if he did train with them he would be in his grave soon enough and no matter how attractive a grave may seem to old people or to heroes or as an alternative to sin to religious mothers it is no place for a nineteen year old kid. (MS. I, 8)

This emphasis on death makes sense only if one of the characters in the novel were to die. In the sixth notebook, by which time Niño's name had been changed to Guerrita, a seemingly gratuitous aside is cut:

> This is not a story about bull fighting. There is not any big final bull fight scene. Guerrita does not get killed. Nobody gets killed. (MS. VI, 10)

Cancelling these lines as soon as he wrote them, Hemingway then relates the final corrida, including a detailed description of Guerrita's two bulls. The assurance that the bullfighter was not going to die was, perhaps, a vestige of the story he had intended to write.

Eliminated, along with the Paris background, is an early passage which bears on the problem:

> Now you can see. I looked as though I were trying to get to be the hero of this story. But that is all wrong. Gerald Cohn is the hero. When I bring myself in it is only to clear up something. Or maybe Duff is the hero or Niño de la Palma. He never really had a chance to be the hero. Or maybe there is not any hero at all. Maybe a story is better without any hero. (MS. II, 7)

Niño could not be the hero. He never had a chance because he could not sustain his performance. To perform well once is not enough. A hero must be able to do it well each time he goes into the ring, even under the worse circumstances. Hemingway knew that Niño de la Palma was incapable of sustained excellence. To replace him, he created Pedro Romero, who sustains his performance well under pressure.

By the time the first draft circled back to Pamplona, Niño de la Palma's name had been changed to Guerrita. In a passage deleted from the fifth notebook, Jake says:

> The story is Guerrita. For a time Guerrita is the hero. Mr. Gerald Cohn is not the hero. He was the hero for a time but he has been chopped. (MS. V, 15)

Rafael Guerra, who fought under the name Guerrita, was a well known torrero whose first professional appearance was on September 27, 1887. Although he was alive in 1925, Guerrita had retired from the bullring. Hemingway had never seen him fight. In *Death in the Afternoon*, Hemingway wrote:

> When in the accounts we come to Guerrita, another golden-age hero, who corresponds to the period just before, during and after the Spanish-American war you read that the bulls were small and young again; . . . finally Guerrita retires and every one is relieved; they have had enough of him, although once the great Guerrita is gone bullfighting is in a profound depression. (DIA, p. 240)

The name Guerrita is used throughout the final three notebooks of the first draft. It does not become Pedro Romero until Hemingway's revised typescript.

Romero was an even more historical figure than Guerrita. In *Death in the Afternoon*, Hemingway said:

> According to historians Pedro Romero, who was a matador in Spain at the time of the American revolution, killed five thousand six hundred bulls recibiendo between the years 1771 and 1779 and lived to die in bed at the age of ninety-five. If this is true we live in a very decadent time indeed when it is an event to see a matador even attempt to receive a bull. (DIA, p. 239)

Hemingway associates the slightly decadent Guerrita with the Spanish-American War, a slightly decadent war. Pedro Romero, the purist, is linked with the American Revolution. These political associations do not appear in the novel, but the decline and corruption of the bullfight becomes a metaphor describing our time. Belmonte, who was once great but decadent, comes out of retirement with only his decadence and his contempt for the crowd. At the bullfights, we can see what a falling off has occurred because we have Pedro Romero for comparison. He becomes the standard of measurement that Niño de la Palma was not.

Hemingway changed all of the names from his first draft. That he changed Niño's is not in itself significant. But by changing his name to progressively more historical, more classical, and less corrupt bullfighters, Hemingway also changed the moral fiber of his character. The extent of this change can be measured in a deleted scene from the opening pages of the first draft. In Pamplona, Ernest is awakened:

> At six our door was banged open and three men came in carrying a fourth, his legs hanging. I woke as the door opened and my first thought was that I must have overslept and missed the morning amateur fight and someone was being brought in wounded. Then one of the men said, "It's not here," and they went out. As they turned I couldn't see the face of the man they were carrying. But it looked like it was Niño. Anyway they put him in Number Eight. (MS. 5-6)

Although most of the opening chapter was recycled in the typescript, this scene was eliminated, for it carries the seeds of Niño's corruption, which Hemingway had decided not to portray.

Pedro Romero becomes the only idealized figure in the novel, but he is still not the central character, nor is he the hero, as Hemingway emphasized in his deleted asides and in his correspondence with Perkins. After the fact, he suggested that the earth was the abiding hero of the novel, but it is not the Spanish earth that is clearly in focus at the novel's end—it is Jake Barnes and Brett Ashley. In his other fiction from the period, Hemingway always left his readers looking directly at his central concern without always telling them what they were seeing. It took readers several years to read some of his stories properly, to understand what had been left out.

Buried in the first draft of the Burguete section there is an exemplum of the principle. After fishing Jake relaxes by reading a collection of A. E. W. Mason mystery stories. All we are told in the printed version is:

> I was reading a wonderful story about a man who had been frozen in the Alps and then fallen into a glacier and disappeared, and his bride was going to wait twenty-four years exactly for his body to come out of the moraine, while her true love waited too, and they were still waiting when Bill came up. (SAR, p. 120)

In the holograph there is a two-page synopsis of the story, some of which appears to be direct quotations. Recovering the frozen husband, the wife's lover chips the ice away from his still youthful face. As the wife watches:

> The airs of heaven beat upon Mark Frobisher, and suddenly his face seemed to quiver and his features to be obscured. Stella uttered a scream of terror, and covered her face with her hands. Just as you thought. But there was something else. While he crumbled a small trifle tinkled on the ice with a metalic sound. I read on about the trifle. The trifle was the point of the whole story. (MS. IV, p. 11)

Even in the holograph Hemingway does not say that the "trifle" was the bullet that had killed the husband twenty-four years earlier. What the wife had thought an accident had been a murder committed by her lover. "The trifle was the point of the whole story."

One might argue that Hemingway cut this passage as being extraneous. But why didn't he cut the entire reference? I suggest that by leaving out even more than Mason left out, Hemingway illustrates his principle of underplaying the most important point of his story. In *Death in the Afternoon* he told us: "If a writer of prose knows enough about what he is writing about he may omit things that he knows and the reader, if the writer is writing truly enough, will have a feeling of those things as strongly as though the writer had stated them" (DIA, p. 192). In "Ten Indians," written immediately after the first draft of *The Sun*, Hemingway does not need to tell us that Nick has had sexual relations with the Indian girl. What is left out of *The Sun Also Rises* is the loss that Jake Barnes suffers.

Critics have long been aware that Jake is the only real loser in the novel. The other wanderers exit no worse off than they began. Brett's self-congratulatory chatter at the end does not deceive either the reader or Jake. She may not have completely corrupted the bullfighter, but she has not been saved by her charity. Jake asks her not to talk about it, not because he admires her action, but because he does not want to think about what happened in Pamplona. He knows he can never go back. By pimping for Brett, he has canceled his membership in the select club of aficionados. Montoya may have once forgiven him his drunken friends, but he will never forgive him for assisting in Pedro Romero's corruption. The novel's most understated passage occurs when Jake pays his hotel bill. He tells us: "Montoya did not come near us" (SAR, p. 228). This, the cruelest line in the book, goes without comment. Here is the "trifle" dropping on the ice. Jake, who started with so few assets, now has even fewer to get him through the night. If the novel "is such a hell of a sad story," as Hemingway said it was, the sadness resides in Jake's loss.[19]

Hemingway's initial intention was to describe the corruption of a promising bullfighter. The novel he wrote is the corruption of Jake Barnes. In that "special moment" in the hotel dining room, both stories are implicit.

This preliminary analysis is a working paper. It does not test all of the critical theorums. It does not begin to examine the textual changes in kind or magnitude. It is merely an example of the difficult work that remains to be done. We have reached the end of one critical era. Another is beginning. It will take at least twenty years to complete the literary biography of Ernest Hemingway. The materials are now available to begin the work. I do not suggest that the manuscripts will disprove our critical heritage. But like Descartes, we must begin by doubting all and thereby confirming or modifying that which we have inherited.

NOTES

[1] EH to Max Perkins, June 5, 1926. (Hemingway-Perkins correspondence is in the Firestone Library, Princeton University.)

[2] All of the manuscript materials are to be found in the Hemingway Collection at the Kennedy Library.

[3] George Plimpton, "The Art of Fiction, XXI: Ernest Hemingway," *Paris Review*, 5 (Spring, 1958), p. 83.

[4] EH to Max Perkins, November 19, 1926.

[5] Ernest Hemingway Collection, Item 194. All parenthetical references will be to items in this collection. The principal manuscripts for *The Sun Also Rises* are contained in Items 193-202.

[6] EH to Fitzgerald, April, 1926 and September, 1926.

[7] Michael Reynolds, *Hemingway's First War* (Princeton University Press, 1976, pp. 53-54.

[8] Reynolds, pp. 17-18.

[9] EH to Max Perkins, August 26, 1926.

[10]*Paris Review*, 5 (Spring, 1958), pp. 76-77.

[11]*Hemingway's First War,*

[12]Sylvia Beach Collection, Firestone Library, Princeton University.

[13]Hemingway Collection, Kennedy Library, Item 489.

[14]"The Art of Fiction," *Paris Review*, p. 81.

[15]Philip Young, *Ernest Hemingway A Reconsideration* (Harcourt Brace, 1966), p. 185.

[16]Hemingway Collection, Item 200, p. 1.

[17]Carlos Baker, *Hemingway, The Writer as Artist*, 4th ed. (Princeton University Press, 1952, 1972), pp. 182-185.

[18]Hemingway Collection, Item 805, pp. 6-7.

[19]EH to Fitzgerald, September, 1926.

Hemingway and Faulkner on the Road to Roncevaux

by H. R. Stoneback

Perhaps the most memorable scenes in Ernest Hemingway's *The Sun Also Rises* take place in the shadow of Roncevaux, or Roncesvalles, Spain. Perhaps the most memorable lines in William Faulkner's *Flags in the Dust* appear at the end of the novel, in the haunting evocation of the "dying fall of horns along the road to Roncevaux." The significance of the Roncevaux interlude in the Hemingway novel, in spite of a great deal of critical attention lavished on the book, seems to have been altogether missed. Similarly, the thrust of the conclusion of the Faulkner novel has been overlooked or misunderstood. It is the business of this paper to consider just what both Hemingway and Faulkner were doing on the road to Roncevaux, to demonstrate the similar allusive use made of Roncevaux by the two writers, and finally to adduce further evidence that Faulkner, as usual, had read his Hemingway carefully.

It seems to be generally agreed that the fishing scenes around Burguete serve to demonstrate that Jake, the wounded hero, is searching urgently for renewal. He is, perhaps, as Malcolm Cowley and Philip Young and many others have pointed out, the Fisher King seeking the redemption of, or fleeing from his post-war Wasteland. That he is lacking T. S. Eliot's "hint of rejuvenation," however, is one of the questions to be reopened here.[1] Most commentators have been content to praise the freshness of these fishing scenes, to congratulate Hemingway for the vivid immediacy with which the mountains and the streams of the magical Pyrenees landscape are rendered, as in the following passage:

> As the bus ground slowly up the road we could see other mountains coming up in the south. Then the road came over the crest, flattened out, and went into a forest. It was a forest of cork oaks,

and the sun came through the trees in patches, and there were cattle grazing back in the trees. We went through the forest and the road came out and turned along a rise of land, and out ahead of us was a rolling green plain, with dark mountains beyond it. These were not like the brown, heat-baked mountains we had left behind. These were wooded and there were clouds coming down from them. The green plain stretched off. It was cut by fences and the white of the road showed through the trunks of a double line of trees that crossed the plain toward the north. As we came to the edge of the rise we saw the red roofs and white house of Burguete ahead strung out on the plain, and away off on the shoulder of the first dark mountain was the gray metal-sheathed roof of the monastery of Roncevalles.

"There's Roncevaux," [Jake] said.[2]

As Emily Stipes Watts has observed, "the entire vista is given life and movement by Hemingway's choice and placement of color . . . an amazing achievement." She notes, too, that "the gray of the monastery is also contrasted to the dark of the mountains; it moves the monastery out from its mountain background."[3] Hemingway has indeed paid keen attention to his Cézanne, as his mastery of color and chiaroscuro in this and other passages makes manifest. Watts, however, is only concerned with the *how* of this passage, not with the *why*. No one, in fact, has bothered to ask why Roncevaux is so strikingly centered here in the reader's line of vision, when, after all, Burguete is closer and is the ostensible destination of the fisherman. Jake, however, does not say "There's Burguete," which is where they are to stay and which is what lies directly in front of them as they clear the rise; he says "There's Roncevaux." Thus it would seem obvious that Hemingway is trying to fix our vision on matters other than their imminent disembarkation from the bus in Burguete. We have, in short, entered a symbolic landscape, a *paysage moralisé*.

But before we give that *paysage* its due, there is one small but crucial piece of concrete business to tend to: when the traveller comes into Burguete on the bus on the road from Pamplona, it is *impossible* to see the monastery of Roncevaux in the distance. It is only necessary to be there, and to look.[4] We have heard a great deal over the years about Hemingway's concern to tell what was truly seen. We have also talked perhaps a a bit too much about his "theory of omission," whereby what is left out makes the reader feel more than he understands. In this case, it would appear, we have in operation what might be called Hemingway's "theory of interpolation." Some readers indeed may have felt a great deal about the action in the area of Burguete, and not understood at all without the interpolation of Roncevaux. Nevertheless, even with this crucial guidepost manipulated and placed conspicuously in our way, we have still missed it.

What, then, is the importance of Roncevaux? It was, of course, the site of one of the great battles of history, where Roland made his stand on August 15, 778, and courageously fought to the last against overwhelming numbers of pagans. After treachery at Saragossa, Charlemagne began his withdrawal to France, by way of Pamplona, where he destroyed the city walls, and then went up to the pass of Roncevaux. It was there that the rearguard under Roland was ambushed and slain to the last man. After several centuries, "La Chanson de Roland" as we have it now appeared, the French national epic which has been "ranked with the first stained-glass window, the first Gothic arch, or the first troubadour lyric as one of those unexplained miracles of the Middle Ages."[5] To imagine that Hemingway would not have known of the deeds of Roland at Roncevaux, indeed to think that he had not read the *Chanson* during his time in Paris or before, is to posit the illiteracy of an extremely literate young novelist. Even if he had not carefully read the *Chanson*, he could have read about it in his friend Ezra Pound's *The Spirit of Romance* or in Henry Adams' *Mont-Saint-Michel & Chartres* to name only two of the familiar and fashionable manifestations of "medievalism" and discussions of the *Chanson* that were current in the early twenties. Pound noted its poetry and dignity, and its "championship of Christianity against Paganism [which] makes it almost as much of Christendom as of France." Adams discussed at length its "directness, simplicity, absence of self-consciousness," and noted Roland's folly as well as his "courage, loyalty and prowess."[6] Roland, then, is type and paradigm for Jacob Barnes who wrestles courageously with the angel of his fate in the country around Roncevaux.

One of the rare commentaries which attempts a minimal reading of this symbolic landscape of Roncevaux has rather badly missed and distorted the point:

> As Jake and Bill *drive* from Pamplona to Burguete, they see high in
> the mountains the *castle* Roncevaux, and suddenly we have two
> worlds superimposed on each other: the *simplicity* of peasant
> Spain and the *elaborate* romance of Roland, whose story is inex-
> tricably connected with the *castle*. So also the novel superimposes
> upon the jaded scenes in Paris and Pamplona the clean, simple
> activity of Burguete and San Sebastian. The first scenes seem to
> partake of death, the second of life; the first are connected with a
> dying order, the second with the *elemental* and *primitive*.[7]

While it may be encouraging to see that explication has recently
advanced to the point of noticing the Roland association, it is
not at all edifying to have both Hemingway's text and history
radically altered in the space of one sentence: clearly, as Jake
and Bill approach Burguete in the bus, what they see is a monastery. There is not now and there never has been a castle at
Roncevaux, just the monastery and the old chapel mentioned in
Hemingway's text. Even more disconcerting than the egregious
textual misreading here are the larger implications of the passage. The fantastical contrast of the "jaded" and "dying" worlds
of Paris and Pamplona with the "elemental" and "primitive"
worlds of Burguete and San Sebastian does not exist in Hemingway's text. The action and the behavior in all of these places is
indeed complicated, and governed by the sense of ritual and discipline which enables the primary characters, some of them, and
the readers of the novel, some of them, to acknowledge and begin to deal with that complexity. The religious fiesta of San
Fermin is of course concerned with "dying" and death, but it is
most concerned with life and grace.

It comes quite naturally to speak of the novel as quest: it
deals straightforwardly with characters who are "lost," who are
seeking to "know the values," as Count Mippipopolous puts it
(p. 60). Yet it is more than just the deep form, or the general
thrust of the book which suggests a quest, a desperate crusade to
find values, to find action and behavior that will signify. The
very structure of the novel, to the minutest detail, is that of
quest, or pilgrimage. Philip Young was perhaps one of the first
to note that the structure of this apparently informal novel,
when considered closely, is a matter of "scrupulous and satisfy-

ing orchestration." He fails, however, to examine that very structure which he notes and ultimately concludes that it is all "motion which goes no place."[8] We have perhaps been to different symphonies, to different countries. Indeed motion is the main business of the novel—motion with a precisely calculated destination and resolution.

The first chapter of the novel has Jake and Robert Cohn in Paris discussing, significantly, which of the engagingly medieval cities of Strasbourg, Bruges and Senlis they should visit the next day. The second chapter presents Jake and Cohn discussing motion again, in more ultimate terms. Cohn is sick of Paris and wants to run away to South America. Jake advises him: "Listen, Robert, going to another country doesn't make any difference. I've tried all that. You can't get away from yourself by moving from one place to another . . . Why don't you start living your life in Paris?" (p. 11). Chapter three continues the discussion of Paris: Georgette does not like it, and Robert Prentiss, the rising new novelist, seems bored by it:

> "Do you find Paris amusing?" . . .
>
> "For God's sake," [Jake] said, "yes. Don't you?" (p. 21).

Thus, in the early chapters, the nature of one's response to place is established as an important touchstone.

Relationships and behavior are delineated in chapters four, five, and six, but as if in response to the negative remarks about Paris made in the first three chapters by Cohn, Georgette and others, we are shown much of the magic of Paris in the descriptions of Jake's taxi rides and morning walks. By chapter six, the landscape begins to take on thematic complexity:

> The river looked nice. It was always pleasant crossing bridges in Paris . . . The Boulevard Raspail always made dull riding. It was like a certain stretch on the PLM between Fontainbleau and Montereau that always made me feel bored and dead and dull until it was over. I suppose it is some association of ideas that makes those dead places in a journey. There are other streets in Paris as ugly as the Boulevard Raspail. It is a street I do not mind walking down at all. But I cannot stand to ride along it. Perhaps I had

read something about it once. That was the way Robert Cohn was
about all of Paris. I wondered where Cohn got that incapacity to
enjoy Paris. Possibly from Mencken. Mencken hates Paris, I believe. So many young men get their likes and dislikes from Mencken (pp. 41-42).

Jake's impatience with Cohn's "literary" dislike for Paris is
underlined at the end of chapter six in the scene where Frances
Clyne devastates Cohn, with his precious "all for literature"
sacrifices:

> I know the real reason why Robert won't marry me, Jake. It's just
> come to me. They've sent it to me in a vision in the Cafe Select.
> Isn't it mystic? Some day they'll put a tablet up. Like at Lourdes
> (p. 51).

Frances Clyne's ironic allusion to Lourdes, the most popular of
all modern pilgrimage sites, ties in neatly with the already well-
established theme of Cohn's "romantic" but directionless de-
sires to travel. Jake, who knows that you "can't get away from
yourself by moving from one place to another," is well aware
that precision and care and purpose are necessary in journeys as
in everything else. As Book I concludes, then, we find the well-
travelled Count alluding to the "secret," that one must get to
"know the values." That is precisely the business of Jake's impending journey to Burguete and Pamplona, which we hear about
in some detail for the first time as Book II begins. When Bill
Gorton returns from Vienna, they plan to "leave for Spain to get
in some fishing and go to the fiesta in Pamplona" (p. 70).

Soon after Bill gets back to Paris, and before they leave for
Spain, they go to the Ile Saint Louis to eat, after which Hemingway gives a rather long, detailed description of their walking
route from Ile to the cafe in Montparnasse. Professor Carlos
Baker has discussed that walk:

> Sometimes, especially in the early work, the facts seem too many
> for the effect apparently intended, though even here the reader
> should be on guard against misconstruing the intention of a given
> passage. It is hard to discover, never-the-less, what purpose beyond
> the establishment of the sense of place is served by Barnes's com-
> plete itinerary of his walk with Bill Gorton through the streets of

> Paris . . . The walk fills only two pages. Yet it seems much longer and does not further the action appreciably except to provide Jake and Bill with healthy after-dinner exercise . . . To the native Parisian, or foreigner who knows the city, the pleasure in the after-dinner itinerary would consist in the happy shock of recognition. For others, the inclusion of so many of the facts of municipal or gastronomic geography—so many more than are justified by their dramatic purpose—may seem excessive.[9]

It may be hard to discover the purpose of this detailed itinerary, yet, far from constituting excess in the service of a sense of place, it is at the very center of the novel's concerns. In the first place, it speaks directly to the theme so carefully developed in the preceding chapters concerning Paris and Cohn's dislike of it. In the pleasure that Jake and Bill take in the walk we have an adumbration of the similar pleasure they will take in the Spanish landscape, again something which Cohn will miss. But far more important than this are the actual details of this itinerary and what they suggest. When they left the Ile Saint Louis they

> . . . stopped on the bridge and looked down the river at Notre Dame. Standing on the bridge the island looked dark, the houses were high against the sky, and the trees were shadows.
>
> "It's pretty grand," Bill said. "God, I love to get back."

They continue up the Rue du Cardinal Lemoine, then, and through the Place Contrescarpe:

> We came onto the Rue du Pot de Fer and followed it along until it brought us to the rigid north and south of the Rue Saint Jacques and then walked south, past Val de Grace, set back behind the courtyard and the iron fence, to the Boulevard du Port Royal (pp. 77-78).

Hemingway's topography is for the most part very precise here, and very pointed. What he calls the "rigid north and south" of the rue Saint Jacques does indeed pass the Val de Grace, a former monastery converted to a military hospital, with its famous church and dome and remarkable complex of buildings. Thus both the monastery of Roncevaux, in another valley of grace, and Jake's war wound are suggested. The rue Saint-

Jacques continues through the Port Royal district with its many
associations with Pascal, another 'wounded' quester, paradoxical
man of the courts and the monastery (who died at no. 67 rue du
Cardinal-Lemoine, also on Jake's itinerary). But by no stretch of
imagination is the rue Saint-Jacques a "rigid north and south"
here. In fact, as anyone who has walked it might remember, it
bends and narrows just before Val de Grace. In comparison,
moreover, with the neighboring broad straight boulevards cut
through this medieval section in the 19th century, the 13th century rue Saint-Jacques has many bends and inclinations. Again,
we seem to have the "theory of interpolation" in operation,
hand-in hand with the "theory of omission." What does Hemingway, usually the master of topographical precision, have in mind?
I believe he is thinking of the crucial historical importance of the
rue Saint-Jacques as the road which led south on the long pilgrimage to Santiago de Compostela, in northwestern Spain.
Santiago was well-known to Hemingway and for someone aware
of the importance of this historical highway as a pilgrammage
route, it might indeed seem, symbolically, a "rigid north and
south." It hardly comes as a surprise, then, to learn that Roncevaux and Pamplona were two important stations on the pilgrimage itinerary to Santiago. Thus, Professor Baker to the
contrary, Jake's after-dinner walk is not mere padding, and it is
not casual fact that it begins in the shadow of Notre Dame, on
the Ile Saint Louis, with its suggestions of the great crusading
king and saint, and then follows the ancient pilgrimage route to
Spain.

A few pages after this detailed description of the walk,
skillful adumbration of the pilgrimage south, Bill and Jake are on
the train for Bayonne where they encounter seven cars of Americans who have "been on a pilgrimage to Rome" and are now on
their way to Lourdes. Bill's ironic banter—"So, that's what they
are. Pilgrims."—underscores the true nature of Jake's journey
and connects with the earlier pilgrimage allusions. There is a
disparity here that is important to note in the attitude of Bill
and of Jake toward the pilgrims. In response to Bill's mockery,
Jake says nothing (as is usual with Jake and other Hemingway
first-person narrators when they disagree with something another
character says). Jake quietly notices the "pilgrims, with their
priests" filing through the corridor to the dining car. After
Hubert, the 'protestant' non-pilgrim American has conned his

way into getting served he boasts to Bill and Jake:

> "They thought we were snappers, all right . . . It certainly shows
> you the power of the Catholic Church. It's a pity you boys ain't
> Catholics. You could get a meal, then, all right." "I am," [Jake]
> said. "That's what makes me so sore." (pp. 86-87).

Thus the pilgrimage theme has received multiple development by
the time they approach Pamplona, one day and a few pages later.
Jake observes "the plateau of Pamplona rising out of the plain,
and the walls of the city, and the great brown cathedral, and the
broken skyline of the other churches" (pp. 93-94). Jake and Bill
are moved by this prospect of Pamplona and Robert Cohn, who
has joined them in Bayonne, is of course asleep. As so often in
the novel, a church or a cathedral or a monastery holds the
central position in the *paysage moralisé*, and reminds us here that
Jake, at least is aware of the religious nature of the imminent
fiesta.

Jake knows, too, the careful preparation and meditation
necessary to ensure a satisfactory resolution of the pilgrimage.
Thus he goes alone to the cathedral to pray as soon as he and Bill
and Cohn have settled into the hotel:

> I knelt and started to pray and prayed for everybody I thought of,
> Brett and Mike and Bill and Robert Cohn and myself, and all the
> bullfighters, separately for the ones I liked, and lumping all the
> rest, then I prayed for myself again, and while I was praying for
> myself I found I was getting sleepy, so I prayed that the bull-
> fights would be good, and that it would be a fine fiesta, and that
> we would get some fishing.

As his thoughts wander, he feels ashamed, regretting that he is
"such a rotten Catholic," and hoping that it will be better the
next time he prays (p. 97). Unwarranted conclusions are usually
drawn from this passage concerning the failure of prayer and religion in the Wasteland; that is hardly the point here, and could
only seem so in a superficial and bemused view of prayer and
Christianity. The fact that Jake says "there was nothing I could
do about it," for example, is hardly intended to mean that Jake
gives up on religion. It is rather a thoroughly orthodox Au-
gustinian reflection regarding the operation of grace. Jake affirms

here that it is "a grand religion," and hopes that prayer will be better the next time; and indeed he continues to pray, to confess, and to attend Mass throughout the novel. The point remains that of the quest, the pilgrimage undertaken in order to grow in grace.

The quest continues the next day as they go up to Burguete for some fishing before the fiesta begins. Hemingway continues to develop carefully the pilgrimage theme in these two important fishing chapters. In chapter nine, we have the approach to Burguete discussed in some detail above, and the interpolation of the monastery of Roncevaux. Once settled in Burguete, Jake notices the "big, framed steel-engraving of Nuestra Senora de Roncevalles" in his room (p. 109).[10] That night, then, for the first time in the novel, he sleeps well, waking only once. The next day, after some good fishing, Jake and Bill have their long humorous and complicated discussion of William Jennings Bryan, who had just died suddenly in Dayton, Tennessee, in the wake of the famous Scopes trial. The thrust of this rich sequence has entirely escaped the notice of commentators on the novel, and it is indeed so involved that we can only glance at it here.

First of all, the Scopes trial was generally felt to be, at the time, a contest between fundamentalism and modernism.[11] For Jake, as for Hemingway, a recent convert to Catholicism, such a view would certainly seem to oversimplify the question, omitting the possibility, for example, of an orthodox Roman Catholic stance that would find serious fault in the positions taken by both Bryan and Darrow, as with the sensibilities they seemed to represent. Thus in Hemingway's complicated satire, both Bryan the fundamentalist and Mencken the anti-fundamentalist "boob-baiter" take their licks. Indeed, if the irony has a center, if the satire has a norm, it shines dimly through such hilarious dialogue as the following:

> "What's the matter?" [Jake] said. "Didn't you like Bryan?"
>
> "I loved Bryan," said Bill. "We were like brothers."
>
> "Where did you know him?"
>
> "He and Mencken and I all went to Holy Cross together."

"And Frankie Fritsch."

"It's a lie. Frankie Fritsch went to Fordham."

"Well," [Jake] said, "I went to Loyola with Bishop Manning."
(p. 122).

It should be with some trepidation that the explicator approaches this humorous mélange. Yet there is meaning discernible here, and if we bear in mind the dominant concerns of the novel thus far, it becomes clear that his long-neglected passage is more than comic relief. The humor ends suddenly as Bill asks Jake how he feels about Brett and, then, asks him if he is "really a Catholic," which is the underlying business of the entire sequence. Jake's response—"technically"—has usually been misconstrued. Robert W. Lewis, for example, regards this answer as an indication that Jake is a "skeptic."[12] To the contrary, if we consider the sense of the word "technically" in the root sense of pertaining to the careful practice of an art or craft, and if we recall Hemingway's pervasive sense of ritual and his observation that "the only way he could run his life decently was to accept the discipline of the church," it is clear that the word "technically" here means the opposite of what is has generally been taken to mean. Jake Barnes is not a skeptic. Rather, he is a pilgram seeking a deeper participation in grace through the careful practice of ritual and discipline.

That this serious conclusion should wrap up the humorous Bryan sequence is no accident. In fact, Jake's earlier whimsical observation that he went to Loyola with Bishop Manning is resonant with meaning and analogue when considered carefully. Bishop Manning was one of the leaders of the Oxford Movement who finally left the Church of England for the Roman Church over a doctrinal dispute on the question of baptismal regeneration. Insofar as Jake's spiritual progress may be said to parallel Hemingway's (and Manning's), the drift of this is clear. The apparent whimsy, moreover, that places Jake with Manning at Loyola signifies crucially here because, as they fish and talk at Roncevaux, they are not far from the birthplace of St. Ignatius Loyola, the founder of the Society of Jesus. It should by now come as no surprise to discover that it was the leg wound which Loyola received during the siege of Pamplona in 1521 which led

Loyola to give up the life of a soldier, and—after a period of contemplation and pilgrimage—to become as he put it a "soldier of Christ" and the founder of Jesuits. Jake, another wounded soldier, has undertaken his pilgrimage to Pamplona, "the same town where Loyola got his wound that made him think," as Hemingway put it a few years later.[13] This long and complicated chapter at the center of the book is rich with suggestion regarding Jake's role as pilgrim. The rest of the five day fishing interlude at Burguete receives only a paragraph or two of attention, including the description of Harris the Englishman "who had walked over from Saint Jean Pied de Port" (p. 125), which is yet another of the important way stations on the ancient pilgrimage route from Paris to Santiago de Compostela.

The final business in the mountains, before they go into Pamplona for the fiesta, is a visit to the monastery of Roncevaux. After they have gone through it, they discuss it as follows:

> "It's a remarkable place," Harris said, when he came out. "But you know I'm not much on those sort of places."
>
> "Me either," Bill said.
>
> "It's a remarkable place, though," Harris said.
>
> "I wouldn't not have seen it. I'd been intending coming up each day."
>
> "It isn't the same as fishing, though, is it?" Bill asked. He liked Harris.
>
> "I say not."
>
> We are standing in front of the old chapel of the monastery (p. 128).

A careless reading of this passage might suggest that the monastery has little effect on the three men and it has often been read in that fashion. At the most, it might be said that it has little effect on Bill. Harris, however, insists that it is remarkable. Presumably Harris says this from a lively sense of its historical associations with Roland and its importance as a way-station on the pilgrimage route which he has just, in part, traversed. What is perhaps most remarkable about the above conversation is Jake's silence. As is usual, when Jake differs profoundly with or finds egregious folly in another's remarks, he says nothing. One of Jake's basic texts, and Hemingway's, concerning any deep feeling is "You'll lose it if you talk about it" (p. 245). It should also be remarked that Hemingway is careful to mention the "old chapel" which is set apart some distance from the monastery proper and which, according to tradition, is built over the bones of Roland, on the place where he fell.

After the monastery scene and the farewells with Harris, the next significant action is the well-known "aficionado" passage, in which Jake and Montoya seem to share a secret that must not be exposed to "people who would not understand." Jake describes the recognition of this "afficion," this passion among aficionados:

> When they saw that I had aficion, and there was no password, no set questions that could bring it out, rather it was a sort of oral spiritual examination with the questions always a little on the defensive and never apparent, there was this same embarrassed putting the hand on the shoulder, or a "Buen hombre." But nearly always there was the actual touching (p. 132).

The language employed here, as well as the laying on of hands, serve to remind us of the connections between Jake's pilgrimage and the bullfight. It is at this point in the novel that the fishing and the pilgrimage themes converge with the bullfight theme.

For the remainder of Book II, our attention is focused on the fiesta of San Fermin, in particular, the behavior of a group of expatriates and the moral elucidation of that behavior by analogy with the ritual and discipline of the bullfight. This aspect of the novel has perhaps been discussed too much and too little understood, because it has been discussed in a vacuum, that is, without awareness of the overarching frame of spiritual reference. Far from being a pointless sequence of sordid events in the lives of vulgar people, as it has often been viewed, the action during the fiesta represents the coming together and embodiment of the book's several themes.

Before the fiesta began, Jake tells us,

> I went to church a couple of times, once with Brett. She said she
> wanted to hear me go to confession, but I told her that not only
> was it impossible but it was not as interesting as it sounded, and,
> besides, it would be in a language she did not know (pp. 150-151).

On the morning that the fiesta begins, Jake goes to mass again in
the cathedral, and reminds us that "San Fermin is also a religious
festival" (p. 153). Jake then describes the religious procession
going from church to church, with thirty foot figures of San
Fermin, the King and Queen and Moors, and the whirling dancers
behind. Jake and Brett start to follow the procession into the
chapel but Brett is turned away because she is not properly at-
tired. Then she is claimed "as an image to dance around" by
some hard-drinking singers and dancers and, emblematically, the
final movement of the novel is initiated (p. 155). Indeed, Jake,
Mike, Cohn and Romero will spend much of the rest of the book
"dancing" around Brett, until the choreographer of this pagan
ritual finally frees Jake, as well as Romero, from the spell of the
bitch goddess.

At no time, however, does Jake relinquish his role as pilgrim
or indeed as spiritual and aesthetic guide to Brett, his apprentice
and initiate in the mysteries of the bullfight. He helps her to
see that, just like his pilgrimage, the bullfight is something "going
on with a definite end, and [not] a spectacle with unexplained
horrors." He points out that "Romero never made any contor-
tions, always it was straight and pure and natural in line" and that
he "had the old thing, the holding of his purity of line through
the maximum of exposure" (pp. 167-168). Later, the day after
Brett has been with Romero and Cohn's fights with Jake and
Romero, Jake and Brett go into the chapel of San Fermin to pray
for Romero. Brett urges Jake to leave:

> "Never does me any good. I've never gotten anything I prayed for.
> Have you?"

> "Oh, yes."

> "Oh, rot," said Brett. "Maybe it works for some people, though.
> You don't look very religious Jake."

"I'm pretty religious."

"Oh, rot," said Brett. "Don't start proselyting to-day" (p. 209).

Jake is indeed a rather insistent proselytizer, for religion as for the bullfight, through which, in this novel, one may best come to know the "values."

In *Death in the Afternoon*, Hemingway said "the bullfight is very moral to me because I feel fine while it is going on and have a feeling of life and death and mortality and immortality." He stresses the aspects of the bullfight which are "well ordered" and "strongly disciplined by ritual." He points out that the "emotional and spiritual intensity" of the bullfight gives an ecstasy, "that is, while momentary, as profound as any religious ecstasy" (pp. 4, 8, 206-207). Now it has usually seemed reasonably clear to most readers of *The Sun Also Rises* that the bullfight is meant to convey an emblem of moral behavior. For conduct to be moral, then, it must be rooted in courage, honor, passion, and it must exhibit grace under pressure. Much of this is contained in the Spanish notion of "pundonor," which as Hemingway says "means honor, probity, courage, self-respect and pride in one word" (*Death*, p. 91). Measured by these rigorous standards, the behavior of every important character except perhaps Romero is found waiting. Cohn, of course, falls most flagrantly into the sins of *démesure* and gracelessness. But Mike, Brett, and all the others, including Jake, are sinners, too, for as Jake reminds us: "Everybody behaves badly . . . Give them the proper chance" (p. 181). It is Jake, however, who as "proselytizer" for the bullfight and religion is most aware of these failings and most concerned to correct them. It is Jake, in his role as pilgrim, who never forgets that San Fermin is a religious festival, and that the code of behavior figured forth by the bullfight is more fully embodied in the ultimate "grace under pressure" with which the Church is concerned. Thus when we find Jake back with Brett in Madrid, after she has renounced Romero, it is necessary to read with great precision the most memorable passage of the book:

"You know it makes one feel rather good deciding not to be a bitch."

"Yes."

"It's sort of what we have instead of God."

Many readers of the novel have been content to stop there, concluding their discussions with some windy effusion about the "lost generation." But it is crucial, as always, that we read the understated text with the care we would give to a poem. Jake, then, responds to Brett: "Some people have God . . . Quite a lot" (p. 245).

Early in Book II, it should be recalled, Jake prays in the cathedral and regrets that he is such a "rotten catholic." Toward the end of Book II, after Jake has "behaved badly," he tells Brett that he is "pretty religious." At the end of Book II, Jake asserts three times that he feels "like hell" (pp. 222-223). He has, that is, just engaged in a harrowing of hell, necessary to look evil directly in the face, necessary to gain his measure of grace. Here at the end of the novel, after the rather obvious and often noted rebirth and baptismal regeneration scenes of Book III, Jake clearly seems to indicate the next step in the progression: "quite a lot." It is the natural sequence and resolution for a pilgrim who has undertaken the arduous journey, who has fished in the mountains around Roncevaux, who has prayed throughout a religious fiesta, who has acted as guide and proselytizer in matters concerning the bullfight and religion. Perhaps the others get something from the fiesta, learn or attain something, but it is Jake who comes through, finally, with his measure of grace under extreme pressure.

It will simply no longer do to misread the text of this novel in the fashion that has prevailed for some fifty years now. A recent commentator has written that in *The Sun Also Rises*:

> We get the tension between an inability to believe in anything and a longing for the old certainties. Dante was able to believe that in God's will is our peace, but that was a long time ago and the Middle Ages have passed. Jake cannot let himself go to God because, in a sense, he knows too much. Jake is of his time and reflects the difficulty of accepting God in a secular age.[14]

We get nothing of the sort in the book Hemingway has actually written, but this is merely the latest variation of an old familiar theme in Hemingway criticism. It would be a thing well worth doing if in observance of the fiftieth anniversary this year of *The Sun Also Rises* we could forever lay the ghost of such time-honored misreadings of Hemingway. The "inability to believe," it seems, belongs to the commentators in most such cases, since it clearly does not belong to Jake or Hemingway, who believe in a great many things, including the Church and a militant quest for values, not a "longing for old certainties." In fact, the deepest thrust of this novel is radically spiritual, and it is addressed directly to the radically "secular age" (most tellingly reflected in the tone of the preceding passage) which has seemed for the most part incapable of deep engagement with Hemingway's vision. It is now time that we begin to deal with Hemingway's version of the life of the spirit, his prescriptions for burning "the fat off [the] soul," and call a moratorium on the old, weary circular discussions of the "code."[15]   It is time that we address ourselves carefully to Hemingway's texts to discover and elucidate what Lionel Trilling (in *The Liberal Imagination*) called the feeling of *piety* at the center of the work. Jake Barnes participates fully in this *pietas*, and the rue Saint-Jacques and the pilgrimage route to Roncevaux and Pamplona and Compostela may skirt the edge of the abyss, and it may have *nada* for another one of the way-stations, in the twentieth century just as in the twelfth; and a proper pilgrimage still requires a dark night of the soul, and perhaps even a harrowing of hell.   But with courage, with honor, with *pundonor*, with ritual and discipline, the motion does go somewhere.   Indeed as the novel so eloquently tells us, there can be grace under the darkest pressures, in spite of the fact—or because of the fact—that every generation is, to be sure, lost.

Thus far, I have avoided invoking certain biographical information because it is my feeling that the deep *pietas* of this novel flows copiously from the text itself. Yet since it has been missed so often, it might be useful here to call attention to a few crucial matters. Hemingway was, of course, a convert to Roman Catholicism from Protestantism. At the time of the composition of *The Sun Also Rises*, apparently, he attended mass regularly. Shortly after the novel was published he described himself as a "very dumb Catholic," with more faith than intelligence. In fact, he had "so much faith" that he "hated to examine into it," but he was "trying to lead a good life in the Church and was very happy."[16]   It is at this time, on his Italian trip with Guy Hickok just after the publication of *The Sun Also Rises*, that we see Hemingway stopping "at a roadside shrine, where he knelt and prayed for what seemed a long time, returning to the car with tears on his cheeks." All during this trip, the "praying and weeping" continued. (Baker, p. 236). When, in 1927, Hemingway and Pauline spent their honeymoon at Grau du Roi, in southern France, he took particular pleasure in the fact that the canal there had been built by Saint Louis "as a launching place for his thirteenth-century Crusades." They went on then to Santiago de Compostela, whose cathedral was among Hemingway's "favorite things" and which Hemingway thought "the loveliest town in Spain." (p. 239). Earlier, during the composition of *The Sun Also Rises*, he had been thinking of writing a book with the title *A New Slain Knight*, a notion and a title that stayed with him for years and almost attached itself years later to *Across The River and Into the Trees* (p. 215). Even more significantly, some of the composition of *The Sun Also Rises* was accomplished in Chartres, one of Hemingway's favorite cathedral cities. As Baker notes: "In Chartres he toyed with the idea of calling it *The Lost Generation* . . . [but] the chief result of his trip to Chartres was the decision to change the name of his first novel to *The Sun Also Rises*."[17]   In the light of the foregoing discussion, this was a most telling change, accomplished in terrain that signifies. Years later, in 1953, when Hemingway made the trip from Paris, through Chartres, and on south to the Basque country, he "amused himself by imagining that he was a medieval knight riding his horse along the riverbank" (p. 648). Finally, in his last years, as late as 1959, he would revisit the "magical region" around Roncevaux, and dream one more time in what he called "the last great forest of the Middle Ages" (p. 693).

Hemingway the medievalist?   In whatever fashion we respond to such a refreshing query, I suggest that the rubric is at least as illuminating as Hemingway the "tough guy." The above details serve, at any rate, to confirm and reinforce what the text of the novel makes quite clear: that the structure and the deep form of *The Sun Also Rises* is that of pilgrimage and quest. The spirit of the quest, moreover, is imbued with medievalism, if that is a useful term here. We might also describe this spirit so central to Hemingway's work as a scrupulously discriminated romanticism. Whatever the label applied to the matter, the spirit of knighthood and cathedrals and the shrines that were so important to Hemingway in life are at the center of Jake Barnes' sensibility and provide the shaping details, the controlling *pietas* of the novel.

If Pedro Romero's conduct of the bullfight provides the most obvious *exemplum* for Jake and for the reader, the more profound and inclusive *exemplum* is the Church, and quite specifically, the medieval, crusading Church, as suggested by the cluster of Roncevaux-Roland images and allusions. In Chartres, where Hemingway decided on the final title for his novel, and where he knew the cathedral well, he surely would have remarked carefully the young Roland conspicuously present among the saints and martyrs at the South Doorway of the Cathedral, depicted as "the Christian champion, the epitome of thirteenth-century chivalry."[18] Since Santiago de Compostela, the most romantic of medieval pilgrimage centers, was one of his favorite towns, and the cathedral there perhaps his favorite, he was certainly aware that, as one observer puts it, "the enormous popularity of Santiago was due . . . to the spirit of the age. The chansons de geste, which flourished in the eleventh century on the pilgrimage routes to Santiago, fired the imagination with stories of heroes, especially that of Roland."[19] Roland's courage and valor and death while fighting the Moors (San Fermin was also martyred by the Moors) must have been the inspiration for many pilgrimages to Santiago. It was, of course, a heroic, fighting spirit that was at the center of these pilgrimages to Compostela, as it is the center of Hemingway's pilgrimages and pilgrims, from Jake Barnes to Colonel Cantwell, who founds *El Ordine Military, Nobile y Espirituoso*, named in Spanish "since that is the best language for founding orders."[20] Here Hemingway is still remembering Loyola, with his "wound that made him think" received at Pamplona, and the *Regimini Militantis Ecclesiae* which established the Society of Jesus with Loyola as its first general. The highly particularized vision, then, is of the militant, crusading, questing, heroic Christianity of Roncevaux and Compostela, rather than the tepid, modern, petitionary, and meekly visionary Christianity of Lourdes. Thus the point of Hemingway's two ironic allusions to Lourdes in the novel is now clear.[21] It is, finally, what Henry Adams called the "courage, loyalty, and prowess" of Roland that Jake Barnes and Hemingway (and a host of other Hemingway heroes) seek and attain in various measure. And, like Roland, as Adams saw him, the Hemingway hero cares mainly for that courage, heroic spirit, and prowess, and in matters of the spirit, as Hemingway said of himself, he "accepts the discipline of the Church."

All of these concerns, then, medievalism, romance and Roland, Compostela and Roncevaux, precisely appropriated, are central and abiding throughout Hemingway's life and works and they must receive, in the next half century of Hemingway criticism, a great deal of attention. Jake Barnes gets us to Pamplona, more than halfway to Santiago de Compostela. It is perhaps not until the last major work, *The Old Man and The Sea*, that Hemingway takes us all the way to Santiago. But in the words of the Church calendar and Colonel Cantwell and Hemingway's last lyrical reminiscence, the entire canon, the long pilgrimage, consists of moveable feasts.

Right from the beginning, Faulkner read his Hemingway carefully, and served his apprenticeship well. It was in the novel which marked the end of his apprenticeship, *Flags in the Dust*, that Faulkner made his initial bows to Hemingway, to Roncevaux and the spirit of Roland. The last pages of the novel contain this memorable paragraph:

> The music went on in the dusk; the dusk was peopled with ghosts of glamorous and old disastrous things. And if they were just glamorous enough, there would be a Sartoris in them, and then they were sure to be disastrous. Pawns. But the Player and the game He plays—who knows? He must have a name for his pawns, though, but perhaps Sartoris is the name of the game itself—a game outmoded and played with pawns shaped too late and to an old dead pattern, and of which the Player Himself is a little wearied. For there is death in the sound of it, and a glamorous fatality, like silver pennons downrushing at sunset, or a dying fall of horns along the road to Roncevaux.[22]

Cleanth Brooks has called this a "purple passage" but has said nothing else about it. Lawrance Thompson discusses it as Miss Jenny's recapitulation of the Sartorises' "religious romanticism," and urges us to hear "the ambivalent Faulknerian tone, predominantly anti-romantic," in the last sentence of the passage. It would accomplish little here to discuss the "purple"

writing charge, but it might suffice to note that any apprentice
novelist who could so skillfully echo Shakespeare, Eliot, Hemingway and the *Chanson de Roland* in one phrase—"a dying fall of
horns along the road to Roncevaux"—and at the same time accomplish a resonant recapitulation of major motifs and images
recurring throughout the novel can risk, I reckon, a "purple
passage." There is certainly "ambivalence" in Faulkner's tone
here and throughout the novel, but I doubt that it is most accurately or most usefully characterized as "antiromantic." To
the contrary, the deepest thrust of the work resides in the highly
particularized romantic sense with which we are here concerned.
What is important is that this passage sums up the business of the
novel, suggests abiding concerns in Faulkner's work, and echoes
Hemingway's use of Roncevaux a year earlier in *The Sun Also
Rises*.[23]

Flags in the Dust, which Faulkner called the "germ of [his]
apocrypha," is centrally concerned with the Sartoris family, and
especially the courage, pride, and glamorous fatality of the male
Sartorises.[24]   Tales of the family are told and retold until a reck-
less prank becomes in the telling "a gallant and finely tragical
focal-point to which the history of the race had been raised from
out the old miasmic swamps of spiritual sloth by two angels
valiantly and glamorously fallen and strayed, altering the course
of human events and purging the souls of men" (p. 14). One of
the Sartoris ancestors, "that Carolina Bayard," had a

> high-colored face [that] wore that expression of frank and high-
> hearted dulness which you visualize Richard First as wearing be-
> fore he went crusading, and he once hunted his pack of fox hounds
> through a rustic tabernacle in which a Methodist revival was being
> conducted; and thirty minutes later (having caught the fox) he re-
> turned alone and rode his horse into the ensuing indignation
> meeting (p. 14)

This Bayard might serve as an emblem, his act described above
might serve as the blazon on the shield carrying the legend of
Faulkner's, and Hemingway's, juxtaposition of the medieval and
modern Church. This Bayard, whose namesake is obviously the
legendary Chevalier de Bayard, the *"chevalier sans peur et sans
reproche,"* is clearly, as Faulkner calls him, a "paladim out of
romance" (p. 22). When Aunt Jenny speaks of the old days, her

voice is "proud and still as banners in the dust" (p. 23). For the current generation of Bayards, after the experience of World War I, the burden of this "glamorous fatality" is a complicated one, and difficult to bear.

In one of the novel's most highly charged scenes, Old Bayard goes to the attic and opens an old chest that has not been opened since 1901:

> While he struggled with the still lock it seemed to him that a legion of ghosts breathed quietly at his shoulder, and he pictured a double line of them with their arrogant identical faces waiting just beyond a portal and stretching away toward the invisible dais where Something sat waiting the latest arrival among them; thought of them chafing a little and a little bewildered, thought and desire being denied them, in a place, where, immortal, there were no opportunities for vainglorious swashbuckling. Denied that Sartoris heaven in which they could spend eternity dying deaths of needless and magnificent violence while spectators doomed to immortality looked eternally on. The Valhalla which John Sartoris, turning the wine glass in his big, well-shaped hand that night at the supper table, had seen in its chaste and fragile bubble (p. 94).

When Old Bayard gets the trunk open, the most important object he takes out—after the family Bible—is "a Toledo, a blade delicate and fine as the prolonged stroke of a violin bow," which is the "symbol of his race" (p. 95). Toledo, of course, suggests—both the sword and the place—the crusading spirit and the central role of Toledo in the long effort to drive the pagans from the Iberian Peninsula. The next thing Old Bayard withdraws from the trunk is a derringer, "a stubby, evil-looking thing with its three barrels; viciously and coldly utilitarian." He places this between the Toledo and a cavalry sabre, "and between the other two weapons it lay like a cold and deadly insect between two flowers" (p. 95). Faulkner need say no more about the modern weapon, or indeed the modern spirit: any reader of Faulkner knows which of the weapons a Snopes—and it is here that we first meet the Snopeses—would use.

The weight of the chivalric tradition, however, is unbearable and perhaps incomprehensible to young Bayard, who like Jake Barnes has just been through the shattering experience of the

Great War, an experience, as Horace Benbow says, "that pretty well shook the verities and the humanities" (p. 177). Young Bayard, again like Jake, drinks a great deal, has trouble sleeping, and stays in motion. It is hunting rather than fishing which provides his only repose, a momentary grace under pressure. But unlike Jake, he never learns "to dream high enough not to lose the dream in the seeking of it" (p. 75). After Old Bayard's death in the car young Bayard drives too fast, and after a final idyllic hunting interlude with the MacCallums, young Bayard runs off to die in a test flight near Dayton. The last feeble gesture of this ironically diminished and failed knight, with much fear, and much reproach, is to refuse the favor of a woman's garter just before takeoff.

No, Bayard Sartoris the younger is not Jake Barnes, he does not seek and in some measure find grace after the shattering experience of the abyss, after *nada*, after the insufferable wound of the war. But their problem is the same, and the deepest feelings, the *pietas* of the two writers are shared. *Flags in the Dust* is a loose, sprawling novel, and many things are attempted which are not to the question here, but unmistakably the novel tells us that there has been some terrible loss of spirit in the "viciously and coldly utilitarian" modern, mechanized world, far gone in a condition beyond "spiritual sloth." It tells us also that the old courage and recklessness and proud spirit of the Civil War Sartorises, of the medieval knights, the Chevalier de Bayard, Roland, the crusading spirit of romance symbolized by the Toledo blade and Roncevaux, sometimes led to the sin of *démesure*, to headstrong folly, yet it is infinitely preferable to and necessary to combat with the insidious spiritlessness of modernism and Snopesism. In Faulkner, clearly, if we are to find a way to come out the other side of the modern abyss, we must hear the "dying fall of horns along the road to Roncevaux" and, like Jake Barnes and Bayard Sartoris (or later Ratliff and Gavin Stevens), set out on the quest.

Before *The Sun Also Rises* was published, apparently on the basis of *In Our Time* and whatever short stories Faulkner had seen in the little magazines (for example, *The Double Dealer*, where he had been published in the same number as Hemingway), Faulkner felt that "Ernest Hemingway is so far the greatest American fictionist."[25] *The Sun Also Rises*, which Faulkner admired, certainly reinforced this opinion. Faulkner's experience and preoccupations, moreover, from the time of World War I to the time of writing *Flags in the Dust*, prepared Faulkner to find the concerns and the spirit of Hemingway's first novel very congenial indeed—in fact, amazingly close to Faulkner's concerns and spirit. In 1918, for example, Faulkner's ideal was the Chevalier de Bayard. His imagination "was captured by the image" of this French knight "who had fought gallantly for his king in Italy, falling finally before overwhelming numbers." (Blotner, p. 109).

In August, 1925, while Hemingway was in Spain and Paris working on *The Sun Also Rises*, Faulkner was walking through northern Italy, pondering the places where "mailed knights once rode" and writing letters imbued with a tone of awe, at the Milan Cathedral for example, "all covered with gargoyles like dogs, and mitred cardinals and mailed knights and saints pierced with arrows" (Blotner, pp. 448-449). As he travelled through France, viewing with wonder the cathedrals and historical sites, he also came to admire the "heroic" spirit of the French in the present, in the wake of the devastating war. When he settled in Paris in the fall, near the Luxembourg Gardens and the cathedral of Saint-Sulpice (not far from where Hemingway and Pauline would settle a year or so later), he enjoyed especially talking occasionally with an old priest and going to mass at Saint-Sulpice. He sent his mother a post card of Saint-Sulpice which "may have caused some slight disturbance to her Methodist sensibilities. 'Be a good catholic soon,' he wrote" (Blotner, p. 464). How curious, how engaging and paradigmatic (in the several senses of the word) it is to entertain the image of the two greatest American novelists of this century, the ex-Methodist from Mississippi and the ex-Congregationalist from Illinois, as communicants at the same French cathedral within a year or so of each other.[26]

In late 1926, then, probably a month or so after the publication of *The Sun Also Rises*, Faulkner began working on the manuscript that would become *Flags in the Dust*. Significantly, it began with the crucial attic scene with old Bayard Sartoris musing over the family Bible, the Toledo blade and other relics. In a passage finally cut from the novel, Faulkner wrote that the Toledo blade had been brought to Virginia by a Sartoris in the time of Charles I along with "little else save the romantic fatality of his name and the jeweled poniard which Aylmer Sartoris, having followed Henry Plantagenet to Rouen and there met and married the Provencal lady who had borne him the first Bayard Sartoris, had slung about the young hips of that first Bayard Sartoris who carried it to Agincourt . . ." (Blotner, p. 532). Thus, Faulkner's "medievalism," his highly particularized romantic sense, carried him into the beginning of his first important novel, with the genealogy neatly in place for his first heroes and, obliquely, for himself. Such preoccupations together with the reinforcement and echoes picked up from Hemingway set the stage for the "dying fall" of Roland's horn which would in fact reverberate through much of Faulkner's work, most notably in the omnipresent hunting horn. Late in his career, when he was asked if Snopesism would win the battle, Faulkner answered in terms that we might now expect:

> No, the impulse to eradicate Snopes is in my opinion so strong that it selects its champions when the crisis comes. *When the battle comes it always produces a Roland (Faulkner in the Univeristy, p. 34, emphasis added).*

The battle has indeed come, has long since been joined. Whether we calculate the onset of the battle with Snopesism, with modernism, with spiritual sloth or accidie, from some dissociation of sensibility which set in sometime in the Seventeenth century or from the so-called Enlightenment, from the Industrial Revolution or from the near triumph of Logical Positivism, or whether we feel more simply that the battle began with World War I, it has come and it has produced a Roland—at least two of them in Hemingway and Faulkner.

When Scott Fitzgerald began writing his series of medieval stories in the thirties, which he hoped to make into a novel, he was most perspicacious in selecting as "the hero of his melodrama, a Frankish knight of the ninth century . . . *modeled on Hemingway*."[27]   His old friend Fitzgerald, it appears, saw with far greater clarity and much richer vision that the modern industry of Hemingway criticism has yet seen the deepest thrust of Hemingway's work, as of his life. So, too, I think, did Faulkner.

From start to finish, both Hemingway and Faulkner are concerned to reinvest the verities—as Faulkner named them in his

Nobel Prize address; courage, honor, hope, pride, compassion, pity, sacrifice—and it was the "dying fall" of Roland's horn along the road to Roncevaux which first struck the tone, the forbidden interval in the modern scale, the reverberation of the spirit which has been resonant across the symbolic landscape from Paris to Mississippi, from Roncevaux and Pamplona to Yoknapatawpha, the *paysage moralisé* of some of the greatest fictions we have known.

NOTES

[1] See Malcolm Cowley's introduction to the *Viking Portable Hemingway* (New York: The Viking Press, 1944) and Philip Young, *Ernest Hemingway* (New York: Rinehart & Co., 1952), especially pp. 59-60, and Arthur Waldhorn, *A Reader's Guide to Ernest Hemingway* (New York: Farrar, Straus & Goroux, 1972), pp. 93-112.

[2] Ernest Hemingway, *The Sun Also Rises* (New York: Charles Scribner's Sons, 1926), p. 108. All subsequent references to the novel are indicated in the text. Hemingway's use here of the Spanish and the French spelling of Roncevaux is probably meant to indicate that the associations with Roland, the French national hero, and upper-most in Jake's awareness. Thus I will follow Jake, and use the French spelling.

[3] *Ernest Hemingway and the Arts* (Urbana: University of Illinois Press, 1971), pp. 144-145.

[4] In May, 1974, the lay of the land as well as the intervening greenery made it impossible to see the monastery of Roncevaux from the vantage point in question. The foilage would of course be even thicker in late June and early July when Hemingway's action occurs. An old villager, who had never heard of Hemingway and who was mystified by my questioning, said that it would have been impossible to see the monastery from the Pamplona road even in the 1920's, when the line of trees between Burguete and Roncevaux was of a lesser growth.

[5] D. D. R. Owen, *The Legend of Roland: A Pagent of the Middle Ages* (New York: Phaidon Press, 1973), p. 34.

[6] Ezra Pound, *The Spirit of Romance* (New York: New Directions, n. d.), p. 75. Henry Adams, *Mont-Saint-Michel And Chartres* (Garden City: Doubleday Anchor, 1959), pp. 34-35.

[7] Richard Lehan, "Hemingway Among the Moderns," in Richard Astro and Jackson J. Benson, eds., *Hemingway In Our Time* (Corvalis: Oregon State University Press, 1974), p. 198. Emphasis added.

[8] Young, p. 58.

[9] Carlos Baker, *Hemingway: The Writer as Artist* (Princeton: Princeton University Press, 1952, p. 52.

[10] What may be the same engraving was still (in 1974) hanging in the inn where Jake and Hemingway (and the present writer) stayed in Burguete. Indeed, pilgrimages—formal and informal—still follow the ancient route. In May, 1974, I observed a long procession of men in black hooded pilgrim's garb, arriving after an arduous journey, at the monastery of Roncevaux.

[11] For the best recent treatment of the Scopes trial, the major American news story of the Twenties, see William B. Gatewood, Jr., ed., *Controversy in the Twenties: Fundamentalism, Modernism & Evolution* (Nashville: Vanderbilt University Press, 1969).

[12] *Hemingway on Love* (Austin: University of Texas Press, 1965), pp. 30-31.

[13] *Death in the Afternoon* (New York: Charles Scribner's Sons, 1932), pp. 274-275. All subsequent references to the work are indicated in the text.

[14] Samuel Shain, *Ernest Hemingway* (New York: Frederick Ungar Publishing Co., Inc., 1973), pp. 48-49.

[15] The phrase is from *The Snows of Kilimanjaro*.

[16] Carlos Baker, *Ernest Hemingway: A Life Story* (New York: Bantam Books, 1970), p. 238.

[17]Baker, p. 201. One anecdote about Hemingway and Chartres tells us a great deal about the man. When his friend Morley Callaghan was about to leave for London without having visited Chartres, he insisted on driving him down the next day, when he "was highly critical of Morley for concentrating on the stained glass while forgetting to genuflect before the high alter" (Baker, p. 262).

[18]Owen, p. 33.

[19]George Zarnecki, *The Monastic Achievement* (New York: McGraw-Hill Book Company, 1972), p. 56.

[20]*Across the River and Into the Trees,* (New York: Charles Scribner's Sons, 1950), pp. 56-57.

[21]Regarding Lourdes, one guidebook states: "Lourdes est devenu, depuis les apparitions de la Vierge à Bernadette Soubirous en 1858, le Compostelle des temps modernes." See Guy Michaud, *Guide France* (Paris: Classiques Hachette, 1964), p. 76.

[22]*Flags in the Dust* (New York: Random House, 1973), pp. 432-433. In the much cut version of the novel, *Sartoris,* which was all we had from 1929 until 1973, there are just a few insignificant variations of the text of this crucial passage. Faulkner completed his novel a little less than a year after the publication of *The Sun Also Rises.* Even the titles suggest, contrapuntally, Hemingway influence here.

[23]Cleanth Brooks, *William Faulkner: The Yoknapatawpha Country* (New Haven: Yale University Press, 1963), p. 114. Afterword by Lawrance Thompson in *Sartoris* (New York: New American Library, 1964), pp. 314-315.

[24]Frederick Gwynn & Joseph Blotner, eds., *Faulkner in the University* (New York: Random House, 1965), p. 285.

[25]Joseph Blotner, *Faulkner: A Biography* (New York: Random House, 1974), p. 448.

[26]Hemingway regularly attended mass at Saint Sulpice for several years. See Baker, p. 263. Sometime after Faulkner came home from France, he had cut ties with the Methodist Church and was attending the Episcopal Church.

[27]Andrew Turnbull, *Scott Fitzgerald* (New York: Charles Scribner's Sons, 1962), p. 248.

Frederic Henry's Escape and the Pose of Passivity

by Scott Donaldson

I

Sheridan Baker distinguishes between the early Hemingway hero, a passive young man somewhat given to self-pity, and the later, far more active and courageous hero.[1] Nick adams is a boy things happen to, Robert Jordan a man who makes them happen. This neat classification breaks down, however, when applied to the complicated narrator-protagonist of *A Farewell to Arms*. Frederic Henry consistently depicts himself as a passive victim inundated by the flow of events. "The world" was against him and Catherine. "They" caught the lovers off base— and killed Catherine as one of "the very good and the very gentle and the very brave" who die young. But Frederic, who survives, belongs to another category, and his determinism is hardly convincing. Assign blame though he will to anonymous scapegoats, he is still deeply implicated in the death of his lover.[2]

It is the same in war as in love. At the beginning, Frederic tells us, he simply goes along. An American in Rome when World War I breaks out, he joins the Italian ambulance corps for no particular reason: "There isn't always an explanation for everything." He falls into the drinking and whoring routine of the other officers at Gorizia largely out of inertia. He follows and gives orders as required, but hardly as a consequence of patriotism or dedication to any cause. He suffers a series of disillusionments—his wound, the "war disgust" of his comrades, the overt pacifism of his men, the theatricality and incompetence of the Italian military generally, the final moral chaos of the retreat from Caporetto—which reach a climax with his plunge into the Taliamento to avoid summary execution.

When he emerges from the river, Frederic is presumably

reborn.[3] But is he? Now he is on his own, and he must *act* to escape. Yet he has not sloughed off his old skin, and before completing his flight he will cover himself with that same cloak of passivity he donned when describing his relationship with Catherine—and for much the same reason. Rinaldi was right about Frederic Henry. He is the quintessential "Anglo-Saxon remorse boy," so driven by guilt that he is unwilling—even when telling his story years later—to accept responsibility for his actions.[4] This view, implicit in the text of the novel, gains added authority in those fragments which Hemingway chose to delete before publishing.[5]

II

Consider Frederic's behavior after he escapes the murderous carabinieri—a part of the novel that has received little critical attention. While still being swept along by the swollen waters of the river, he begins to map out a course of action. He considers taking off his boots and clothes but decides against it, since he would be "in a bad position" should he land barefoot. He will need his boots, for he already knows where he is going—to Mestre—and that to get there he will have to hike to the main rail line between Venice and Trieste. Why must he reach Mestre? He does not tell us at once, but it comes out later in conversation with Catherine: because he has an old order of movement authorizing travel from Mestre to Milan, and he needs only alter the date. In Milan, of course, he expects to find Catherine at the hospital.

When he reaches shore safely, Tenente Henry begins "to think out" what he should do next. He wrings out his clothes, and before putting his coat back on cuts off the cloth stars that identify him as an officer. The battle police (who were shooting officers indiscriminately) have taken his pistol, so he conceals his empty holster underneath the coat. Encountering a machine-gun detachment, he limps to masquerade as one of the wounded and is not challenged. He crosses the flat Venetian plain to the rail line and jumps aboard a canvas-covered gondola car, avoiding one guard's notice and "contemptuously" staring down another, who concludes he must have something to do with the train. He clambers inside the car, bumping his head on the guns within. He washes the blood away with rainwater since he will have to get off before the train reaches Mestre and he does "not want to look conspicuous." He is on his way back to his lover, and tries to think of nothing but their reunion and escape: "Probably have to go damned quickly. She would go. I knew she would go. When would we go? That was something to think about. It was getting dark. I lay and thought where we would go. There were many places."

The next day in Milan, Frederic engages in three different conversations that confirm Switzerland as their destination. The first of these occurs when he goes to the wine shop in Milan for early morning coffee and bread. The owner of the wine shop realizes at once that Frederic has deserted: he has seen the lieutenant come "down the wall" from the train and notices the bare spots on the sleeves where the stars have been cut away. But he is sympathetic and offers to put Frederic up, to arrange for false leave papers, and to help him leave the country. Nothing comes of this proposal, for the understandably cautious fugitive keeps insisting that he is in no trouble and needs no assistance.

In an earlier draft, Frederic actually did contract for forged papers.[6] This is the deleted passage, which originally followed the wine shop owner's offer of leave papers midway on P. 239 of the text:

> "I have no need for papers. I have papers. As for the stars, they never wear them at the front."

> I thought a minute.

> "I will be back."

> "Only you must tell me now."

> "A Tessera [identity card]," I said, "and leave papers."

> "Write the name."

> "Give me a pencil." I wrote a name[7] on the edge of a newspaper. "Some one will call for them."

"Who?"

"I don't know. He will bring the photograph for the Tessara. You will know me by that."

"All right. That will be one hundred and fifty lire."

"Here is fifty."

"Do not worry Tenente."

"What do you say?"

"I say do not worry."

"I do not worry. I am not in trouble."

"You are not in trouble if you stay with me."

"I must go."

"Come back. Come again."

"I will see you."

"Come at any time."

"Don't forget I am your friend," he said when I went out. He was a strange enough man.

"Good," I said.

Sheldon Norman Grebstein and Michael S. Reynolds have both observed that when Hemingway cut this passage he tightened the plot of the novel. With an identity card and leave papers, Frederic might have remained in Italy and avoided arrest for some time. Without them, he must leave the country very soon. But the deletion also functions in two other ways: to avoid a lapse in credibility and to flesh out the character of the protagonist. A man on the run, Frederic would be unlikely to repose trust in the first stranger who accosts him after his desertion. Furthermore, to go through the spy-story machinations outlined here—giving "a name" apparently not his own, sending an intermediary to pick up the counterfeit papers, paying but one-third down to encourage delivery, and maintaining despite this damning evidence that he has nothing to worry about—would war against the lieutenant's nature. He already feels guilty, as we shall see. Active participation in illegal intrigue would only exacerbate that guilt.

Leaving the wine shop, Frederic skirts the train station, where there were sure to be military police, and goes to see the porter of the hospital and his wife. They tell him that Miss Barkley has gone to Stresa, on Lake Maggiore, with "the other lady English." After extracting a promise ("It is very important") that they tell no one he has been there, he immediately takes a cab to see Simmons, an American singer trying to break into Italian opera he'd met while recuperating from his wounds. Lieutenant Henry's plan is now taking shape. He has visited Lake Maggiore before—earlier, he and Catherine had planned to vacation at Pallanza, as preferable to Stresa because further from Milan—and surely knows that the lake extends into Switzerland. So upon awakening Simmons, he wastes no time in coming to the point. He's in a jam, he tells the singer, and asks about "the procedure in going to Switzerland." He knows that the Swiss will intern him, but wonders what that means. "Nothing," Simmons reassures him. "It's very simple. You can go anywhere. I think you just have to report or something."

Even with Simmons Frederic is somewhat evasive. It's not yet "definite" that he's fleeing the police. He "think(s)" he's through with the war. But Simmons does not insist on the details, and like the wine shop owner he's more than willing to help. When Frederic asks him to go out and buy civilian clothes for his use, Simmons won't hear of it; take anything of mine, he commands (Frederic probably decided to call on Simmons rather than some other acquaintance because they were of a size). Thus the lieutenant is relieved of the danger of traveling around Italy in an officer's uniform with his stars cut off and his holster empty, without leave papers or proper orders. The way is clear for escape, and before leaving Frederic ascertains the means. Yes, he tells Simmons, he still has his passport.

"Then get dressed, my dear fellow, and off to old Helvetia."

> "It's not that simple. I have to go to Stresa first."

> "Ideal, my dear fellow. You just row a boat across."

Once in Stresa, Frederic continues to lay the groundwork for his flight. He takes a carriage to the hotel, since it "was better"—less attention-provoking—"to arrive in a carriage" than on foot. He looks up Emilio the barman he used to fish with, lies to him about his civilian clothes ("I'm on leave. Convalescing-leave"), discovers where Catherine and Miss Ferguson are staying, and—most important of all—chats with him about fishing. The next morning, he persuades Emilio to leave the bar and take him out into the lake to troll. They catch no fish, but after two vermouths at the Isola dei Pescatori—the fisherman's island, which was not a tourist attraction like the Isola Bella they row past, and hence a safer stopping place[9]—he learns of Emilio's disaffection with the war (if called, the barman says, he won't go) and admits that he himself had been a fool to enlist. Little else of consequence passes between them, but they have reached a tacit understanding. "Any time you want it," Emilio remarks after padlocking his boat, "I'll give you the key."

Up to this point, Frederic has moved purposefully toward his goal. As a fugitive from military justice, he has repeatedly been forced to act, in both senses of the verb. He has calculated his chances, and calculated well. Finally he has located Catherine and found where he can get a boat to take them to the neutral country down the lake. Yet with his lover he is all wide-eyed innocence and passivity; now he will "act" only in the theatrical sense. He understands precisely what must be done, but waits for her—and then for Emilio—to tell him what that is. By adopting this pose, he appears far less calculating in her eyes. By involving her and the barman, he tries to parcel out shares of his guilt.

After a long night of love-making, Catherine queries Frederic about his status.

> "But won't they arrest you if they catch you out of uniform?"

> "They'll probably shoot me."

"Then we'll not stay here. We'll get out of the country.

He has, he confesses, "thought something of that," but continues his charade, waiting for her to drag the scheme out of him.

"What would you do if they came to arrest you?"

"Shoot them."

"You see how silly you are. I won't let you go out of the hotel until we leave here."

"Where are we going to go?"

But Catherine will not cooperate: "Please don't be that way, darling. We'll go wherever you say. But please find some place to go right away." So Frederic reluctantly reveals his plan: "Switzerland is down the lake, we can go there."

That midnight, as a rainstorm sweeps across Lake Maggiore, Emilio comes to announce that the military police will arrest Frederic in the morning, and the lieutenant once again plays the game of "tell me what to do." When the barman knocks, Frederic takes him into the bathroom (so as not to waken Catherine, or alert her to his deviousness), and disingenuously asks, "What's the matter Emilio? Are you in trouble?" No, it is the Tenente who is in trouble, and this incredible dialogue ensues:

"Why are they going to arrest me?"

"For something about the war."

"Do you know what?"

"No. But I know that they know you were here before as an officer and now you are here out of uniform. After this retreat they arrest everybody."

I thought a minute.

"What time do they come to arrest me?"

"In the morning. I don't know the time."

"What do you say to do?"

He put his hat in the washbowl. It was very wet and had been dripping on the floor.

"If you have nothing to fear an arrest is nothing. But it is always bad to be arrested—especially now."

"I don't want to be arrested."

"Then go to Switzerland."

"How?"

"In my boat."

"There is a storm," I said.

"The storm is over. It is rough but you will be all right."

"When should we go?"

"Right away. They might come to arrest you early in the morning.

"I thought a minute," is an exact repetition of a phrase used before, when Frederic—in the deleted passage—determined to purchase false leave papers. In both places, it is a sign that he is about to embark on a course of deception. In this case, the deception consists of suggesting to Emilio—in the questions italicized—that the notion of crossing to Switzerland in his boat has never occurred to Lieutenant Henry. This is patently untrue, as the barman, like Hemingway's readers, must realize. But Frederic's purpose is not simply to fool Emilio. He is after bigger game: the raging tooth of conscience within.

III

Lieutenant Henry, in the version of the tale he presents, is provided with every possible reason to bid a farewell to arms. As an officer with a foreign accent separated from his men, he faces almost certain death from the carabinieri unless he runs. But long before that climactic moment, Frederic has brought up example after example of soldiers trying to opt out of the war. Rinaldi, we learn, has few real wounds to treat early in the war, except for self-inflicted wounds. Frederic meets an Italian soldier with a hernia who has slipped his truss, and advises him to bloody his head as well to avoid being sent back to the front lines. The soldier does so, but the ruse does not work. When the lieutenant himself is wounded, the doctor dictates as he works: ". . . with possible fracture of the skull. Incurred in the line of duty. That's what keeps you from being court-martialed for self-inflicted wounds." Later, Miss Van Campen accuses him of contracting jaundice to avoid return to active duty; in denying the charge Frederic admits that both he and Miss Van Campen have seen plenty of self-inflicted wounds. When he eventually rejoins his unit, things have gone so badly that even the Major talks of desertion: "If I was away I do not believe I would come back."

During the retreat Frederic serves as a kind of moral policeman. He not only prevents his men from looting, but goes so far as to shoot one of the two sergeants who hitch a ride with the ambulances but refuse to help when the vehicles mire down in mud. Bonello, who finishes off the wounded man (he's always wanted to kill a sergeant, he says), slips away himself the next day to surrender to the Austrians. In the confusion, Aymo is gunned down by "friendly fire" from Italian bullets. Frederic and the faithful Piani are left to plod along with the rest of the retreating soldiers, who chant "Andiamo a casa" and cast aside their weapons. "They think if they throw away their rifles they can't make them fight," Piani explains, but his lieutenant disapproves. Despite all the precedents he's cited, then, Frederic sticks to his mission and his men up to the moment when he must either escape or be executed.

Furthermore, once he has escaped nearly every civilian he meets either assists him in his flight or reinforces his conviction that the war is senseless and badly managed. The wine shop owner's offer of forged papers is only partly attributable to the profit motive. "Don't forget that I am your friend," he tells

Frederic, in the text as well as in the deleted passage. Is he
through with the war? Simmons inquires. "Good boy. I always
knew you had sense." Emilio the barman has served in Abyssinia
and hates war. The wise Count Greffi thinks the war is, really,
"stupid." And Catherine, especially, reassures Frederic that he
has done the right thing. Yet no amount of reassurance can
shake him free of his nagging sense of guilt. Hemingway conveys
the persistence of this debilitating emotion in two ways: through
Lietuenant Henry's unsuccessful attempts to rationalize his desertion, and through his equally unsuccessful attempts to shut
the war out of his consciousness.

On the train to Mestre, Frederic calls up an analogy to justify his flight:

> You were out of it now. You had no more obligation. If they
> shot floorwalkers after a fire in a department store because they
> spoke with an accent they had always had, then certainly the
> floorwalkers would not be expected to return when the store
> opened again for business. They might seek other employment; if
> there was any other employment and the police did not get them.

The analogy seems curious until one reflects that Frederic had
functioned during the retreat much as a floorwalker functions—
to prevent thievery.[10] Then he goes on, in internal monologue,
to discuss "the outward forms" of soldiery. He would like to
take the uniform off, and he has removed the stars "for con-
venience," but it was "no point of honor." The abstract word
"honor," rising to Frederic's mind at this moment, comes from
the conscience which will not let him stop "thinking"—a code
word, in this novel, for the functioning of the superego. He
wished the Italians "all the luck": some good and brave and
calm and sensible men were fighting for their cause. "But it
was not my show any more and I wished this bloody train would
get to Mestre and I would eat and stop thinking. I would have to
stop."

That he cannot stop is shown on the next train ride Hemingway describes, when Frederic is en route from Milan to Stresa
in Simmon's civilian clothes. Presumably he should be happy:
he is on his way to Catherine. But he misses the feeling of "being
held" by his clothes that a uniform has provided, and feels "as

sad as the wet Lombard country" outside the window. He shares
the compartment with some aviators:

> They avoided looking at me and were very scornful of a civilian
> my age. I did not feel insulted. In the old days I would have
> insulted them and picked a fight. They got off at Gallarte and I
> was glad to be alone. . . . I was damned lonely and was glad when
> the train got to Stresa.

"In the old days"—two days before—Frederic would not have
stood for the scornful attitude of the aviators. Now he accepts
their view of him as a slacker, a point emphasized in a sentence
Hemingway cut from the novel as, undoubtedly, belaboring
the obvious. "I did not feel indignant [vs. insulted]," he originally wrote. "I felt they were right."[1][1]

Ensconced at the bar of the Grand Hôtel & des Isles Bor-
romées, his nerves and stomach soothed by three cool, clean
martinis, the same number of sandwiches, and olives, salted
almonds, and potato chips, Frederic begins to feel "civilized,"
by which he means that he "did not think at all." But the
barman asks some question that starts the thought processes
going again:

> "Don't talk about the war," I said. The war was a long way
> away. Maybe there wasn't any war. There was no war here. Then
> I realized it was over for me. But I did not have the feeling that
> it was really over. I had the feeling of a boy who thinks of what
> is happening at a certain hour at the schoolhouse from which he
> has played truant.

The pattern is the same in the bar as on the train to Mestre. The
fugitive insists to himself that he is through, that the war is over
for him, that it isn't his show any longer, but then he cannot
help touching the wound, striking a note of self-recrimination.
Even when pleasantly fuzzy on gin, he is reminded of childhood
truancies. Thus he tells Count Greffi like Emilio that he does
want to talk about the war ("About anything else"), but soon
brings up the subject himself. "What do you think of the war
really?" he asks the ancient nobleman.

Nurse Catherine Barkley provides the best medication—sex—

to enable Frederic to forget.[12]   That she is later to perform
this function is foreshadowed on their second meeting, when
Lieutenant Henry initiates this exchange:

> "Let's drop the war."
>
> "It's very hard. There's no place to drop it."
>
> "Let's drop it anyway."
>
> "All right."

He then kisses her, is slapped, and the kiss and the slap succeed:
at least "we have gotten away from the war," he observes. But
they haven't, nor will they ever, despite the oblivion-inducing
therapy she administers. Immediately after telling her that they
will go to Switzerland, Frederic seeks and gets her reassurance:

> "I feel like a criminal. I've deserted from the army."
>
> "Darling, *please* be sensible. It's not deserting from the army.
> It's only the Italian army."
>
> I laughed. "You're a fine girl. Let's get back into bed. I feel
> fine in bed."
>
> A little while later Catherine said, "You don't feel like a crimi-
> nal do you?"
>
> "No," I said. "Not when I'm with you."

But they cannot make love all the time, and when Frederic
returns from fishing and finds Catherine gone, he "lay down on
the bed and tried to keep from thinking" without success until
Catherine came back and "it was all right again." His life, he
tells her, used to be full of everything. His job in the army had
given purpose to his existence. "Now if you aren't with me I
haven't a thing in the world."

Safe in Switzerland, the two lovers ride a carriage to their
hotel, where Hemingway introduces an ironic commentary on
Frederic's problem. He is still groggy from the long night of

rowing, and neglects to tip the soldier who has brought them and their bags to Locarno. "You've forgotten the army," Catherine remarks, and for the moment she's right. But very soon, during the idyllic first days at Montreaux, the narcotic begins to wear off: "We slept well and if I woke in the night I knew it was from only one cause," Frederic observes. What was the cause? "The war seemed as far away as the football games of some one else's college. But I knew from the papers that they were still fighting in the mountains because the snow would not come."[13] Later, when Catherine urges him to fall asleep simultaneously with her, he is unable to do so and lies "awake for quite a long time thinking about things." What things? "About Rinaldi and the priest and lost of people I know," he tells Catherine, adding, "But I don't think about them much. I don't want to think about the war. I'm through with it." This is wishful thinking, for Frederic's declaration, "I don't think about them much" is undercut by his next sentence, "I don't want to think about the war."

Hemingway emphasizes Frederic's continuing absorption in the war through repeated references to his newspaper reading.[14] While convalescing in Milan after his operation, the wounded Tenente read all the papers he could get his hands on, including even the Boston papers with their stale news of stateside training camps. After he deserts, however, he tries to repudiate the habit. Riding the train to Stresa, "I had the paper but I did not read it because I did not want to read about the war. I was going to forget the war." Catherine is surprised, the morning after their reunion, to find that Frederic does not want to read the news. He'd always wanted the paper in the hospital. With characteristic understanding, she asks, "Was it so bad you don't want even to read about it?" Not for the moment, but he promises that he'll tell her about what happened if he "ever get(s) it straight" in his head. He never does tell her, yet that very afternoon when she is away he sits in a lounge chair at the bar and reads the bad news in the paper. "The army had not stood at the Tagliamento. They were falling back to the Piave." At the Guttingens' cottage in the mountains, no papers are available, so he catches up on the news when they come down to Montreaux. While Catherine is at the hairdresser, he drinks beer and eats pretzels and reads "about disaster"—the war was going badly everywhere—in "the *Corriere della Sera* and the

English and American papers from Paris." The night they move
to the hotel in Lausanne, he lies in bed drinking a whiskey and
soda (liquor like sex makes him feel better temporarily) and
reads the papers he has bought at the station. "It was March,
1918, and the German offensive had started in France." During
the three weeks they spend at the hotel, his days fall into a
routine. In the morning he boxes at the gym, takes a shower,
walks along the streets "smelling the spring in the air," stops at
a café "to sit and watch the people and read the paper and drink
a vermouth," and then meets Catherine at the hotel for lunch.
During the afternoon of her protracted labor, Frederic kills time
reading the paper. Sent out to eat supper, he takes a seat across
from an elderly man with an evening paper and, "not thinking
at all," reads about "the break through on the British front."
When the man, annoyed that Frederic is reading the back of his
paper, folds it over, he considers asking the waiter for one of
his own but decides against it: "I could not concentrate." He
has been unable to forget the war; now Catherine's Ceasarean
has given him something else to shut his mind to. "It was the
only thing to do," the doctor assures him when she has hemor-
rhaged and died. "The operation proved—." But Frederic cuts
him short: "I do not want to talk about it."

IV

Eventually Frederic Henry does bring himself to talk about
his tragic love affair and about the horror of the war: ergo, *A
Farewell to Arms*. But it is important to remember that we
have the story *as he tells it to us*. Maxwell Perkins, Hemingway's
editor at Scribners, thought like some others that the novel was
insufficiently integrated. "The serious flaw in the book," he
wrote Owen Wister on May 17, 1929, "is that the two great
elements you named—one of which would make it a picture of
war, and the other of which would make it a duo of love and
passion—do not fully combine. It begins as one thing wholly,
and ends up wholly as the other thing."[15] But Perkins and
Wister missed the point. The subject of the novel is not love
and war, in whatever combination, but Frederic Henry.

Hemingway was careful, in commenting on the novel, to
refer to his protagonist as "the invented character," thus distin-

guishing between author and narrator. And he issued a further warning: that he was not to be held accountable for "the opinions" of his narrators.[16]

Both Frederic Henry and Ernest Hemingway were Americans wounded on the Italian front and both fell in love with nurses. Otherwise, they have not much in common. Frederic is certainly older than his creator, for one thing. Hemingway was only 18 when he came to Italy—not as an officer in any army but as a Red Cross ambulance driver—in the last summer of the war. Frederic, on the other hand, had enlisted in the Italian army three years earlier, and even before that he had been studying architecture in Rome. Unlike the raw youth only a year out of Oak Park high school, he has been around enough to acquire a good deal of knowledge. He knows the geography of Italy very well indeed, as his movements after deserting testify. He even knows how the war should be fought: as Napoleon would have fought it, by waiting until the Austrians came down from the mountains and then whipping them.

Despite his background of experience, however, the lieutenant does not conduct himself bravely or intelligently as a warrior. He is no Othello, nor even a Hemingway. After Frederic is wounded, Rinaldi tries to get him the Medaglia d'Argento. Hadn't he done anything heroic? Rinaldi wants to know. Didn't he carry anyone on his back? No, Frederic replies, he was "blown up while eating cheese." It hardly matters. He has been wounded, he is an American, the offensive has been successful, and Rinaldi thinks they can get him the silver. Hemingway was in fact awarded the silver, but for better reasons. Unlike his narrator, young Hemingway *did* carry another soldier on his back while wounded himself. During the retreat Lieutenant Henry is given his one chance to command, and makes a botch of it. He orders his three ambulances onto side roads where they bog down permanently. He shoots the uncooperative sergeant to no particular effect for when the others proceed on foot, the lieutenant leads good soldier Aymo to a senseless death and Bonello surrenders to save his skin knowing Frederic will not turn him in. In sum, the Tenente loses his ambulances and all his men but one, and it is—as he reflects—largely his own fault.

By showing Frederic's lack of courage and competence,

Hemingway aimed to achieve a certain distance from his narrator. That he was determined to maintain this separation is illustrated by his decision to delete reflective passages in which the narrator's thoughts too closely resemble his own. In one of these, Frederic in conversation with the priest asserts that he loves lots of things: "The night. The Day. Food. Drink. Girls. Italy. Pictures. Places. Swimming. Portofino. Paris. Spring. Summer. Summer. Fall. Winter. Heat. Cold. Smells. Sleep. Newspapers. Reading." All this, Frederic remarks, "sounds better in Italian." It also sounds very much like the vigorously alive Hemingway, in love with all that life had to offer.[17] So does an excised digression on the subject of fear:

> (When I had first gone to the war it had all been like a picture or a story or a dream in which you know you can wake up when it gets too bad . . . I had the believe [sic] in physical immortality which is given fortunate young men in order that they may think about other things and that is withdrawn without notice when they need it most. After its withdrawal I was not greatly worried because the spells of fear were always physical, always caused by an imminent danger, and always transitory . . . I suppose the third stage, of being afraid at night, started about at this point . . .)[18]

Fear and how to combat it was a topic that obsessed Hemingway, but did not much concern his narrator.

In two other eliminated passages, Frederic demonstrates a capacity for love that is missing from the novel. In the first, the protagonist says that he felt a sense of oneness with Catherine the moment she appeared at the hospital in Milan. "We had come together as though we were two pieces of mercury that unite to make one . . . We were one person." Then, in an attempted revision, Hemingway wrote this dialogue:

> "You sweet," I [Frederic] said. "You were wonderful to get here."

> "It wasn't very hard. It may be hard to stay."

> "Feel our heart," I said.

> "It's the same."[19]

These sentiments are transferred in the novel to Catherine. When Frederic sees her, he says that he is in love with her, that he's crazy about her, that he wants her. But when *she* says, "Feel our hearts beating," he only replies, "I don't care about our hearts. I want you. I'm just mad about you." It is she who insists on their being "one person" throughout. The effect of the change is to transfer sympathy from Frederic to Catherine, since he emphasizes physical satisfaction, while she alone is so romantically smitten as to lose herself in their love. The other excision shows Frederic thinking long and bitter thoughts about loss and the inadequacy of conventional religious consolation. What follows is but part of an extended interior monologue:

> . . . They say the only way you can keep a thing is to lose it and this may be true but I do not admire it. The only thing I know is that if you love anything enough they take it away from you. This may all be done in infinite wisdom but whoever does it is not my friend. I am afraid of god at night but I would have admired him more if he would have stopped the war or never have let it start. Maybe he did stop it but whoever stopped it did not do it prettily. And if it is the Lord that giveth and the Lord that taketh away I do not admire him for taking Catherine away . . . [20]

Here was the kind of stitchery, linking love and war, that Perkins might have applauded. But Hemingway left it out, probably because its inclusion might have aroused undue empathy with his narrator.

On yet another discarded page of manuscript Hemingway typed a sentence that might stand as a motto for his novel: "The position of the survivor of a great calamity is seldom admirable."[21] Indeed it is not, since no special glamour—rather the reverse—attaches to simply having survived, and when one's friends and lover are not so fortunate, one is liable like Frederic Henry to suffer from excessive guilt.

"There is generally nothing to which we are so sensitive," Karl Jaspers observed in his study of collective guilt in Germany during and after World War II, "as to any hint that we are considered guilty." Such sensitivity finds expression in more than one way, however. Most Germans, Jaspers discovered, reacted aggresively by accusing their accusers. When wall posters went

up in German towns during the summer of 1945, with pictures
from Belsen and "the crucial statement, You are the guilty!
consciences grew uneasy . . . and something rebelled: Who
indicts me there? . . . It is only human that the accused, whether
justly or unjustly charged, tries to defend himself."²² But when
the accusation is not public but comes from within, the tendency
may be, as with Frederic, to internalize the guilt, hug it to one's
bosom, and retreat into inactivity.

Actually, Frederic does twice face accusations after his
desertion. The first takes the form of the aviator's silent scorn,
and he mutely accepts their judgment. The other, more overt
accuser is Catherine's friend Miss Ferguson, who lashes out at
Frederic in Stresa. What is he doing in mufti? she asks. He's
"sneaky," she tells him, "like a snake" for getting Catherine
with child and then turning up unexpectedly to take her away.
Though Catherine makes a joke of it ("We'll both sneak off"),
Frederic is not amused, probably because he is reminded of the
dissimulation he has just gone through to avoid capture. So he
remains quiet, and since no one else points a finger, he has no
one to lash out against. Yet it *is* "only human" to defend oneself, even against one's own accusations. All of *A Farewell to
Arms*, from this point of view, may be considered the narrator's
apologia pro vita sua.

Throughout the book Frederic paints himself as a man more
sinned against than sinning, as a passive victim of circumstances.
Yet the portrait is not, finally, to the life, as Hemingway shows
by daubing in occasional brush strokes of his own. One of these
is the analogy between Frederic and (not the guileful snake but)
the crafty fox. Walking one evening in the brisk mid-January
cold of the mountains above Montreux, Frederic and Catherine
twice see foxes in the woods. This is unusual, for foxes rarely
show themselves. And when a fox sleeps, Frederic points out, he
wraps his tail around him to keep warm. Then he adds:

> "I always wanted to have a tail like that. Wouldn't it be fun if
> we had brushes like a fox?"

> "It might be very difficult dressing."

> "We'd have clothes made, or live in a country where it wouldn't

make any difference."

"We live in a country where nothing makes any difference."

This peculiar exchange suggests a good deal about Hemingway's protagonist. Catherine has done all anyone could to protect him: she pulls his cloak around the two of them, makes a tent of her hair, administers the soporific of sex and humor ("It's only the Italian army") to his hyperactive superego, urges him off to "old Helvetia," a neutral country where to her, at least, "nothing makes any difference." But it has not been enough, and Frederic still thinks conspiratorially of disguises and how to keep himself safe and warm. Like the wily fox in the woods, he pretends to an innocence he does not possess; the comparison itself constitutes a *caveat* against accepting as gospel Frederic Henry's presentation of himself. In the end, his pose of passivity cannot hide the guilt underneath, nor can he dissipate the guilt by play-acting or by writing about it. Hemingway's untrustworthy narrator remains a principal agent of both his farewells—to war as to love.

NOTES

[1]Sheridan Baker, *Ernest Hemingway: An Introduction and Interpretation* (New York: Holt, Rinehart and Winston, 1967), p. 2.

[2]This was the subject of "Frederic Henry, Selfish Lover," the paper I presented at the Alabama conference. In slightly amended form that paper constitutes a portion of the chapter on love in *By Force of Will: The Life and Art of Ernest Hemingway* (New York: Viking, 1977).

[3]Malcolm Cowley first proposed the idea of Frederic's rebirth in his introduction to *The Portable Hemingway* (New York: Viking, 1944).

[4]Delbert E. Wylder discusses Frederic Henry's guilt at length, but does

not elaborate on the narrator's strategy of passivity nor his behavior during his flight.　See Wylder, *Hemingway's Heroes* (Albuquerque:　University of New Mexico Press, 1969), pp. 66-95.

[5]These deletions were made from the pencil manuscript, Ms-64, now among the Hemingway papers at the Kennedy library.　I am indebted to Mary Hemingway for permission to examine the manuscript, and to Jo August and William Johnson of the library for their generous assistance. Michael S. Reynolds's *Hemingway's First War: The Making of "A Farewell to Arms"* (Princeton:　Princeton University Press, 1976) contains a definitive discussion of Hemingway's alterations.　Sheldon Norman Grebstein's *Hemingway's Craft* (Carbondale:　Southern Illinois University Press, 1973) comments on several of the deletions.　Both books reproduce some of the deleted passages.

[6]Ms-64, pp. 470-471.

[7]Reynolds incorrectly renders "a name" as "the name."　Reynolds, p. 291.

[8]Grebstein, pp. 211-212; Reynolds, pp. 35-36.

[9]Reynolds, p. 233, calls attention to this point.

[10]Hemingway may have been thinking of a 1921 fire in a Paris department store that took the lives of 150 people.　See "142 French Youths Killed in Fire at Dance Hall," *International Herald Tribune* (2 November 1970), p. 2.

[11]Ms-64, p. 477.

[12]Stanley Cooperman, in "Death and *Cojones*: Hemingway's *A Farewell to Arms*," *South Atlantic Quarterly*, 63 (Winter 1964), pp. 85-92, sees Frederic as requiring of Catherine not love "but medication and in this respect he is less the Byronic lover than patient."　Cooperman also writes: "The hyena of passivity—always a nightmare for Hemingway—reduces Frederic Henry to a spiritual *castrado*."

[13]While rowing across Lake Maggiore in the rain, Frederic thinks that it must be snowing in the mountains, but he is apparently mistaken.

[14]See Reynolds, pp. 101-103, for observations on the "motif of news-

paper reading."

[15] The letter from Perkins is quoted in Reynolds, p. 76.

[16] Quoted in Arthur L. Scott, "In Defense of Robert Cohn," *College English*, 18 (March 1957), p. 309.

[17] Ms-64, pp. 168-170.

[18] Ms-64, pp. 235-236.

[19] Ms-64, pp. 201-209.

[20] Ms-64, pp. 586-588.

[21] This motto is noted by Reynolds, p. 60.

[22] Karl Jaspers, *The Question of German Guilt* (New York: Dial, 1947), pp. 47-107.

Hemingway as Artist in *Across the River and Into The Trees:* A Revaluation

by W. Craig Turner

Across the River and into the Trees, though not one of Ernest Hemingway's best novels, presents for us in Richard Cantwell one of Hemingway's most complex and interesting characters. Unfortunately, since the novel's intitial, highly unfavorable reception by the critics in 1950, *Across the River* has received scant attention.[1] However, at least one critic, Philip Young, has referred to it as among Hemingway's "most revealing" works, and another, John Atkins, has classified its protagonist as Robert Cohn's only rival as Hemingway's best character creation.[2] Though in some ways the novel forms a composite of earlier Hemingway themes, characters, and situations, it also incorporates experimental techniques and indicates other areas into which Hemingway sought to expand his art.[3] Particularly noteworthy are his achievements in the structure, narrative technique, and characterization of this most maligned novel.

As Carlos Baker has pointed out in *Hemingway: The Writer as Artist* (p. 266), the circle dominates the structure of *Across the River*. The Colonel's journeying to Venice to die exemplifies the fast-closing circle of his life, for it was in defense of the city during World War I that the young Lieutenant Cantwell first lost his illusion of immortality. Venice is his home: the city he fought for when a boy and partly owns now; the city of his youth and happiness as well as of his "last and true and only love"; and the city that he loves and where he is loved and treated well. In the Venice of Richard Cantwell, Peter Lisca notes (pp. 245-246), opposites meet and things come full circle. Life and Death, Youth and Age, Past and Present, Old World and New World, Love and Hate, and War and Peace all come together in Cantwell's final weekend. The Colonel fittingly returns to the place where his mature life began, both to complete the circle of his existence and to end his journey through life.[4]

Also, certain actions occurring entirely during the weekend (and not partially in the past and thus remembered) function as completed circular movements. The lovingly kept, radiantly varnished speedboat with the dilapidated motor transports Cantwell from the garage to the Gritti Palace Hotel (pp. 43-52) and back to the garage again; Renata, who accompanied Cantwell on the Gritti-to-garage trip, chooses to return in the same "displaced engine boat" instead of "a good one" (pp. 274-277).

Other images somewhat incidentally emphasize Hemingway's concern with the circle in *Across the River*. In an interior monologue passage centering on his entrance into the Gritti, Cantwell remembers, "Didn't Giotto describe a circle,   he thought? . . . 'It was easy,' said Giotto as he drew the perfect circle" (p. 54). Similarly, but more significantly, the Colonel recalls Dante's circles when Renata accuses him of sounding like Dante: " 'I am Mister Dante,' he said. 'For the moment.' And for a while he was and he drew all the circles. They were as unjust as Dante's but he drew them" (p. 246).

The fact that Hemingway uses circular structure in both *For Whom the Bell Tolls* and *Across the River and into the Trees* has been noted by Baker;[5] however, while Hemingway employs concentric circles focused on the bridge in his development of Robert Jordan's story, in Richard Cantwell's story he draws a series of separate circles interconnected at the point of the Colonel's final weekend in Venice—the pattern is much like a daisy, with the yellow center as the Colonel's last days and the connected petals extending outward as his remembrances. The primary viewpoint is that of the Colonel looking around at the disparate actions and memories of a lifetime—all of which must be seen from the perspective of the final days of his fifty-one-year life. The reader must look at the whole through the circle of the narrative framework, the duckhunt which begins and ends the novel. Thus, the reader first sees the yellow core of the weekend, and then the connecting circles as they interlock with that center. Much as the bridge stands at the very core of *For Whom the Bell Tolls*, Richard Cantwell's failing heart—in its several capacities—provides the focal point for *Across the River*.

Like Robert Jordan in the earlier novel, Cantwell seeks to extend his circle of existence through the woman he loves. The name Renata, "the reborn one," and Cantwell's frequent references to her as "daughter" emphasize the idea of such perpetuation. Once he even notes her ambivalent situation as both lover and offspring as he speaks to her portrait: "Boy or daughter or my one true love or whatever it is; you know what is is, portrait" (p. 173). As Cantwell was initiated into his adult life at Fossalta in his eighteenth year, so Renata symbolically joins the ranks of the experienced—at the same age—with her membership in the Order of Brusadelli (p. 270). The circles of Richard and Renata interlock, and hers becomes a meaningful extension of his. Cantwell's Venice serves as a city for new beginnings as well as old endings; Hemingway's circular structure serves as an appropriate artistic device for Cantwell's story.

In his article "the Structure of Hemingway's *Across the River and into the Trees*," Peter Lisca raises the question of Hemingway's "narrative strategy" in the novel.[6] Lisca asserts that even though the story is told in the grammatical third person throughout, only in the first chapter and in the last thirty pages—those sections dealing with the duck-hunting frame—do we encounter an omniscient third person who can occasionally tell us things the Colonel cannot know. The rest, Lisca argues, Colonel Cantwell tells himself in "an uninterrupted interior monologue": "Thus, the novel is really a first person narration of events in the past, like *The Sun Also Rises* and *A Farewell to Arms*, but disguised as third person narration through the device of using the shooter as a *persona* through whom the Colonel thinks about himself." Therefore, Lisca concludes, the objections raised by the critics to the absence of any difference of sensibility between the narrator and the Colonel is surmounted: the narrator *is* the Colonel.

Lisca's two-narrator theory, however, fails to take notice of more than a dozen separate passages within the frame which initiate *outside* the Colonel's mind and *inside* the thoughts of a half dozen other characters (including the one and only narrator). The omniscient narrator enters the minds of T5 Jackson ("I wonder what he's riding me for now, the driver thought", p. 27; see also pp. 37; 57-58); the garage bar-tender ("I hope there is nothing wrong with him, the bar-tender thought";

p. 41; see also 39); the *Gran Maestro* (". . . he wished the Colonel would return to things they both knew together when they were a lieutenant and a sergeant": pp. 62-63; see also pp. 108, 269); the hunting host Andrea (who "looked into the mirror . . . and decided that he did not like what he saw there": p. 81); and Renata (who in "the room for women . . . said to herself . . . 'Don't think at all"; p. 269; see also 112). In one passage the narrator calls attention to three different viewpoints simultaneously, telling us that "The Colonel was conscious of using the word, and so was the *Gran Maestro*, and so was the girl. But to each one it meant a different thing" (p. 107). One of the most obvious passages outside the Colonel's thought processes occurs when the narrator points out that the Colonel "did not notice the old used steel of his eyes nor the small, long extending laugh wrinkles at the corners of his eyes, nor that his broken nose was like a gladiator's in the oldest statues. Nor did he notice his basically kind mouth which could be truly ruthless" (p. 112).[7]

As in the later *The Old Man and the Sea*, *Across the River and into the Trees* employs only one narrator to relate its contents throughout, even though most of the novel lies within the range of consciousness of its protagonist. Though there is no confusing narrative strategy, Hemingway does give us an artful demonstration of his skill at handling the possibilities of a shifting point of view within the limitations of a single narrative voice. In the following five paragraphs, taken from the passage relating Cantwell's Friday night alone with the portrait of Renata, Hemingway uses four different methods of exposition, though the whole is technically spoken by the narrator:

> "Here's to you, Daughter," he said. "You beauty and lovely. Do you know, that, among other things, you smell good always? You smell wonderfully even in a high wind or under a blanket or kissing goodnight. You know almost no one does, and you don't use scent."

> She looked at him from the portrait and said nothing.

> "The hell with it," he said. "I'm not going to talk to a picture."

What do you think went wrong tonight? he thought.

Me, I guess. Well I will try to be a good boy all day; starting at first light. (p. 165)

That Cantwell speaks the first paragraph is obvious through Hemingway's use of quotation marks (a signal for all spoken matter) as well as the use of the third person "he said" (a practice which Hemingway almost always uses in one of its forms in this novel). The third person narrative voice gives us the information in the second paragraph, and the Colonel speaks again in the third paragraph. The fourth paragraph renders Cantwell's interior monologue through the use of the third person "he thought," while the final paragraph continues the interior monologue in an unsignalled first person voice. Hemingway so skillfully handles this blending of narrative modes that the shifting of perspective from the poles of third person omniscient narrator to first person interior monologue occurs with no sense of intrusion upon the reader. Hemingway explores and develops this technique even further in *The Old Man and the Sea*.[8]

Since so much of *Across the River* is the narrator's presentation of the thoughts and feelings of the characters, Hemingway feared that his novel would be criticized for its lack of action. He was, of course, right. In an interview with Harvey Breit in the *New York Times Book Review* (September 1950, p. 14), Hemingway argued that action pervades the novel, "Only it is all done with three-cushion shots." Hemingway has certainly added a new dimension to his narrative techniques by having the action of *Across the River* reported in a second-hand manner: the ball of action must first be bounced off the cushion of Cantwell, then onto the cushion of the narrator, and finally into the cushion of the reader.

The quiet, relatively calm reminiscences found in the thoughts and conversations of the professional soldier add a new dimension to the horror of war. That the soldier is a veteran of three wars and thirty-three years of military service furnishes the story with the all-important element of experience; that the man faces death and has nothing to gain by lying suggests for the novel truth; that the confessions of this dying man are

ultimately overheard by no one lends to the narrative the dignity of soliloquy.[9] While the critics were correct in observing
this lack of action, they were not necessarily correct in counting it as a negative criticism. Artiscally, the second-handed,
three-cushion method of revealing "action" functions consistently with the novel's situation: Cantwell faces an inner
threat of death (not outward violence), and the problems of
his final weekend are inner hurdles (not overt obstacles) which
he must psychologically fight to overcome. In *Death in the
Afternoon* Hemingway relates that at the time of his first bullfight he "was trying to learn to write, commencing with the
simplest things, and one of the simplest things of all and the
most fundamental is violent death. It has none of the complications of death by disease, or so-called natural death. . . ."[10]
Hemingway saw in "death by disease" a complicated subject,
and his three-cushion narrative is a complicated technique to
match it.

In this complicated novel so tightly wrapped around one
central character, Hemingway uses a broad range of character
revelation modes. The Colonel's actions, his dialogue and interior monologues, his relations with others (including their
thoughts and comments about him), and the symbols, images,
and motifs with which he comes to be identified all function
to delineate the character of Richard Cantwell. Although he
recalls many past actions in his thoughts and conversations,
Colonel Cantwell actually engages in few actions during the
course of the story. In brief, a fifty-one year old career soldier,
confronted with imminent death from heart disease, goes to
Venice to spend his final weekend eating and drinking well,
courting his mistress, and shooting ducks—the whole while
behaving alternately as a "mean son of a bitch"   and a "God
damn nice" chicken Colonel (p. 37).

The Colonel's return to Venice to close the circle of his
life, discussed earlier, serves as part of the larger circular movement of the novel. His preoccupations with eating and drinking
and making love have too often been interpreted by critics
as mere sensual self-indulgence. As is usually the case with
Hemingway, however, there is more to the iceberg than meets
the eye. Hemingway often associates eating and drinking with
the basic life force, and it is psychologically appropriate that a

man in Cantwell's hypersensitive mental state should devote special attention to such seemingly mechanical actions. The substance of Cantwell's eating and drinking also demonstrates his connoisseurship in those areas, and point toward his general artistic sensibilities.[11] The Colonel's love-making is not only associated with the life force, but also serves as a physical bond between Cantwell and Renata, and functions as part of the larger motif of procreation and perpetuation. The entire weekend—and the whole story—grows out of the "best run duck shoot" at which the Colonel has ever shot. In *Death in the Afternoon* (pp. 232-233), Hemingway points out that one of the greatest pleasures of killing is the feeling of rebellion against death. Though Cantwell shoots fewer ducks than anyone else, he does shoot well and according to the rules, and therefore enjoys his last bit of rebellion against the death which hovers so near.

Throughout *Across the River and into the Trees* the Colonel vacillates between behaving like a "mean son of a bitch" and acting "God damn nice." Baker identifies this with the Yeatsian Ille and Hic—the tough and the tender, fighter and lover.[12] The Colonel's "wild boar blood" often causes loss of patience, but his conscious preparation for death, and the semi-conscious castigation-purgation principle make Cantwell apologetic and prompt him to want to extend understanding and acceptance to others.[13] His remorse reveals itself as he ponders, "why am I always a bastard and why can I not suspend this trade of arms, and be a kind and good man as I would have wished to be" (p. 65). While the Colonel's roughness extends even to Renata at times, only with the incompetent, the uncomprehending, or the unscrupulous does his sonofabitchness come through with full and unrelenting force.

Most of the character development in *Across the River* derives from the conversations and thoughts of Colonel Cantwell. From these we learn, among other things, that the embittered Colonel is a demoted ex-general who has suffered through three wars, three bitch-women, the loss of three countries, and three heart attacks. These conversations and thoughts also aid in the thematic development of Cantwell's confessional preparation for death. Such ritual preparation necessitates Cantwell's putting into words—whether spoken aloud or merely formed in thought—those dark, foreboding, subconscious horrors which have left his heart so full of rancor: after being forced into consciousness, his malice dissipates and his rancor is purged.

Hemingway incorporates more allusion into *Across the River and into the Trees* than into any of his other novels. And through this constant allusiveness Hemingway provides us with another important means of evaluating his protagonist's character. Though critics have strenuously objected to the contemporary references to military, political, and artistic figures, the lack of action and the largely self-revelatory technique of character delineation make such pronouncements an integral part of Hemingway's creation of Cantwell as a "living person," not just a "character."[14]　Since the novel focuses in Cantwell's mind, an essential aspect of understanding and evaluating the man rests in understanding and evaluating the judgments of the man of action in politics and the military and of the man of artistry in the written and pictorial arts. On another level, incidental allusions—such as to the gray of a Degas painting in association with the mood in the mind of the man approaching death—add to the deployment of atmosphere, setting, and theme.

The language which the Colonel unconsciously uses in both speaking and thinking also contributes to his characterization. His preoccupation with honorific words (such as "honor," "true," "truly," "honest," "well," "straight," and "good") reveals the obsession of a super-sensitive mind preparing for death. Such words seek to lend credibility both to Cantwell's own mind—self-assurance that his words, thoughts, actions, and motives are indeed honest—and to the reader. Their overuse, however, becomes intrusive and offensive to the reader, and even suggests a parody of the so-called "Hemingway style." The Colonel also constantly thinks and speaks in military terminology; though appropriate for a thirty-three year infantry veteran, such shoptalk has been objected to as obscure by the critics and presents an obstacle for readers.

Hemingway further develops the character of Cantwell through the Colonel's relations with other people in the novel. On the one hand, the Colonel's relations with T5 Jackson reveal his impatience with provincial Americans who lack artistic sensibility, who are "sad, self-righteous, and over-fed and under-trained," and who, in essence, have merely "eaten and slept and eaten and slept" (pp. 14-16, 58-59, 301). On the other hand, the *Gran Maestro* brings out the true comradeship which the Colonel can share, for the *Gran Maestro*, like the Colonel himself, "had received the castigation that everyone receives who goes there long enough" (p. 71).

The Colonel shares his most important relationship, however, with Renata. She functions in several capacities which are necessary for an understanding of the thematic significance of the protagonist. She serves as the prompter who continually urges him to tell her (pp. 122, 124, 143); the confessor who encourages him to purge his bitterness (p. 240); and the thermostat which continually checks Cantwell's rising ire with her "don't be rough" and "don't be brutal" (e.g., p. 136, et passim). Renata's name, "the reborn one," and the Colonel's constant references to her as "daughter" hint at his perpetuation through her, an idea suggested by Robert Jordan to Maria in *For Whom the Bell Tolls* [15] Similarly, Renata plays pupil to his teacher, innocence to his experience. She also comes to represent Cantwell's own lost youth (pp. 142, 146). Most of all, however, Renata stands as Cantwell's idealized love, Venus rising out of the sea (p. 97). As his lover, Renata seeks to prepare the Colonel for a "happy death" by relieving him of his loneliness and his feeling of spiritual nakedness (pp. 240, 128-129).

The association of Richard Cantwell with symbols, images, and motifs operates as Hemingway's most successfully artistic and complex method of character delineation. Hemingway introduces one of the most important of these motifs in his early description of Cantwell's return to Fossalta (where he was wounded as a nineteen year old lieutenant) and his ritual purgation: "The river was slow and muddy blue there, with reeds along the edges, and the Colonel, no one being in sight, squatted low, and looking across the river from the bank where you could never show your head in daylight, relieved himself in the exact place where he had determined, by triangulation, that he had been badly wounded thirty years before" (p. 18). With the addition of money—he buries a ten thousand lira note—and the already present blood, the place becomes his monument. The Colonel exorcises the bitterness and pain of his first death, and now looks toward his last one.

Like the rain in *A Farewell to Arms*, the wind of *Across the River* throughout implies death. The wind is repeatedly associated with cold, snow, mountains, north, and late afternoon-night—all symbols of death to the Colonel. In his guise as the man of courage bravely facing death, the Colonel orders the windows of his hotel room opened to allow the cold, north wind to enter (p. 68). The image of a gondola struggling against the wind represents for the Colonel his own fight against death (pp. 72-73); wind imagery also pervades the love scene in the gondola as the excitement and exertion threaten his weakened heart (pp. 149-157).[16]

The use of boats—such as the gondola struggling against the wind—serves as part of the larger journey motif. There are suggestions of a journey inward, in the vein of Conrad's *Heart of Darkness*, and the traditional journey through life, but Hemingway primarily emphasizes the journey toward death. The quietness, cold, darkness, wind, ducks, and Charon-like boatman of the first chapter initiate this motif which continues throughout the novel to Cantwell's death in his oversized Buick (which also has its Charon figure in T5 Jackson).

Bridges—like the boats a natural and important part of the Venetian setting—often function, in Carlos Baker's words, as "symbolic reminders of certain milestones in [Cantwell's] youthful experience."[17] But perhaps Hemingway's most masterful use of symbol occurs in the powerful passage focusing on the two mooring stakes and the five bridges passed in route to the Gritti (p. 46). Baker points out that the two stakes symbolically suggest the two Richard Cantwells—the Lieutenant of 1918 and the Colonel of 1950. The stakes may almost as readily be associated with the Richard-Renata relationship: chained together by their love; separated by their age differences (and Cantwell's impending death); pulled and worn by the tides of time and death. Again, the stakes also call to mind two sides of the protagonist's character—Richard Cantwell, the man of artistic sensibility, and Colonel Cantwell, the man of brutal action.

The scars which mark the body of the old soldier stand out as obvious signs of his experience. The most emphasized of these, his maimed right hand, points toward another area of imagistic significance—the repeated religious, particularly Christian and Easter, overtones of *Across the River*.[18]   Though Cantwell seems doubtful of any turning to Christianity "toward the end" (p. 291), the frequent use of Easter imagery does function effectively as part of his ritualistic, personally religious preparation for death as a martyr-hero.

There are obviously many other symbols and images at work in the novel, such as The Order of Brusadelli (a coterie for the experienced only), the uniform (worn as a badge of duty and courage, not as a costume), the emeralds and the portrait (youth and freshness given by Renata to Cantwell and which he must return), the Negro pin (experience given by the Colonel to Renata which she may keep), water (rivers and canals work especially as purifying agents), and Venice itself (the city built beside and reborn out of the sea).   The images and symbols throughout the novel function most significantly in portraying the aging Hemingway hero as he recalls his fifty year life in the face of death.

In his discussion of *Death in the Afternoon*, Carlos Baker points out that the ideal Hemingway protagonist must stand "somewhere between the hero as man of action and the hero as artist."[19]   While working on *Across the River and into the Trees*, Hemingway wrote to Buck Lanham that his new hero was "most of all himself as he might have been if he had turned to soldiering instead of writing"; what Hemingway sought was "a picture of a highly intelligent fighting man deeply embittered by experience."[20]   Examined in light of Hemingway's statements, and with Hemingway's own heroic models of the bullfighter Maera (man of action) and the painter Goya (the artist), Cantwell functions as the hero who attempts to span the poles of brutal action and artistic sensibility.[21]

Colonel Richard Cantwell serves as a professional soldier in the infantry, but his is a trade which he does not always relish.   In one of their discussions focusing on his "sad science," Renata comments, " 'I hate it but I love it.' "   The Colonel immediately replies, " 'I believe we share the same emotions' " (p. 126).   The conflict which gnaws at the Colonel's heart does not arise from an art versus life dilemma, but rather involves his being a man of artistic sensibilities who has served for more

than thirty years in the most brutal of professions: " 'It is
always disheartening as hell. But you are not supposed to have
a heart in this trade' " (p. 135). Appropriately enough, it is
Cantwell's heart which kills him, not the violence of his trade,
for Cantwell has been the dislocated hero all his adult life;
his conflict—as he looks back over that life—grows from the
contrast between what he was and what he wanted to be. At
one point Cantwell asks himself, "why am I always a bastard
and why can I not suspend this trade of arms, and be a kind and
good man as I would have wished to be" (p. 65). But Cantwell
constantly slips into his trade "unconsciously," and though
he tries "always to be just," he is too often "brusque and brutal"
(pp. 83, 65). Thus, Jackson can wonder at Cantwell's sometimes
acting like "a mean son of a bitch" while "he can be so God-
damn nice" (p. 37).

Cantwell's brutality, however, cannot be entirely blamed
on his trade, for the Colonel's diseased heart pumps "wild boar
blood" (p. 65). Such "wild boar blood" prompts Cantwell not
only to be short-tempered with Jackson, but also to participate
in three wars against Fascism, to fight with two soldiers in a
chivalric defense of Renata's idealized womanhood, and to face
down two young Fascists for the sake of his own honor. Cantwell regrets each time this "wild boar blood" betrays his sensibility toward the innocent, but he feels no remorse for his ill
treatment of the likes of unscrupulous war profiteers, unre-
formed Fascists, the dishonest in all walks of life, incompetent
leaders, and those who lack sensitivity. This part of Cantwell's
nature causes him to remain intrepid and undaunted in the face
of all enemies, even Death. His "wild-boar truculence" thus
works both for and against the Colonel. Unfortunately for
Cantwell the artist, the Colonel is half-a-hundred years old and
has seen three wars fought: his participation in the "sad science"
has embittered and brutalized him so that he unwantingly and
unconsciously lives his *triste metier*, though in his heart he never
wants to practice it at home (p. 83).

The artistic side of Cantwell's nature exhibits itself in his
numerous allusions to the literary and pictorial arts. In her
book *Ernest Hemingway and the Arts*, Emily Stipes Watts refers
to *Across the River* as "a moveable feast of art history and art
appreciation," pointing out that "this is the novel which most

fully explores and illustrates Hemingway's own interest in the arts." Ms. Watts recognizes that the Colonel is a connoisseur of both good paintings and good food: his retirement dreams, for instance, focus on daily viewing the Tintorettos at the Accademia and eating "in good cheap joints behind the market" (p. 45). *Across the River* "is Hemingway's most intellectual novel," Watts concludes, "just as the Colonel is Hemingway's most intellectual protagonist."[22]

Cantwell's connoisseurship also manifests itself in his general dislike of Americans because of their lack of artistic sensibility and their artifices. T5 Jackson best exemplifies the unartistic Americans in his "bambini-Madonna" art theory, his description of the "local museum" (with the "photographs of Liver Eating Johnston, and the skin of some bad man that they hanged him and some doctor skinned him out"), and his seeming preference of K-rations and Ten in One over Italian food (pp. 14-16, 25). When Cantwell refers to his provincial chauffeur as "Sad, self-righteous, over-fed and undertrained" (pp. 58-59), the "undertrained" betokens his lack of artistic education as well as his incomplete military schooling. Jackson's eating and sleeping and eating and sleeping—with only a comic book tossed in for excitement—contribute to his boorish portrait. Like Goya, the artistic Cantwell dislikes artifice and costume. He finds the wire and sponge rubber of American women offensive, and he informs the *pescecani* of the garage bar, "I am sorry that I am in uniform. But is is a uniform. Not a costume."[23] Such disgust at artifice and costume also suggests the artist's preoccupation with truth (Hemingway's "one true sentence" approach to writing) and helps explain the strong concentration of honorific words in the novel.[24]

Several more subtle suggestions to the artist-action conflict within the Colonel occur in the duck hunt and in his comments on Shakespeare. In *Death in the Afternoon* Hemingway describes wing shooting as a "purely aesthetic" form of killing (*DIA*, pp. 232-233). Thus, Cantwell's final duck hunt is more than a rebellious action against death; it is also an artistic exercise. Cantwell—the soldier with artistic sensibility—sees his qualities reversed in Shakespeare—the artist who writes like a soldier: "Soldiers care for Mister Shakespeare . . ." (p. 171). Significantly, Cantwell sees Shakespeare—the man of art and action—as "The winner and still the undisputed champion" (p. 171).

More obvious allusions to the dichotomous pull within Cantwell are the mooring stakes passage and his legacy. Though also pointing toward the young and old Cantwells, and the Richard-Renata relationship, the two mooring stakes suggest the sensitively artistic Richard Cantwell and the brutally active Colonel Cantwell: the stakes are chained together as the two sides of the same person; they are separated because they are opposites; they are both worn by the tides of time and conflict. Cantwell's meager material legacy for Renata consists of two shotguns and the wrapped painting, an obvious contrast. Nowhere, however, are the two sides of Cantwell's character more explicitly brought out than in one of his conversations with Renata: " 'I know how to fight forwards and how to fight backwards and what else?' 'About pictures and books and about life,' " Renata replies (p. 211).

Richard Cantwell's knowledge of life—like that of Goya—derives from experience, for the Colonel, the narrator informs us, is a "quite practical" man (p. 40). Though Cantwell is an art connoisseur, he appreciates the real thing infinitely more than its artistic reproduction. To the portrait he says, " 'I love you very much because you are beautiful. But I love the girl better, a million times better, hear it?' " (p. 174). The old soldier gives his young mistress only one material gift before his death, but this one gift—the small pin of the confidential Negro servant—functions symbolically as the more important intangible legacy which he bequeaths to Renata (p. 105). This favorite, most trusted servant which the Colonel gives to his lover is the cutting edge of experience—a gift she will accept only from her half-a hundred year old lover.

Across the River and into the Trees is not one of Hemingway's best novels—not on a level with *For Whom the Bell Tolls* or *A Farewell to Arms* or *The Sun Also Rises*. Nevertheless, it is, as Carlos Baker has pointed out, "a genuine contribution to the Hemingway canon," and, therefore, deserves further specialized studies such as have been accorded most of Hemingway's other works.[25]   In some ways the novel forms a composite of the earlier Hemingway's themes, characters, and methods. But

Across the River also incorporates such devices as interior monologue (more than any other Hemingway novel prior to 1950), an experimental—for Hemingway—narrative technique, and the most complex, extended use of imagery and symbolism in the Hemingway canon. In *Across the River and into the Trees* Ernest Hemingway consciously sought to extend his art into hitherto unexplored territory; if he was not completely successful, at least Hemingway must be credited with an "attacking," not a "defensive," novel.

NOTES

[1] Few studies have been devoted to any kind of formal analysis of *Across the River and into the Trees*; the three most important articles seem to be: Peter Lisca, "The Structure of Hemingway's *Across the River and into the Trees*," *Modern Fiction Studies*, 12 (1966), pp. 232-250; Horst Oppel, "Hemingway's *Across the River and into the Trees*," trans. Joseph M. Bernstein, *Hemingway and his Critics*, ed. Carlos Baker (New York: Hill and Wang, 1961), pp. 213-226; and Robert O. Stephens, "Hemingway's *Across the River and into the Trees*: A Reprise," *University of Texas Studies in English*, 37 (1958), pp. 92-101. Also, Carlos Baker's *Hemingway: The Writer as Artist*, 4th ed. (Princeton, New Jersey: Princeton University Press, 1972) contains an indispensable chapter-length study entitled "The River and the Trees" (pp. 264-288; Baker's book will hereafter be cited as "Baker"). Delbert Wylder's *Hemingway's Heroes* (Albuquerque, New Mexico: University of New Mexico Press, 1969) devotes a lengthy chapter to Cantwell subtitled "The Tyrant Hero," pp. 165-198. I am heavily indebted to the above studies in my discussion, especially in my section dealing with symbols and images. For a sampling of critical reviews, see Ben Ray Redman, "The Champ and the Referees," *Saturday Review of Literature*, October 28, 1950, pp. 15, 16, ff.

[2] Philip Young, *Ernest Hemingway: A Reconsideration* (University Park, Pennsylvania: Pennsylvania State University Press, 1966), p. 120; John Atkins, *The Art of Ernest Hemingway* (London: Spring Books, 1952),

p. 71.

[3] For further discussion of *ARIT* as a recapitulation of the earlier Hemingway, see Robert Stephens, "Hemingway's *ARIT*: A Reprise," and Young, *EH: A Reconsideration*, passim.

[4] For references to Venice in this circular function see *Across the River and into the Trees* (New York: Scribner's, 1950), pp. 26, 45, 86, 301; 33, 34. Subsequent references in both text and notes will be to this edition.

[5] Baker compares *FWBT* and *ARIT* on p. 266; his discussion of the concentric circles of *FWBT* occurs on pp. 245-247.

[6] See Lisca, pp. 235-236.

[7] Wylder's *Heroes*, pp. 175-180, calls attention to the narrative experiment—which he lables "limited omniscience"—and its attempt "to bring the reader, the omniscient author, and the protagonist of the novel all together at the same level of involvement."

[8] *The Old Man and the Sea* (New York: Scribner's, 1952); note particularly Hemingway's skillful handling of modes on p. 45.

[9] Renata falls asleep at the Colonel's side, and he falls into an interior monologue: see pp. 248, 252, 254. The soliloquy idea I owe to Horst Oppel, p. 221.

[10] *Death in the Afternoon* (New York: Scribner's, 1932), p. 2.

[11] Cf. the use of eating as a life force in *A Farewell to Arms* (New York: Scribner's, 1929), pp. 47, 54, 113, 171, 190-199, 233, 276. For a discussion of Cantwell's "intense state of awareness," see Baker, pp. 274-275. The relation of Cantwell's eating and drinking with his artistic temperament will be further explored below.

[12] Baker, pp. 268-271.

[13] See Oppel, pp. 220-225, for a complete exposition of the castigation-purgation theme.

[14] Hemingway's ideas on the "living person" as opposed to the "charac-

ter" are found in *DIA*, pp. 191-192. For a further apology for the contemporary allusions, see Lisca, pp. 248-249.

[15]*For Whom the Bell Tolls* (New York: Scribner's, 1940), p. 463.

[16]For a more complete discussion of Hemingway's use of the wind see Lisca, p. 240, and Richard K. Peterson, *Hemingway: Direct and Oblique* (Paris: Mouton, 1969), pp. 50-57.

[17]For a complete explication of this function, see Baker, pp. 278-279.

[18]Lisca, pp. 247-248, discusses this area more completely; see Peterson's *Hemingway*, pp. 208-210, for a non-Christian explanation of the significance of the scars.

[19]See Baker, pp. 154-155.

[20]For the Contents of Hemingway's letter to Lanham, see Carlos Baker, *Ernest Hemingway: A Life Story* (New York: Bantam Books, 1970), p. 603.

[21]Hemingway's discussions of Maera and Goya are found in *DIA*, pp. 78-83, 205.

[22]Watts, *Hemingway and the arts* (Urbana, Illinois: University of Illinois Press, 1971), pp. 176-178, 166. The Colonel's seemingly overactive interest in food and drink serves not only as an association with the life force, but also functions as a psychological link with painting; see Watts, p. 166: ". . . psychologists tell us the two often go together." See also *A Moveable Feast* (New York: Scribner's, 1964), p. 69, in which Hemingway says that for a writer, "Hunger is a good discipline and you learn from it."

[23]*ARIT*, pp. 113, 38; see also pp. 103, 186, 237-238.

[24]See *Moveable Feast*, p. 12, for Hemingway's statement on the "one true sentence." Notice how the two strongest objections to the novel's language—honorific words and military jargon—point to this artist-action dichotomy.

[25]Baker, p. 264.

Hemingway's Poor Spanish: Chauvinism and Loss of Credibility in *For Whom the Bell Tolls*

by F. Allen Josephs

It would be difficult to imagine any American writer, or perhaps any writer in our time, to whom style was more crucial than to Hemingway, or to think of any writer who so consciously made pronouncements regarding proper style, or ultimately to name a writer of English who has been as influential in matters of style as he has been. One wonders how such an ostensibly careful writer could have allowed such excessive sloppiness in his Spanish, especially in *For Whom the Bell Tolls*, which is marred by over sixty errors (not counting repetitions of the same error which would put the figure well into the hundreds) ranging from obvious typographical mistakes to errors which seriously undermine the novel's credibility.

Apparently no one pointed out to Hemingway or to Scribners the embarrassing irony of a novel about a Spanish professor containing errors on virtually every page. The errors are not corrected in subsequent editions, and the latest Scribners edition, with a renewal copywright in 1968 by Mary Hemingway, has the same errors as the first edition (1941). An examination of these errors reveals more than Hemingway's linguistic ignorance because it begins to expose a chauvinism which is not in keeping with Carlos Baker's view of Hemingway as a citizen of the world, nor with Hemingway's image of himself.

One does not feel picayunish in the least about taking Hemingway to task here since his use of Spanish is rather analogous to his use of Spain: the Spanish in *For Whom the Bell Tolls* bears a relationship to the novel not unlike that which Spain and Spanish culture bear to Hemingway's work as a whole. If the words are wrong, if the characters say things wrong, if verbal concepts are wrong, may we not begin to question other and larger issues? Hemingway told Malcolm Cowley: "But it wasn't just the civil war I put into it . . . it was everything I had learned about Spain for eighteen years."[1] An examination of the errors may begin to call into question just how sound that knowledge was.

The errors themselves are easily categorized. The great majority are matters of accents, capitalization, and spelling, which would not be so important if they did not undermine the novelist's authority. But Robert Jordan makes his living teaching Spanish at the University of Montana, and although he is only an instructor, he is an exceptional one since he speaks the language "completely . . . and idiomatically" (Scribners Library edition, p. 135). As Anselmo says: "He speaks Spanish as we do" (p. 209).

The problem of authority arises because Robert Jordan can speak Spanish perfectly, but Hemingway, whose Spanish is far from perfect, cannot transmit that perfection. Thus Jordan, or Hemingway-Jordan, and ultimately Hemingway himself, lose credibility. The problem is compounded by the fact that most of the dialogue is supposedly taking place in Spanish although it is written in English. To achieve the effect of Spanish, Hemingway invents a hybrid language and liberally sprinkles it with Spanish words. That this sprinkling is so often incorrect erodes the narrator's authority to a considerable degree. Hemingway needed to be bilingual, which of course he was not. Since he was not, he seems to have chosen to use Spanish as he pleases, correctly or incorrectly, without regard to the sensibility of the reader who does know Spanish and, evidently, without regard to the unfortunate consequences.

María, for example, is spelled wrong throughout: Maria.[2] It is possible that Hemingway intended to leave off the accent, but if he did, why did he bother to use the accent with Joaquín, Andrés, and Agustín? And why did he leave it off the name of the town, Puerto de Santa María, spelling it Santa Maria (p. 230), a name which cannot be anglicized?

Robert Jordan is frequently referred to as Inglés, which is also incorrect. It should be *inglés* since nationalities are not capitalized in Spanish. Even the assumption that Hemingway considers *Inglés* to take the place of a name does not solve the problem since once again he is not consistent. Jordan calls María *guapa*, but Hemingway is careful not to capitalize that. Also, when *Inglés* is used clearly as a nationality (p. 67 and p. 159) and as the English language (p. 27 and p. 248), and is in no way connected to Jordan, why is it capitalized, contrary to Spanish practice? It seems pretty clear that a little English interference was at work since *Ruso* (p. 141) and *Escoceses* (p. 106) are also incorrectly capitalized.[3]

Proper nouns get perhaps the shoddiest treatment of all. Aside from the errors already pointed out, Rincon (p. 375), Sanchez (p. 376), Gomez (p. 396) and Lopez (p. 372), all need accents: Rincón, Sánchez, Gómez and López. Elias ought to be Elías (p. 145). Gran Via—the main street of Madrid—should be Gran Vía (p. 228). And yet, and it is the inconsistency that is so annoying, on the same page, in fact only a line above Gran Via, we read Mantequerías Leonesas *with* its proper accent even though Vía and Mantequería are accented for exactly the same reason.[4]

Robert Jordan, while thinking about what sons of bitches many Spaniards have been, spells—that is Hemingway-Jordan, for Hemingway is artful and purposeful at erasing the distinction between them—Cortés the English way: Cortez (p. 354).[5] While Robert Jordan is thinking that *Fuenteovejuna* is not the greatest play in the world, we are wondering just how qualified he is to judge Lope de Vega's work since we are faced on the page with "fuente Ovejuna" (p. 231). Jordan, the Spanish professor, has his literary criticism undone by Hemingway's spelling and apparant belief that the play is a one-act.[6]

Some forms are strange indeed. *Déjamos* (p. 270) we can understand as a purely typographical error (it should be *Déjanos*), but what is Andalucia (p. 230) supposed to be, Andalucía in Spanish, Andalusia in English, or some new Hemingway hybrid? Judging from the form Andalucian (p. 112), it would seem to be the latter. In *Death in the Afternoon*, Hemingway says: "If a man writes clearly enough any one can see if he fakes. If he mystifies to avoid a straight statement, which is very different from breaking so-called rules of syntax or grammar to make an effect which can be obtained in no other way, the writer takes a longer time to be known as a fake. . . ." (p. 54). One wonders if this rule applies only to English? In any case, Hemingway certainly gets some effects "which can be obtained in no other way."

In the category of different effects is the word *Busnes* (p. 175), which is an incorrect—and for all but specialists utterly obscure—form of *caló* or *romaní*, the Spanish dialect of Romany, an ancient Indic language, a few words of which are still used by the Spanish gypsies. Pilar orders María: "Shut up. *Busnes* of thy age bore me." The term *busnó*, the plural of which is *busné*, or macaronically, *busnés*, not *busnes*, is one that Robert Jordan would have encountered in his reading of George Borrow's books on Spain (p. 248). But how the reader is supposed to deduce the meaning of this incorrect and obscure usage remains a mystery (it means non-gypsy). In fact, it is such an obscure form that Lola de Aguado, in the best Spanish translation (Barcelona: Planeta, 1968, p. 214), translates it out of incorrect *caló* into Spanish, rendering it as *las chicas*. Perhaps lamentably, this rendition loses the original intended meaning of non-gypsies; on the other hand it does not mystify the reader. Just as he pretends to know Spanish, Hemingway pretends to know *caló*. Pilar, for example, asks Jordan, "You have no *Calí* blood, *Inglés*?" (p. 174). This common *caló* term meaning gypsy, Lola de Aguado leaves in but correctly has it read *calé* (p. 212).

In another instance, Hemingway uses a term which seems to be *caló* or French:

> Then, as he thought, he realized that if there was any such thing as ever meeting, both he and his grandfather would be acutely embarrassed by the presence of his father. Any one has a right to do it, he thought. But it isn't a good thing to do. I understand it, but I do not approve of it. *Lache* was the word. But you *do* understand it? Sure, I understand it but. Yes, but. You have to be awfully occupied with yourself to do a thing like that. (p. 338)

The entire paragraph is reproduced so the reader can appreciate the confusion. This passage dealing with suicide is obviously important, so important that the word "suicide" is never mentioned. Instead we get "it" six times and "a thing like that" at the end. In the middle, surrounded by the use of "it", we get: "*Lache* was the word." The *word* for what? *Lache*, in a Spanish context, can only be a known variant of the *romaní* form *lacha* which means by extension *vergüenza*, or something like the English "shame." Thus *Lache* would refer quite logically to the acute embarrassment Jordan and his grandfather share. But if this is indeed the case, Hemingway did not understand, or forgot, that the term originally meant female chastity and specifically virginity and its physical manifestation in the hymen, a subject which Borrow discusses at length in the seventh chapter of *The Zincali: an Account of the Gypsies of Spain*.

It is more probable, even though Jordan tells us Borrow wrote one of the "good books" (p. 248) on Spain, given the context and Hemingway's penchant for disregarding diacritical marks, that he means *lâche*, the French word for "cowardly." What purpose the use of the French term—or the obscure gypsy word—serves, is unclear and puzzling, especially since, as if in unconscious parody, at the bottom of the same page, Jordan, who is clearly using English in an interior monologue, thinks ". . . there is never any point in referring to a son of a bitch by some foreign term." Foreign terms they are to be sure: Lola de Aguado, apparently stumped, leaves the word just as it was, in italics, indicating that it is a foreign term in Spanish as well. She seems unsure that it is French, however, since she does not add the necessary circumflex.

Clearly the worst mistake actually in Spanish is the following:

> "How art thou called?" Robert Jordan asked.
>
> "Agustín," the man said. "I am called Agustín and I am dying with boredom in this spot."
>
> "We will take the message," Robert Jordan said and he thought how the word *aburmiento* which means boredom in Spanish was a word no peasant would use in any other language. Yet it is one of the most common words in the mouth of a Spaniard of any class (p. 45)

Arturo Barea has already objected to this passage which he calls an example of ". . . artificial and pompous English which contains many un-English words and constructions, most of which cannot even be admitted as literal translations of the original Spanish."[7]   As Barea points out, it is an abstract word which a peasant would be most unlikely to use.

What Barea kindly does not point out, and what is even more embarrassing, is that Hemingway-Jordan not only gets the concept wrong, he also gets the word wrong.   The word for boredom is not *aburmiento*, it is *aburrimiento*. Hemingway-Jordan's statement "Yet it is one of the most common words in the mouth of a Spaniard of any class," becomes absurd to anyone who knows the correct form. If it is so common, then why is it spelled wrong?   In a famous passage from *Death in the Afternoon*, Hemingway says, laying down the law for generations of writers to come:

> If a writer of prose knows enough about what he is writing about he may omit things that he knows and the reader, if the writer is writing truly enough, will have a feeling of those things as strongly as though the writer had stated them. The dignity of movement of an iceberg is due to only one-eighth of it being above water. A writer who omits things because he does not know them only makes hollow places in his writing. A writer who appreciates the seriousness of writing so little that he is anxious to make people see he is formally educated, cultured or well-bred is merely a popinjay. (p. 192)

Which of his own rules is Hemingway breaking? Obviously he does not know enough about what he is writing about and the discerning reader recognizes it.   Also he is clearly not formally educated in Spanish, although he certainly speaks as though he were an authority.   Finally, one wishes that Hemingway had worried less about what he omitted and more about what he included.   Leaving out things you do not know may cause hollow places, but putting in things you do not know and getting them wrong is even worse.   In the *Paris Review* interview with George Plimpton, Hemingway reiterated his iceberg theory, and he also said: "The most essential gift for a good writer is a built-in shockproof shit detector.   This is the writer's radar and all great writers have had it."[8]   Hemingway may have had such a device, but it was not bilingual.

The most egregious blunder in the novel is not literally in Spanish; that is, the actual Spanish word never appears in the text. Nevertheless it is always as though it were in Spanish since almost all of the dialogue is to be understood as Spanish except as the narrator or narrator-protagonist otherwise indicates. I have saved this error for the last because it is the most important one in that it is the faux pas which most ironically reveals Hemingway's ineptitude: Robert Jordan nicknames María "rabbit".

Robert Jordan, who speaks Spanish so well that "they trusted you on the language, principally. They trusted you on understanding the language completely and idiomatically" (p. 135), who had written a book on Spain and "had put in it what he had discovered about Spain in ten years of travelling in it, on foot, in third-class carriages, by bus, on horse-and mule-back and in trucks" (p. 248), and who, after the war, thought he would write a book "about the things he knew, truly" (p. 248), Robert Jordan, the professor and expert on Spain, chose to call María "rabbit".

In Spanish the word for rabbit is *conejo* which, as Barea pointed out in 1941, is "one of the more frequent and vulgar euphemisms for the female sexual organ."[9] None of the critics seems to have paid much attention to Barea's fine article, perhaps because he was a foreigner. Even though the article is anthologized by Carlos Baker in *Hemingway and His Critics*, one suspects that it is not taken seriously enough. Since Barea's article does have some Spanish wounded pride in it (much of it justifiable), one suspects that this "rabbit" matter is disregarded. It is possible English language critics are not enough "offended" to realize the gravity of the error.

Perhaps the only way to understand just how devastating the blunder is, for those who do not have an idiomatic command of Spanish, is to reverse the situation. Imagine for a moment a Spaniard, an expert on America and an avowed enemy of slavery, who comes to America not so much to aid the Union cause and preserve unity in the U. S. A. as to fight against the slavers. Imagine that he is paid to speak the language perfectly and idiomatically. Imagine, too, that the first night he spends with a group of Yanks behind the rebels' lines, a mountain girl from Pennsylvania, say, is so taken with the Spaniard that she immediately becomes his lover, a fact that she tries to hide from no one. Imagine finally that the American expert chooses to nickname her and call her, publicly and privately, and with apparent disregard for the fact that she had been raped by a gang of slavers, "Pussy." That is precisely what Robert Jordan does when he calls María "rabbit", and there is no escaping it, explaining it or rationalizing it away. Nor is there any possibility whatsoever that "rabbit" means anything else: *"CONEJO* (arg.) *Organo genital femenino,"* (RABBIT [slang]. Female genital organ).[10]

An examination of the instances where Jordan calls her "rabbit" could lead one to begin to form a circumstantial case for irony on Hemingway's part. Is it possible he did it on purpose, that he knew and consciously used "rabbit" as an ironic symbol or commentary? The answer is no, definitely not, both on philosophical and on textual grounds.

When Hemingway is being ironic or funny it is usually very apparent (consider, for example, the ironic conversations in *The Sun Also Rises*, the use of the Old Lady in *Death in the Afternoon*, the "literary anecdotes" in *Green Hills of Africa*, or the "rummy" scene in the first part of *Islands in the Stream*, to mention a few). Then too, he is usually quite serious about his heroines and about sex. If he means to call her "rabbit," or if he is aware of that meaning and expects anyone else to be aware of it, think what it does to the importance of the scene in which the earth moves. No, to have been aware of it would have been to make a parody of all the love scenes. Hemingway is quite capable of the most biting irony, but not that kind. He and Jordan take such matters far too seriously for us long to entertain such notions of irony.

Textually, too, there is proof that Hemingway simply ignored what "rabbit" means in Spanish:

> "Hello, little rabbit," he said and kissed her on the mouth. She held him tight to her and looked in his face and said, "Hello. Oh, hello. Hello."
>
> Fernando, still sitting at the table smoking a cigarette, stood up, shook his head and walked out, picking up his carbine from

where it leaned against the wall.

> "It is very unformal," he said to Pilar. "And I do not like it.
> You should take care of the girl." (p. 92)

What Fernando, who is the soul of seriousness, objects to is not
the use of the word, it is the kissing. However, when Pilar tells
him they are engaged, he replies: "I encounter it to be perfectly
normal" (p. 92). The use of "rabbit," of course, would not be
perfectly normal no matter what the case. Later on, Fernando
is offended by Robert Jordan's saying *los cojones* in front of
women: "Anselmo laughed and so did the others who were
listening; all except Fernando. The sound of the word, of the
gross word spoken before the women, was offensive to him"
(p. 206). Clearly, had Fernando been upset by "little rabbit,"
and he very much would have been had Hemingway known
enough to have him react in character, he would have said so.
But his realistic objection to the kissing and his inconsistent failure to understand the vulgarity do not ring true. "Little rabbit"
in Spanish is *conejito*, a usage Fernando would have been a good
deal more scandalized by than by the word *cojones*.

Later on, Pilar, who refers in anger to María in Jordan's
presence as "your piece" and "thy little cropped-headed whore"
(p. 150), for which she later apologizes, telling María that she
loves her—but being clear to tell her, too, that she is no *tor-
tillera* (p. 155), the slang word for lesbian—Pilar, who obviously
has no compunctions about language, says: "Thou art a very
pleasant little rabbit" (p. 155), and "But I give you back your
rabbit. Nor did I ever try to take your rabbit. That's a good
name for her. I heard you call her that this morning" (p. 156).
Jordan blushes at this point, but it is clearly the sentimentality,
the exposed tenderness of the nickname, not the sexual connotation of the word, that makes him blush. Pilar's foul mouth
could never have let "rabbit", *conejo*, go by without a gibe
(and what Agustín's foul mouth would have constructed is almost unimaginable). Instead, Pilar commends Jordan for the
nickname. There is a wholly accidental kind of humor here for
the bilingual reader, but unfortunately Hemingway-Jordan is
the butt of the joke.

María, the nineteen year old ravished innocent about whom

Jordan felt: "she was all of life there was and it was true" (p. 264), whom he intends to marry and, in fact, does marry verbally: "We are married, now. I marry thee now. Thou art my wife. But go to sleep, my rabbit, for there is little time now" (p. 354), and about whom he feels: "Until thee I did not think that I could love . . . deeply" (p. 344), this María, whom he calls "rabbit" is not meant to be the object of a lewd or puerile play on words.

What "rabbit" is meant to suggest is a kind of identification with the earth and with animals, a natural quality, an innocence and a perfection so pristine that María does not even know how to kiss: "She moved awkwardly as a colt moves, but with that same grace as of a young animal" (p. 25). She has hair that is "the golden brown of a grain field . . . but little longer than the fur on a beaver pelt" (p. 22), which is "the same length like the fur of an animal" (p. 345), and "as thick and short and rippling . . . as a grain field in wind on a hillside" (p. 23). When María and Jordan meet, Jordan shares in the band's meal which was "rabbit cooked with onions and green peppers and there were chick peas in the red wine sauce. It was well cooked, the rabbit meat flaked off the bones, and the sauce was delicious. Robert Jordan drank another cup of wine while he ate. The girl watched him all through the meal" (p. 22-23). Later they share another meal, this time of hares that the gypsy had caught: "Before daylight I heard the male thumping in the snow. You cannot imagine what a debauch they were engaged in. I went toward the noise but they were gone. I followed the tracks in the snow and high up I found them together and slew them both" (p. 274). It is, I think, significant that the hares were mating (not engaged in a debauch as the gypsy's foul mouth would have it) and that they, like the *guerrilleros* were betrayed by the snow. The animals, the snow, the grain fields, the mountains, the earth itself that moves in tellurian empathy, all are meant to be parts of a natural and innocent and pure world of which María, too, is a part. That her name is María is both realistic (María is by far the most common name for women in Spain) and symbolic of her innocence and her "virginity". Jordan tells her before they make love the first time: " 'I love thee María, he said. 'And no one has done anything to thee. Thee, they cannot touch. No one has touched thee, little rabbit' " (p. 71). Had he used any nickname but "rabbit", this romantic conceit of natural innocence destroyed by a mechanized and fratricidal conflict, and of the regenerative, even if ephemeral, power of pure love to overcome the most violent brutality, might have been successful. But all the inadvertent Freudian blunders which become apparent if you know what *conejo* means, mar the novel as distressingly as an impurity spoils the tone of a bell.

It is difficult to imagine how such grave errors were committed. How could so many things go wrong? Castillo-Puche in *Hemingway in Spain* allows that "Ernesto's spoken Spanish was much more fluent and precise than his written Spanish. It was plain to see that he had doubts and misgivings when he wrote in Spanish, and he usually fell into a much more formal sort of diction and made grammatical errors."[11] But that does not explain the extent of the errors in a book that was supposed to contain all he had learned about Spain, a book by the man who, as Salvador de Madariaga said, "revealed to his country and to the world many Iberian aspects until then badly misunderstood."[12]

According to Carlos Baker, Gustavo Durán, an exiled Loyalist commander, read the galleys "to make sure that the Spanish was correct . . . and was not much impressed by the quality of Ernest's Spanish."[13] That he was not much impressed is easily understandable; what is hard to fathom is how or why the errors persisted. Did Durán really read the galleys? Did he make corrections? Whatever actually happened, the galleys did not get corrected. Baker also maintains: "One updated page labeled 'DON'T LOSE THIS FOR CHRIST'S SAKE' gave the printer a checklist of Spanish spellings and accents. . . ."[14] Yet, in spite of the apparent concern, the errors persisted.

Hemingway made errors in Spanish starting with the first pieces on Spain he wrote, if the typography can be trusted. In an article called "Bull Fighting a Tragedy", for example, he spells *banderillas* wrong: banderillos; and the street in Madrid known as the Carrera de San Jerónimo comes out Via San Jerónimó.[15]

There is little Spanish in *The Sun Also Rises* but there

are mistakes in it too.[16]　　The most interesting is the term *desencajonada* (p. 131), which while not strictly incorrect, is at least not idiomatic. The term is properly *desencajonamiento*, which means the removal of the bulls from their individual shipping crates. In a way, this term is typical of the whole problem. When Hemingway does not know the correct usage, he irresponsibly or inadvertently passes on the error. As Hotchner says in *Papa Hemingway*, "From the time I read my first Hemingway work, *The Sun Also Rises* . . . I was struck with an affliction common to my generation—Hemingway Awe."[17] In 1959 when Hotchner is with Hemingway in Pamplona, he observes: "The twenty-five thousand tourists were mainly American college kids. . . . Almost to a student they had been attracted to Pamplona by *The Sun Also Rises*. . . ."[18] To see how a Hemingway error persists, one has only to keep in mind Plimpton's interview with Hemingway and hears Plimpton say ". . . later, during the *desencajonada*, the bull. . . ."[19] The error, however unimportant, has nevertheless become the common usage of the American *afición*.

Just for the record, *The Fifth Column* and most of the short stories that deal with Spain also demonstrate the same kinds of inconsistencies and errors: grammar, spelling, accents, capitalization. And for what may be Hemingway's worst writing, there is the spaghetti-Italian dialect that the Spanish characters, especially the Manager, mouth in *The Fifth Column*. *The Old Man and the Sea*, which has very little Spanish, nevertheless has some errors.

On the other hand, *Islands in the Stream*, which contains quite a good deal of Spanish, perhaps as much as *For Whom the Bell Tolls*, though none of the macaronic language that pervades the latter, has almost no errors in the Spanish (I could find only two and they are not worth listing). The idiomatic Spanish is all neatly italicized, properly spelled, accented and capitalized. Even the upside down question marks are included at the beginnings of questions. But Hemingway never read those galleys, and the book was prepared for publication by Charles Scribner, Jr. and Mary Hemingway who, according to a prefatory note, as well as cutting, took care of "the routine chores of correcting spelling and punctuation."

From all this there begins to emerge a kind of pattern of error. One finally is struck with the notion that Hemingway did not really care whether the Spanish was correct. No matter what he may have said, the facts speak plainly, and if you know Spanish well and look for them, the errors are glaring, too numerous to discount, too persistent to shrug off, too pervasive not to ring false. *For Whom the Bell Tolls* is the repository of an enormous quantity of errors precisely because it is the most Spanish, which is to say the least accurate, of Hemingway's works.

It is quite possible that Hemingway simply did not attribute to this matter of Spanish that much importance. In fact, I suspect—although there is probably no way to prove it—that this was the case. If it is true, it betrays a kind of chauvinism which does not sit well on such an international figure.

In the final analysis, one must conclude that, regarding correctness of Spanish terms, Hemingway either did not care, which is to say that he did not take pains to find out whether he was being correct, or that he wrote essentially for an American public which would not know the difference anyway. If the former is true, his attitude was sloppy and chauvinistic and if the latter, chauvinistic and perhaps patronizing. In either case one begins to see a certain provincialism behind the authority, an authority which the writer abused at times to such an extent that the critics have assumed that he was right where he was in fact incorrect.

Joseph Warren Beach, for example, thinks that in *For Whom the Bell Tolls*: "Hemingway is surely relying on the literary culture of his readers", to appreciate the use of thee and thou as they are used in other languages, and he believes that by the "skillful use of the idioms of a foreign tongue and the poetic associations of the Bible, he has added another 'dimension' to his English prose."[20] I cannot disagree more, if by "literary culture" he has any notion of our having read Spanish literature in the original language. Quite the contrary, Hemingway seems to rely, whether consciously or not, on our not having a knowledge of the language, on our having rather a linguistic ingenuousness which will allow us to accept, or at least not to question, what Hemingway presents as Spanish.

But now we know that much of that Spanish is incorrect and that at least the use of "rabbit," which is translated Spanish, is poor to the point of ridicule. How much of that other translated Spanish is wrong, incorrect, false, invented or at least cockeyed like the speculation about *aburrimiento*? The answer is, a whole lot of it. You cannot translate much of it back into Spanish. Just what is wrong with it and just how serious that is are the subjects for future essays,[21] but the point for now remains that Hemingway invented a good deal of Hemingway-Spanish and tried to pass it off as correct. As Edward Fenimore has quite correctly pointed out, it is "Hemingway's familiar rhythmic patterns that contribute to what we accept as Spanish."[22] It is Fenimore's point that this is Spanish because "as readers we tacitly assume the primitive, in common with all the unfamiliar, to be necessarily Spanish."[23] Mr. Fenimore is only right if you happen not to be able to read Spanish. And yet he is correct that we are supposed to react as he suggests. In other words *For Whom the Bell Tolls* was not written for anyone who reads Spanish. Furthermore, Mr. Fenimore's (and if he is correct, then Hemingway's) assumption that Spanish necessarily equals primitive is not merely chauvinistic, it is ignorant.

What Hemingway attempts to render, the effect of one language in another, is quite ambitious, but it requires wide knowledge of both languages, something Hemingway lacked. Where he did not know, he invented and where he invented he made holes in the story. It was surely unintended, but Hemingway made the lack of knowledge of Spanish a prerequisite to the enjoyment of the novel. The first time I read the novel, in Spain in 1963, this was not apparent since I was just beginning to learn Spanish. Thinking back about it, I realize the novel seemed then to be almost perfect and so true that it was like a virtuoso execution of what Hemingway had called the "writer's problem" in his speech in 1937 to the second American Writers' Congress: "It is always how to write truly and having found what is true, to project it in such a way that it becomes part of the experience of the person who reads it. . . ."[24] Coming back to it in 1975, I was appalled at the mistakes and unable, finally, to take the novel seriously.

The first time I read it I was an American just come to Europe (one of those innocents who considered Spain primitive), waiting to be led by the old master. The second time, I was bilingual and largely bicultural, no longer unknowing enough, and unable to suspend what I had learned. So that what I learned in the second reading was that the novel had been written for an American public and a public ignorant of Spain and Spanish. I was able to see how necessary it is in neo-realistic fiction for the author to know everything his characters are supposed to know. Since Hemingway did not know Spain and Spanish as well as Robert Jordan should have, and since this showed through if you knew the language, parts of the novel seemed falsified: there were some "rotten" places in it and they spoiled all the rest, even the very good parts.

What *For Whom the Bell Tolls* is, then, is not at all *the* novel of the Spanish Civil War written by a "citizen of the world;"[25] it is, rather, a novel about the Spanish Civil War written by an American. In the long run, the errors in *For Whom the Bell Tolls* undermine Baker's contention. Hemingway was more properly an American at large, acting in his writing as well as in his living almost as a Henry James character trying to act as a citizen of the world. That American critics have usually taken him at face value is not so much a confirmation or recognition of his world citizenry as it is an indication of their own lack of expertise regarding Spain, and, in some cases, an indication of their own chauvinism.

There needs to be a book written on Hemingway and Spain, a book written by an American critic precisely because Hemingway is so American. But that American critic is going to have to know Spain better than Hemingway so that he can see over Hemingway and get a clear picture. He will have to know bullfighting better and know a good deal about the Spanish Civil War and about Spaniards in general. A recent study called *Hemingway's Spanish Tragedy*[26] is an illustration of a book which could have been better had its American author known more about such matters.

Until a more comprehensive account is written, we will not have a clear critical picture of Hemingway's work since so much of it deals with Spain and her oldest and closest colony,

Cuba. What this essay does, I hope, by examining Hemingway's misuse of Spanish and some of the consequences involved, is to get us pointed in that direction.

NOTES

[1] "A Portrait of Mr. Papa,"*Life,* January 10, 1949.

[2] Unless otherwise indicated, the terms to be discussed appear in my text as they did in the work or works being discussed.

[3] And who can explain why *Ingles* (p. 27) is both capitalized and unaccented? Or why *Compadre* and *Chico* (p. 55) are capitalized, or why El Sordo is not written *el sordo*? Why is it Rafael el Gallo and El Gallo (p. 187) on the same page instead of Rafael *el gallo* and *el gallo*? Why El Campesino (p. 229) instead of *el campesino*, whose name is also spelled wrong: Valentín Gonzalez instead of González? Why *Cuatro Dedos* instead of *cuatro dedos* (p. 110), and why italicize this name but not El Campesino? There is simply no comprehensible pattern: *camarada*, for example, is correctly not capitalized (p. 153), but incorrectly capitalized at other times (p. 131).

[4] Alcazar (p. 242) needs an accent: Alcázar. So does Irun: Irún (p. 237). San Sebastián (p. 237) ought to be San Sebastian. Sanchez Mejias (p. 253), the famous *torero*, ought to be written Sánchez Majías—but then it is also misspelled in *Death in the Afternoon* as are a good many other names. Garcia (p. 108) ought to be García and Concepcíon Gracia (p. 353), María's friend, needs to be either Concepción Gracia or Concepción García, probably the latter. Café Colon (p. 185) has the correct accent on Café but leaves it off Colon.

There are many other accent mistakes including some superfluous accents, some of them grammatical, most of them too tedious for lengthy discussion but worthy of note nonetheless:

Hemingway		Spanish
Qué no?	(p. 97)	¿Que no?
Qué salga	(p. 109)	Que salga
A mi qué?	(p. 179)	¿A mí qué?
Cómo qué no?	(p. 284)	¿Cómo que no?
Como fué?	(p. 149)	¿Cómo fue?
Si	(p. 149)	Sí
mas	(pp. 249, 409)	más
peon	(p. 251)	peón
vamanos	(pp. 99, 268, 294)	vámanos
util	(p. 152)	útil

Some of the above, for example *vámanos* (p. 406) and *más* (p. 384), are also correctly written at times. Even the obscenity gets poor treatment. Most of the time *cabrón* is written without the accent (pp. 108, 109, 111 and 125 for example) but once in a while the accent is correctly there (p. 453). Other accent errors:

Hemingway		Spanish
picardia	(p. 332)	picardía
bubonica	(p. 418)	bubónica
mania	(p. 419)	manía
tambien	(p. 435)	también
Ojala	(p. 263)	Ojalá
concienzudo	(p. 444)	concienzudo
Ole	(p. 187)	Olé
Tu	(p. 214)	Tú

Anarquia (which should be *anarquiá* with an accent) is strangely capitalized (p. 120). So are *Libertad* (p. 120), Corrida, without italics (p. 128), *Gitanos* (p. 175), and *Gitana* (p. 187), although *Gitana* (p. 255) is correctly written for some reason. *Salvoconducto* (p. 375) and *Novedad* (p. 450) are also incorrectly capitalized.

Other errors: *Sinverguenza* (p. 212) and Siguenza (p. 334) should be *sinvergüenza* and Sigüenza. *Apesar de* is *A pesar de* (p. 418); *guardia civiles* (p. 351) should be *guardias civiles*; *Yo maté uno tambien* (p. 435) should read *Yo maté a uno también*. *El Debate* (p. 398) and *Mundo Obrero* (p. 397), both newspapers, are both correctly italicized, but A.B.C. (p. 398), one of Madrid's most important dailies, is not.

[5]Hemingway-Jordan also gets Velázquez wrong (p. 234) by leaving off the accent. In *Death in the Afternoon*, it is still worse: Velasquez; El Greco comes out worse yet when Hemingway calls him el Rey de los maricones which should read *el rey de los maricones* (Scribners, 1932, pp. 203-205).

[6]In *Death in the Afternoon*, the author is Lope da Vega (p. 73).

[7]Arturo Barea, "Not Spain But Hemingway," *Horizon*, III (May, 1941), p. 358.

[8]In *Hemingway and His Critics*, ed. Carlos Baker (New York: Hill and Wang, 1961), p. 37.

[9]Barea, p. 359.

[10]Jaime Martín, *Diccionario de expresiones malsonantes del español* (Madrid: Ediciones Istmo, 1974), p. 90. Lola de Aguado's diminutive, *conejito*, fails to help.

[11]José Luis Castillo-Puche, *Hemingway in Spain*, trans. Helen R. Lane (Garden City, New York: Doubleday and Co. Inc., 1974), pp. 30-31.

[12]*Saturday Review of Literature*, July 29, 1961, p. 18.

[13]*Ernest Hemingway: A Life Story* (New York: Charles Scribner's Sons, 1969) pp. 350-351.

[14]Baker, p. 352.

[15]*By-Line: Ernest Hemingway*, ed. William White (New York: Charles Scribner's Sons, 1967), pp. 90-97.

[16]*Afición* does not have the accent (Scribner's Library Edition, p. 131), for example. It is left off San Fermín, too, the patron saint of Pamplona (p. 153). *Corrida* is incorrectly capitalized in the middle of a sentence (p. 173). Some of the Spanish words are italicized but many are not. Some are enclosed in quotation marks, for example "quite" (p. 216). Some get made into English as "templed" does (p. 219). The common greeting *muy buenas* is spelled wrong: muy buenos (p. 240).

[17]A. E. Hotchner, *Papa Hemingway* (New York: Random House,

1966), p. 3.

[18]Hotchner, p. 212.

[19]*Hemingway and His Critics*, p. 29.

[20]"Style in *For Whom the Bell Tolls*" in *Ernest Hemingway: Critiques of Four Major Novels*, ed. Carlos Baker (New York: Charles Scribner's Sons, 1962), p. 86.

[21]Barea touched on this point, but it could use a thorough analysis.

[22]"English and Spanish in *For Whom the Bell Tolls*" in *Ernest Hemingway: The Man and His Work*, ed. John K. M. McCaffrey (New York: Cooper Square Publishers, Inc., 1969), p. 218.

[23]Fenimore, p. 218.

[24]*Ernest Hemingway: A Life Story*, p. 314.

[25]Baker's essay called "Citizen of the World" serves as the introduction to his *Hemingway and His Critics*.

[26]Lawrence R. Broer, *Hemingway's Spanish Tragedy* (University of Alabama Press, 1973). Anyone interested in a more Spanish slant on Hemingway's view of Spain may wish to consult my "Hancia un estudio de la Espana de Hemingway," *Insula* (Madrid), no. 363 (February, 1977).

Hemingway: The Writer in Decline

by Philip Young

As experts all in the study of American letters you will
remember how Walt Whitman once paraphrased Emerson:

> Do I contradict myself?
> Very well then I contradict myself
> (I am large, I contain multitudes).

Permit me then a little paraphrase of Whitman:

> Do I repeat myself?
> Very well then I repeat myself
> (I am small, I contain platitudes).

Things are worse than most of you think. I have, for
example, had to use even this opening business before. (That
was when I was outrageously conned, if anyone cares but me,
into writing not for the second but the third time the story of
going through Hemingway's manuscripts in the bank vault.) It
ought to be easy to dodge this sort of thing, but sometimes—as
on the conned occasion and now on this one—it is not. One
does, however, come to wonder what in the world people expect. After writing off and on for over 25 years on the subject
of a single author, what can you possibly have to say that will
be neither stale nor wholly trivial? I don't know, and it won't
happen again. It's been five years since I last even attempted
to accomplish anything fresh with Hemingway; in the mean
time I've done a book which is as far as I can get from my
familiar topic (it isn't even "about literature"), and I'm well
into another that's a sort of sequel to it. But even as I hear me
saying "Never Again" it pops into my mind that I have been
described, in print, as "the Sarah Berhardt of Hemingway criticism." (I took that for some kind of dirty crack, but was calmed

by the explanation that the reference was to this thing she and I appear to have shared about giving Farewell Appearances.)

Well, in thinking how I could conceivably contribute to the present coming-together it occurred to me first that I have never expressed myself publicly on the subject of what I take to be a special reason for Hemingway's general descent as a writer of fiction over his last decade or so. And second that this partial explanation of that falling off has a great deal to do with the next-to-biggest objection he had to my understanding of his work. Further, that although I have told the story of his biggest objection—the complaint that I was psychoanalyzing him alive—I have never said much about his other chief grievances. The concern here is of course not the critic's notions, which some of you know anyway, but how in responding to them the author reveals something of what he thought about his own fiction. My hope is that this will serve.

Arnold Toynbee observed that history shows how the same traits that made nations great eventually led to their downfall. Precisely, it seems to me, the case with Hemingway in my present view of him. What made him great were of course things like extraordinary talent—"gifts"—originality, courage, absolute dedication, and so on, but I am taking these things as givens, common in varying degrees to most important writers. My notion of the special quality, marked in Hemingway from the start, that promoted his early success as a writer of fiction was what I will call "confident self-absorption"; in his decline it became an insecure obsession with self. The very early ability to look objectively to himself for a protagonist, and to write realistically and impersonally of his own experience, while transmuting it to fiction, was an act of daring. To believe that one is significant enough, and what happens to one, too, and to start a career on that basis took guts. I have specifically in mind the recently uncovered "Summer People"—almost certainly the first story Hemingway ever wrote about Nick Adams, his first protagonist. The confidence here was that the reader could be interested, as he generally is, in Nick's youthful thoughts, ambition, conversation—even in the way he swims and dives!—and most of all in his assurance that he is "different": that because of "something in him" he could "have what he wanted" —which is not, chiefly, the girl of the tale, whom he does have, but to be "a great writer."

I would hope to do justice to the early fiction that emerged from such confidence. It took repeated acts of moral courage to break through, in those first stories, so many conventions that people were unwilling even to call them "stories" (they were *contes*, etc.). Here was a new kind of prose, a new objectivity, a brilliant economy, a startling freshness of view—even a willingness to put up with complaints about some of the tales that "nothing happens." It took fantastic discipline, still at the start of a career, to write a long story (I'm thinking of "Big Two-Hearted River") while intentionally omitting the one crucial fact that would explain it. (It's equally astonishing that he got away with it, by which I mean that the story was widely admired long before it was completely understood—if it is yet: I'm thinking about that "tragic" swamp.)

Obviously I am assuming that in both the fishing story and in "Summer People" the author was seeing himself as Nick, in the summer after his return from the war. Thus I am still registering the identification that Hemingway first objected to in me long before my book on him was published, or he had seen any of it. It was two full years before the volume appeared that he wrote saying he had heard from Malcolm Cowley, who had read the manuscript, that I was writing a book which "proved" that he was all his heroes, or protagonists, and that to save me time and effort he had decided to dissuade me. (Except for a few revisions, the book in fact was finished; its two opening chapters would go to considerable pains to distinguish between characters that represent Hemingway and those who were often taken to do so and definitely did not.)

The identification of himself with such of his characters as Nick—and of events in his stories with some of those in his own life—did not, of course, begin with me. Rather, though I didn't know it then, with his parents and siblings. When most of the Nick Adams fiction remained to be written, Hemingway had Nick thinking (in an abortive ending to "Big Two-Hearted River," later published separately) that "Everything good he'd ever written he'd made up. None of it had ever happened. . . . That was what the family couldn't understand." Possibly because, like the fishing trip to that River, some of it had happened. In any event it was immediately after thinking this that the passage goes on to say "Nick in the stories was never himself. He made him up." But in context it is clear that it is "he, Nick," who thinks or says that—which amounts to saying—it does indeed say—that Nick was never Nick: it is precisely at the moment when the author attempts to distinguish writer from character that he confuses them absolutely, which is to say identifies them.

Hemingway must have sensed that I would relate him as well to Jake Barnes, as I did and do.   Not literally, of course; everybody knows how in those Paris days Ernest was married to Hadley and the father of Bumby.   But I did believe that in many real ways—in his attitudes, interests, thoughts and general character—Jake would be hard to tell from the author, who wrote to inform me that he was specifically *not* Jake.   This figure came, he explained, out of his own wounding when some pieces of cloth were driven into his scrotum so that he got to know soldiers with other genito-urinary wounds, in particular a boy who had suffered Jake's special disaster.   He had got to wondering what a man's life would be like in this condition and so took *him* and made him a foreign correspondent in Paris, which is of course what Hemingway had been.   It was at the time as far from his mind as from mine that I would one day be leafing through the start of the first draft of what he was calling FIESTA without encountering the name Jake Barnes: there *was* a young man known as "Ernie" of "Hem."   (The author also thought to mention Francis Macomber in this connection. Was that him?   He knew very well it was not, and I agree.)

It's my belief that it was when Hemingway put on a mask that de-personalized himself—as Nick, Jake, or Frederic Henry— that the autobiographical method worked, and awfully well. Nick, indeed, is almost im-personalized, or played down as a person, at least until he appears in the late-written and post-humously published "Last Good Country."   With these three protagonists, further, it seems pretty much the same mask.[1] No matter.   Hemingway deeply resented my thought (which was scarcely peculiar to me, though I went farthest with it) that these protagonists were based loosely on himself and his experiences.   To take the case of Nick alone for a moment, it is easy to see his position.   "Indian Camp," for instance, does not describe an ordeal that Ernest went through any more than he'd had the adventure related in "The Battler," or run off with his sister following his shooting of a great blue heron as in "The Last Good Country." But many of the stories involving Nick do reflect or build on things that had happened to the author. It was he, not I, who said that the little Nick tale called "The Doctor and the Doctor's Wife" is "about the time I discovered that my father was a coward." (I do not believe that is what the story is "about," and the identification of himself with Nick here is more absolute than I ever made it.)

At the time of the argument over the publication of my book on him I was unaware of how *much* my relating Nick to the author bothered him. It was fifteen years after his first protest that I had the eerie experience, in going through his manuscripts, of finding letters he had written me and never posted. (At one point, nine months before my book was published or he'd seen any of it, he wrote four of them in two days, May 26 and 27, 1952, mailing one.) In another, unposted, he remarks a couple of reasons why he was at the time not happy in general—the chief of them being my assumption that Nick was a persona for the author. Assuming that I was handing this out in the classroom, he took moral exception to teaching students what is untrue. Not realizing that I had no academic employment at the time—or any other job—he asked to be invited to sit in on a seminar of mine some time, and watch me show the students how to write, and see if it was easy, and if they all learned. He also suggested that I take a good look in the mirror prior to going out and hanging myself. (In an undated letter of the same period he had a more awesome thought: my two most sensitive organs were to be nailed to a fence, the whole of me then to be rocked back and forth nice and easy, "critic.") His preoccupation remained the academy: I was poisoning colleges. It was at about this time that he was also writing Charles Fenton, who did have a job, and it was to Fenton and not to me that he explained how I got him so utterly "down": by simply not knowing what things are all about. The basic trouble, as he saw it, was my lack of experience in warfare. Non-combat characters like me, he wrote, will *never* forgive combat characters, so they have to destroy them. I've related this little episode before, but the newspapers somehow missed it and I think it bears repeating for a fundamental insight I'd never had. One day when I was skipping through some letter files to see if any literary manuscript was mixed in (no), I came across perhaps the fifth such reference to myself. Momentarily out of my gourd I charged out of the study where I'd been reading into the living room where Mary worked, flourishing the letter and saying "for crying out loud where do you suppose he got this non-combat stuff? I've got three battle stars and a decoration." Mrs. Hemingway is very quick in the head, and it didn't take her a second to start saying very quietly "Philip, if Ernest had known that there would *never* have been any trouble." I could have lived a hundred years without thinking of such a thing.

Once my attempt to "destroy" him was printed and Hemingway had actually read it, one might think things would have cleared up at least a little. It never happened, as I know best from reading a series of letters the novelist wrote to Charles Poore, who had in the daily *New York Times* given me the only bad review the book ever got. (These letters have been in part published, however improperly, in an auction catalogue—which frees me, I think, to quote a bit from them.) Hemingway wrote Poore that in reading me he was reminded of "the incredible accusations a woman that loves you will make sometimes on the day before she gets the curse. . . . I think we ought to get him to his analyst. . . . I'd say he was pretty well around the bend already. . . ." The trouble in this correspondence was again and still not the psychological business he had so vigorously protested in letters to me but the autobiographical. "Because some character in a story drinks before an attack," he wrote, "Young makes me out a coward." (The character is Nick in "A Way You'll Never Be"; no one else ever misread me so wildly—not that I know of.) It was, however, while writing Poore that the author at least gave up his plans for doing me some dreadful injury: "since I saw the picture on the back of the book," he wrote (in which, all things considered, I thought I looked fairly well), "I'm just going to let him hang and rattle." But he applauded the physical approach in Poore: "I'm glad you body punched him a little . . . you hit him where he hurts." (I think this referred to my own psychological problem, unspecified.) Yet at the end of this exchange, Hemingway was still grousing about the "autobiographical" business—now for a reason that had never dawned on me and which I have never been able to credit:

"what I do hate," wrote the author, "is chicken English instructors constituting themselves detectives and writing about your life and . . . bringing in so many people . . . that you are deprived of making stories . . . because you would expose youself to libel suits." He concluded that Young must be, indeed, "a strange character. If you shot him he'd probably bleed footnotes."

The idea that Hemingway wrote often of himself, in whatever disguise, and out of his own experience needs of course to be qualified. An important qualification is that he often romanticized things—or even more simply "wish-fulfilled" them. This was especially true of his female characters in their relationships with the hero—and right from the start. In "Summer People," for example, Kate gives herself most willingly to Nick. She was in life named Kate, and I once heard from her brother Bill (Smith), who appears in the same story as he did in "The Three Day Blow." The original Kate was much older than Ernest, and seems to have thought of him as a likeable kid; Mr. Smith was absolutely positive that Ernest had never slept with his sister (who became, incidentally, Mrs. John Dos Passos). Likewise, as you will remember, Nick had a colorful introduction to sexual fulfillment in "Fathers and Sons"—in the woods with the Indian girl Trudy; in a brief passage that was removed in editing from "The Last Good Country" it is revealed that Nick indeed had got her pregnant. Carlos Baker reports that in letters Ernest occasionally boasted that Trudy provided his own initiation; it is Baker's conclusion that the whole affair was something the author wished had happened. In *A Farewell to Arms* the same process is at work: Lt. Henry's love affair with Catherine Berkley is what Hemingway in writing dreamed of; what actually and very differently happened in his relationship with Agnes von Kurowski the author presented in a little piece called "A Very Short Story." Similarly Hemingway does not appear to have more than fantasized the affair with the youthful Italian Adriana Ivancich, who became Renata in *Across the River and into the Trees.* And no ex-wife (whom I take to be modeled on Marlene Dietrich) turned up in Havana for the sexual interlude described in the "Cuba" section of *Islands in the Stream.* Which leads me to the third and last thing about my book that got under Hemingway's skin, as again I did not know until I saw the letters he didn't mail.

The sore point here was that I thought the "Hemingway heroine"—meaning Catherine, Renata, and Maria in *For Whom the Bell Tolls*, to which list now might be added Hadley in *A Moveable Feast* and Littless in "The Last Good Country"— seemed day dreams of the author's: as females, too good to be true, submissive and devoted to the hero beyond credibility and to the near-extinction of their own personalities. This, Hemingway explained to me, was because I knew so pitifully little about women. If he wrote of his lovely wife Mary, or of his late wife Pauline, or of Ingrid Bergman or Marlene Dietrich I would call them fantasies. (I note that he did, according to him elsewhere, write of Ms. Bergman: he inscribed her copy of *For Whom the Bell Tolls* "To Ingrid Bergman who is the Maria of this book"; she played Maria in the movie; I did say she was a fantasy.) In another unsent letter he wrote at considerable length about my knowledge and experience of women, remarking that we had moved in different circles. (I had, one night, sat right behind Ms. Dietrich at the movies, but she was with Jean Gabin and paid neither me or the film much attention; I expect that doesn't count.) According to Professors, Hemingway said (how rapid my promotion from Instructor!), women are like professors' wives. Some of them look like Mrs. Whitaker Chambers, others like Priscilla Hiss. Or better, the women I knew were like the Catholic Communist he once met on a ship: instead of a mons veneris she had a mountain of dialectics; one breast was for Marx and the other Engels; the only open orifice was for fouling Trotsky. Professor, he wrote, she would have been your dream girl. (He cut that off remarking that he shouldn't joke with anyone as mentally understaffed as me; especially, I thought, unless he could be funnier.)

He had already made the point that his heroines were "invented from life"; as little as he wanted to hear it, so too were his proper heroes invented out of his own life, in an act of imaginative self-dramatization. As long as the raw material—Hemingway—was strictly under control, disciplined and objective, the method worked. It worked for that matter in *For Whom the Bell Tolls* too, and in the non-fictions called *Green Hills of Africa* and *Death in the Afternoon*. It was in *Across the River and into the Trees* that things got all out of control: it is my argument that this was largely for the reason that as his career moved toward its close, the author was less and less willing or able to turn himself into a protagonist who is anything different from or more than himself. In this novel Richard Cantwell is an almost exact and utterly indulgent self-portrait, and it was out of the assumption that he could be made fascinating—and moving—for those reading about him that disaster struck. There are very fine passages in this book not open to this objection; for the rest we get the Colonel's banal and downright embarrassing conversations with the girl, and worse ones with her portrait. (In her book, Mrs. Hemingway remarks that at the time of writing it was her hope that these parts would be "improved" at Scribner's, but I at any rate am unaware that her husband ever did, alive, get any editing there, though like the rest of us he could sometimes have used it.) In other places, Cantwell appears to be under the curious delusion that he is being interviewed; people hand him implausible questions so that he can pontificate. This book is a parody of the grace of execution which once made its author distinctive. No one has made fun of him as effectively as he does himself; once exposed to it it is hard to forget the moment when Cantwell is having a little wine, and reaches for the champagne bucket "accurately and well."

The Old Man and the Sea seemed at first a happy turn away from the self-absorption that deluded Hemingway into believing that his readers could subsist on portraits of the artist as a middle-aged man. But even here it is my ungenerous reaction that the old Cuban fisherman is distractingly impinged on by the author, who gives him thoughts and phrases characteristic not of such a figure but of the writer. "I am a strange old man," Santiago thinks twice—as Hemingway was much given to saying of himself (to Lillian Ross, among others) in that period of his life. (As *I* read it, this was a way of saying how mysterious, ineffable, are the gifts of the great artists!) At a couple of points, Hemingway intrudes on Santiago to the extent that he seems more a writer (or *the* writer) than a fisherman. His lines are "as thick around as a big pencil," and "He kept them straighter than anyone did." The boy, who stands in for the Hemingway heroine, tells him "There are many good fishermen, and some great ones. But there is only you." He is soon doing "that which I was born for"; he had proved it many times and "now he was proving it again"—which is to say he was writing a book. We recall being told that Santiago lost his prize because

he "went out too far," though he did, after all, catch his fish,
and the sharks who took it from him are also present much
nearer shore. It seems to me that Hemingway is saying that it
was he, in his recent *Across the River and into the Trees*, who
had gone out too far—farther than the critics could go (so he
remarked of their failure with his experiment "in calculus").
They were the sharks who had devoured his enormous trophy.

Thus *The Old Man and the Sea* does not, for me, contradict
my argument: *A Moveable Feast* does. The author is almost
wholly preoccupied with himself in it, and he wrought a minor
masterpiece. What was always needed between himself and his
protagonist was distance. If the triumph of this book is as I
feel it to be enchantment, it is distance that lends it—a distance
of nearly forty years. I was once very mistaken in my understanding of the writing of this memoir. Having read Mary's
story about finding some old notebooks which had reposed in
the Paris Ritz for some thirty years, and believing that the
prose of *A Moveable Feast* was comparable to the prose which
distinguished the artist at the peak of his Paris power, my hunch
was that those notebooks contained at least sketches for what
would become these chapters, and a big leg up on them. The
facts appear to betray me. The only manuscript I found in the
bank that clearly derived from the Paris days and made its way
into the posthumous volume was a single sheet of paper containing what was published as a headnote to the Fitzgerald
chapter. ("His talent was as natural as the pattern that was
made by the dust on a butterfly's wing. . . .") Carlos Baker
found a few sentences in a blue notebook labeled "Paris 1922"
that did not become any part of the *Feast*; they are printed in
his biography. The only notebooks *I* found were marked "Fiesta
a Novel"—the first draft, of course, of *The Sun Also Rises*.
Thus it appears that Hemingway wrote his Paris book from
scratch, as the manuscript also indicates. (The only exception
to this I know of is that until the author in galleys struck the
first chapter and a half of *The Sun Also Rises* the Ford Madox
Ford episode of *A Moveable Feast* was presented, in embryo,
in the novel.) *How* Hemingway managed to write the memoir
when he was, so much of the time, unwell—and was also occasionally working on a long bullfighting piece that I would one
day be unable to get through—I have no idea in the world.

The process whereby the author became increasingly his own, undisguised subject is writ plain in *By-Line Ernest Hemingway*, the 1967 collection of his journalism. At the start a youthful reporter is filing stories on Mussolini, a Genoa conference, Swiss hotels, and a lovely one on Christmas in Paris. By part II he is a famous man writing letters to *Esquire*; by part IV he is himself being interviewed, and part V is entirely about him, his wife, and places where they lived or adventured. The reporter had hit again on his natural topic—sometimes managing very well with it, too. His *Four Stories of the Spanish Civil War*, published in book form in 1969 but written at the time of that struggle, show the same tendency far earlier. They are autobiographical fictions so dominated by the presence of the author that they scarcely seem fictional: personalized feature stories, rather, much like the wire-service dispatches reprinted in *By-Line*.

If *A Moveable Feast* came to me, anyway, as a superb surprise, I have to confess that *Islands in the Stream* brought disappointment. (Not at all in the editing, by the way; from such looks as I had at the manuscript I would say that the very best that could be got from it was gotten.) But the problem of self-absorption and -dramatization was never (unless in the unpublished *Garden of Eden*) more painful than here. Indeed in the "Bimini" section, which I like much the best of the three, it seems possible to say that for the first and only time the authorial ego grew so big it took two characters to contain it. By that I mean that Thomas Hudson is transparently autobiographically drawn, and his friend Roger Davis is whatever of himself the author thought was left over once Hudson was established. (When I first saw the start of the manuscript—which appeared much the least finished part of it—I wondered if perhaps these two men were really a single persona, Hemingway not having yet decided—such was occasionally his practice—which name to use.)

For me the chief weakness of the book is what I have in general been talking about: the lack of distance between writer and hero, the apparent conviction as well that readers could be caught up in this character as the author was. But it is impossible so to be caught. The peerless Hudson assumes the posture of the tragic hero for no assignable reason. He is, further, a

suffering stoic who—save for two failed marriages—has nothing
in his past but success to explain the stoicism; behind the pervasive despair lies a great void. I reread the novel for the present
occasion, but am still at a loss to know what is the "point"
of "Bimini." The "Cuba" section, made up of unfunny high-
jinks in and around Havana, with episodes involving cats, a
bar, and an ex-wife, seem not only pointless for all I can perceive but also ill-related. "At Sea" strikes me as simply that—
"neither here nor there," as we say—a straight adventure story
lacking in excitement, which I thought the purpose of adventure
stories.

Worst of all, to my taste, is the unaccountable adulation
of Hudson in the book—by his sons, women, servants, friends,
and cats. When it dawns on one, as it does very quickly, that
the object of the adulation is the author himself, the response
can be excruciating. Then self-admiration turns to self-pity,
the unloveliest form of charity. As Hudson finally drives himself
half to death in a mission of undemonstrated importance, one
of his men (speaking for their leader) says "the poor son of a
bitch . . . and covered him carefully" in his slumbers. I can find
no meaning in the book beyond this one. The central fact about
Hudson is his despair. One can search the pages forever without
finding the cause of it—not, that is, beyond the desperation-shot
at one which misfires, the deaths of the man's three sons, which
seem utterly fabricated on two separate occasions to substitute
for what is not understood. One way of putting this point
would be to say that Hudson's despair was Hemingway's, but
John, Patrick, and Gregory Hemingway are alive and well and
living all over the place.

Carlos Baker and now Mary Hemingway both make it clear
that among the author's troubles in his last years was the loss
of the very thing I say helped to make him as a writer—confidence—along with a growth in preoccupation with self that I
believe helped undo him. What I am not clear about, however,
is how the author had still, in his last decade, confidence enough
in what he was doing to keep on doing it. The manuscript of
"The Dangerous Summer," written in the late 1950s, runs
over 900 pages; the "African Book," a little earlier, is nearly as
long; *Garden of Eden* runs to 28 chapters. They did not appear
to be going anywhere, and it seems to me that a man who has

begun to lack faith in what he is doing should not have been able to do so *much* of it. I'm missing something here.[2]

What does strike me over and over in reading Mary's book is how the literary problem I've been talking about was so clearly a personal problem—which, when the author is his own topic, is not very surprising. As she and Carlos both show, the ego in life was gigantic. It is Mary who tells how—like Col. Cantwell—Ernest was given to acting as though he were being interviewed, a situation in which he rejoiced. (When he was *actually* being interviewed, I note, he usually complained about it.) There was an obsession with self; the need for flattery at times nearly determined his life—as when in Cuba, expecting the visit of a young lady, "He could barely stand," Mary writes, "the waiting for Adriana's bright, admiring glances." (Which suggests that it was mostly her admiration of him as Col. Cantwell that had the old soldier so gone on her as Renata in *Across the River. . . .*) Leicester Hemingway made much the same point long ago. Hemingway needed the conviction, which was hard to come by, that he was still, like Santiago down on his luck, the Champion. No one will gloat over such a picture, as all these biographers know. One hurts for the man as he gets personally into the trouble his books reflect. Never more than in the unexplained despair of *Islands* . . . that I was just speaking about. When Hemingway told his wife "I'm just a desperate old man" I cannot help remarking that he was seven years younger than I am. "You're not old," she told him, wishing she could help with the rest of it.

At one time "the world," as Gregory Hemingway writes and no one has said much better, "had flowed through" his father "as though through a purifying filter, with the distillate seeming more true and beautiful than the world itself." The son thought that his father drank to cover up the loss of talent; a psychiatrist I once talked to, who was a Hemingway buff and knew quite a bit about his life, remarked that anyone who drank as much as the writer did for so long a time would go into depression if for no other reason (especially if there had also been manic tendencies). It is a great pity that we did not have, fifteen years ago, the likes of lithium, which has brought so many back from the edge.

And that leads me to express, finally, the hope that I have not seemed disrespectful of a great writer in a period when he was no longer great. If I have so seemed, perhaps I can defuse it a little by pointing out that it is no clearer to you than it is to me that what I have been exhibiting is a Hemingway *critic* in decline—who, like his subject, has taken refuge in autobiography. What I really had to say on the subject of this conference I said a long time ago, thanking whatever gods may be that I have another subject now. I conclude in the realization that after twenty-five years of taking a dim view of the Hemingway hero as Richard Cantwell in *Across the River* . . . I feel at this moment very much at one with the character I have ridiculed. Indeed I retreat as Cantwell does—in both humility and pride, that is—into the position assumed by the superannuated Colonel when suddenly it dawns on him that, quote, "Nobody would give you a penny for your thoughts, he thought. Not this morning. But I've seen them worth a certain amount. . . . when the chips were down." Unquote, and thanks if you remember.

NOTES

[1] A very small thing, but has it been noticed that the same three— Henry, Barnes, Adams (as in "In Another Country")—and Hemingway all recuperated in Milan and at the Ospedale Maggiore (the last two going there for physiotherapy)? Several years ago I gave a talk to the faculty and students in American literature at the University of Milan, fatuously remarking for their satisfaction that Hemingway had recovered in that city. After the lecture a professor came up and said "in this city? In this building." As Nick remarks, the "hospital was very old and very beautiful. . . ." It was explained to me that when the bombers completely gutted the structure in World War II, leaving the ancient walls more or less intact, the hospital was rebuilt elsewhere and a modern interior constructed inside the shell, which now houses Milan's university.

[2] In response to this point at the Alabama conference, Mrs. Hemingway suggested that her husband, sensing the decline in quality, may have driven himself to increase the quantity. I believe that this is at least part of the answer.

Islands in the Stream: Death and the Artist

by Richard B. Hovey

There is one point at which the moral sense and the artistic sense lie very near together; that is in the light of the very obvious truth that the deepest quality of a work of art will always be the quality of the mind of the producer.

Henry James

It is easy to make a case against the art of *Islands in the Stream*—and gratuitous. Most of us agree that it is a badly flawed book which adds little if anything to Hemingway's stature.[1] Would it be a satisfactory novel had the author got around to rewriting it? We can never know. What we do know is that is is autobiographical—too much so, as Carlos Baker has documented for us.[2] And as he and other critics have remarked, its flaws derive from Hemingway's failure to transmute the materials of autogiography, whether his personal experiences or the stuff of the legend, into something closer to art. Granted, the failure here does not embarrass us as did *Across the River and into the Trees*. This posthumous book is more interesting and more emotionally compelling. For the fans, it offers nearly all the standard ingredients: weather, seascapes, terrain, boating, fishing, hunting, drinking, love, war, violence, *cojones*, death, grace under pressure, and the magic style. Most of those who have written about it have found in it passages where the prose is as effective as anything Hemingway has done elsewhere. Besides, whatever good or damage our professional accretions may eventually wreak upon the text, one statistician has informed us that this book was a hit with the public: "In 1972 there were six paperbacks that sold over 150,000 copies in American *bookstores*, and he [Hemingway] wrote three of them. Meanwhile *Islands in the Stream* was selling 900,000 copies in the drugstores."[3]

The work has of course attracted those more studious
readers of Hemingway who are curious whether it can lead us
toward a fuller understanding of the man and the artist. None
of us, I suppose, can read its pages without being continually
aware of Hemingway: his troubled life, his adventures, his
courage, his scars, his final illness, his suicide. He has put so
much of himself directly into *Islands in the Stream*, that it is
less a novel than "a valuable documentary."[4]   As to genre,
that, at any rate, is a feasible label and the one I prefer. The
agony of the artist Thomas Hudson is what grips us, makes for
the dark power of the book. This power, as Arthur Waldhorn
reminds us, "lies just beyond the boundaries of the art of fiction."[5]

Whatever those boundaries, we want to know what is wrong
with Thomas Hudson, the malaise which relentlessly gnaws
within him. At the outset, Irving Howe provides us with a
cautionary note: "One looks through him toward the Hemingway psyche, but not into him as a man interesting in his own
right."[6]   This shortcoming in the art of characterization and
this opacity we cannot dodge. We must risk trying to see in the
dark. The only thing we can at once be sure of is that this
protagonist lives by and exemplifies the famous code and that
he is the most miserable of the Hemingway heroes.

He is a study in melancholia, in nearly unbearable depression. In his celibate existance he manages to hold himself together by his daily routines and the discipline of his art. But
in his dread loneliness, Hudson's is a life of unquiet desperation.
His sufferings are the most real thing in the story, an obsessive
gloom from which even the amusing or lovelier passages are
only momentary distractions. Yet Hudson, we are told, "had
been successful in almost every way except in his married life."
(p. 8)[7] He is a painter whose work has brought him fame and
affluence. Allegedly, his pain is due to the loss of love; he has
been twice divorced and he sorely misses the three sons he
greatly cares for. Such a plight, though, is not enough to explain
his almost suicidal mood. If we look for the causes, the book
in its entirety never makes them explicit.

Since *Islands in the Stream* does not offer us the self-
contained imaginary world we expect in a novel,[8] I believe we

are justified in going outside its pages at certain points for light on the motivations and conduct of the hero. Autobiographical considerations afford us some clues. For a few more, I suggest we dip briefly into psychology. For the rest and most important ones, I hope to document my discussion from Hemingway's own published writings—from one book in particular.

We know that he worked on the manuscript at intervals during 1946-1947 and again 1950-1951.[9] *Islands in the Stream* is, then, a product of that half-decade following the author's World War II experience. In these years, it will be recalled, he published *Across the River and into the Trees* (1950), the novel which is his worst. And this was his first work of fiction for a decade. There is considerable evidence that Hemingway's World War II exploits—his scouring the Caribbean in his cabin cruiser in hope of meeting German submarines and later his escapades on the battlefields of Europe—took a toll of his body, nerves, and finer energies.[10] It is not unlikely that the bitter mood of the querulous Colonel Cantwell was also projected into the creation of Thomas Hudson, in of course far grimmer hues.

As to psychology, I want to press only a point or two. One is that most fiction—I'd say, even *Pilgrim's Progress*—has its origins not in moral dicta but in fantasy. Freud, we recall, pointed to analogies between the artist and the daydreamer. Each indulges in fantasies which flatter his egocentricity. When the daydreamer asks us to share his reveries, we are bored or irked by their display of raw egoism. The artist, on the other hand, may please us; because, though his fantasies rise from a similar kind of self-absorption, he can by his gifts conceal their origins. His discipline and technical mastery, his devotion to formal requirements, enable him to disguise and elaborate his fantasies and get them into patterns which win our acceptance. (I have argued elsewhere that this Freudian hypothesis explains, almost too patly, the mess of Colonel Cantwell's sad tale.)[11] Perhaps it goes some distance toward explaining the gaps and gaffes in *Islands in the Stream*. Perforce the daydreamer is subjective and self-indulgent, as in some respects are Hemingway and his hero here. What might be added, incidentally, is that Hemingway, by his own admission, wrote in part with a therapeutic aim: to "get rid of it," as he put it.[12]

Surely he is too closely identified with Thomas Hudson to depict him with objectivity or to penetrate Hudson's psyche at much depth, though his effort to do so wins our respect. Here, I believe, we move toward accounting for the presence of Roger Davis in this book. The fantasy-process is at work in the characterization of Roger in that he functions as the *alter ego*.[13] He has unmistakable similarities to Thomas Hudson: Roger is an artist, is witty and cultivated, is a fighter, is suicidally melancholy and self-punishing, and suffers from a string of unhappy loves—in his case a victim of bitch women. Like Hudson, he is guilt-ridden. But two things about his psyche are in marked contrast to Hudson's. That is, Hemingway makes clear the sources of Roger's malaise. One is that Roger sold out as an artist; he hates himself for having prostituted his talent by formula-writing for the movies. And Hemingway probes for a deeper cause of Roger's guilt feelings: the man blames himself for a childhood accident. Roger was present when his younger brother drowned; and though he tried, Roger was unable to rescue the boy.

Interestingly, Hemingway provides for Roger a way out of his torment. We are given to understand that he will soon be at work on his first "honest" novel; and Hudson recommends that he begin it with the canoeing tragedy. Besides, Roger's salvation —at least a hope thereof—comes through a marvelous contrivance: the arrival on Bimini of lovely, young Audrey Bruce. She has long loved him and comes to rescue him. So, Roger suddenly disappears from the story. With his *dea ex machina* he flies away to love, and presumably, to dedicated work.[14] One thing noteworthy about the episodes in which Roger figures is that he is the only character in the Hemingway canon who finds a loving woman who promises to foster his talent. Further, though far less promising as to what he will do in art as against the past accomplishments of the hero, Roger Davis is given a second chance in life. That chance Hemingway denies to Thomas Hudson. If we regard Roger Davis as the *alter ego*, he embodies the happier wish-fulfillment that Hudson-Hemingway longed for. The nightmare side of the fantasy—whatever our explanation for it—is that the author requires a blacker fate for his hero.

As to the rest of Part I, we may be pleasantly surprised to find Hemingway, through Hudson, revealing himself as a fond father.   The arrival of the three sons to vacation on Bimini brings a respite from Hudson's solitariness.   But before they are gone, he so dreads their departure that he feels "a loneliness coming into him already . . . . [and] the happiness of the summer began to drain out of him." (pp. 179-180)   Whatever warmth this reunion may bring to us readers, I am not among those who admire the author's handling of the father-sons relationship. It lacks verisimilitude and convincingness.[15]   Our credibility is strained when Tom, the oldest son, reminisces with such particularity about his father's early years in Paris.   This bittersweet nostalgia will find a better place in *A Moveable Feast.* What is intended as a climactic rite of puberty, the middle son's, David's, long and unsuccessful fight to land a giant broadbill, wearies us non-anglers because it is too protracted.[16]   Aside from thematic parallels here to *The Old Man and the Sea*—some of the dialogue is similar—our feeling for the boy's skill and courage is damped by the over-sized and over-solicitous cheering section which hangs upon his every exertion.[17]

The Bimini section ends with frightful abruptness: the radio message notifying Hudson that his two younger sons have been killed in a car accident.   The tragedy does more than worsen Hudson's desolation.   To a friend who tries to console him, " 'We've got young Tom,' " the father replies, " 'For the time being!' " (p. 184)   This ominous response is not mere dramatic foreshadowing; it is as if Hudson anticipates the premature death of his remaining son also.   "We'll play it out the way we can," he tells the friend.   "But now he knew he did not have much interest in the game." (p. 185)   When such grief is piled atop an already melancholic disposition, we can expect the worst.   The four pages of the final chapter of "Bimini," describing Hudson's descent into the lower circles of hell, comprise one of the most powerful passages in all of Hemingway.[18] Trying to come to terms with the catastrophe, Hudson thinks: "Time is supposed to cure it, too.   But if it is cured by anything less than death, the chances are that it was not true sorrow." (p. 185)   Those members of the race who have experienced permanent sorrow will recognize how much validity is in this remark.   For anodynes Hudson considers drink and his work. He tells himself, "He had built his life on work for so long now that he kept that as the one thing he must not lose." (p. 185) When we meet him next, however, in Part II "Cuba," Hudson has given up the easel for the bottle—and for battle.

The crux here is, why does Hemingway finish off all three of Hudson's sons? For in "Cuba," whose period is six years later, in the winter of 1943, we learn that Tom, too, has been killed, in World War II. Personal anxieties about his boys at the time of the writing probably colored Hemingway's mood.[19] In the context of *Islands in the Stream* the loss of all three sons by violent death is intended to deepen Hudson's grief and desolation—though, in Huck Finn's language, these events might be called "stretchers." Naturally, the critics have puzzled over this triple killing. Malcolm Cowley remarks "that the sons have served as a blood sacrifice to the exigencies of fiction."[20] "Utterly manufactured," says Philip Young, and "a desperate shot at a reason" for Hudson's subsequent display of stoic endurance.[21] Christopher Ricks declares that the sons are "slaughtered for the cruelest of markets: not commercialized sentimentality, but authorial escape . . . so that Thomas Hudson—alias Ernest Hemingway—may get away."[22] But why must Hudson get away? And get away to where?

Since "Cuba" is the weakest section of the book, perhaps the less said about it, the better. In his torment, Hudson's chief consolations are drink and daydream. The work he is now dedicated to is patrolling Cuban waters in his war-equipped cabin cruiser in search of enemy submarines—after the fact in Hemingway's own experiences.[23] What is striking about the mood here is Hudson's dismal need to be loved. Yes, there can be such love between a human being and a cat, as Hemingway describes Boy's devotion to the hero. But it is only with this animal that Hudson can let down his guard and expose the naked longings of his heart. At the Floridita, his chosen Havana bar, he talks with one of "the fine old whores," his favorite, Honest Lil. All sympathy, she encourages him to tell her stories of "love" and of happy times past and of old sorrows. However, as seemingly quarts of double frozen Daiquiris "without sugar" are downed, the dialogue degenerates into slush. One critic has charged that not only is the Cuba section "unfunny"; it is also "permeated with a particularly unattractive kind of tough self-pity."[24] Hudson is having a hard time of it upholding the proper stoicism of the Hemingway hero and trying with little success not to think. As he pours in more and more alcohol to feed his inward hunger, he remarks to Lil, " 'Maybe I'll be dead.' " (p. 279) The rather frequent and sometimes jocular palaver about suicide in "Bimini"—we hear of a case of a self-killer whose malady was diagnosed as "Mechanic's Depressive"—takes on bleaker connotations here.

Sex-starved, Hudson moons over an illicit affair he had had on shipboard with a European princess. When he considers the paintings he has at his *finca*, especially those by Gris, Klee, and Masson, he muses: "That was the great thing about pictures; you could love them with no hopelessness at all." (p. 244) Lil asks, " 'Tom, why can't you tell me what is the matter?' " (p. 280) He cannot tell her because he himself does not know.

At this juncture we have another free-wheeling contrivance: the arrival of Hudson's first wife. Fantasy wins out again. Young Tom's mother is a composite portrait of Hadley Richardson and Marlene Dietrich.[25] With breathtaking promptitude she beds and makes passionate love with her estranged ex-husband. Only then does she ask about Tom. The father lies at first and is evasive; then in an implausible exchange she gets the news.[26] Shared bereavement draws the couple together. True, in the ensuing dialogue they bicker; and there is some sharp talk about old hurts and frictions.[27] But the conversation is also shot through with expressions of love. In my reading of the episode, Hemingway does not make it a bitter and impossible fight; reconciliation is not out of the question. In fact, anyone who scrutinizes this passage will count that no fewer than five times she offers to stay with Hudson or wait for him. It is he who says it will not work, adding that he must go to sea again as soon as the weather eases.[28] Conveniently, a message comes to recall him for another military mission. So ends their relationship. Why? Because Hudson wishes it so and Hemingway wishes it so. As Hudson goes out, he tells himself: "Get it straight. Your boy you lose. Love you lose. Honor has been gone for a long time. Duty you do." (p. 307)

This is a manly and ringing statement. The trouble is, it makes almost no sense at all. To be sure, the sons are dead. But Hudson has not lost love, he has rejected it. As to honor, except for his marital infidelities—which seem not to weigh heavily in the mass of Hudson's guilt—*Islands in the Stream* provides no explicit evidence whatsoever that he has been false to his sense of honor. Some other force drives Hudson to feel and act as he does.

Typically, the Hemingway hero does not lie down and cry—not for long anyhow. He prefers to stand up and fight. Nor does he, except temporarily, seek the consolation of love. So, Thomas Hudson opts for the heroic role; and here it looks like a conscious choice. Duty? Hudson uses the word. He means it sincerely according to his lights. But, as Edith Wharton once remarked, the trouble with always doing one's duty is that it unfits one for doing anything else. At any rate, Thomas Hudson intends to be heroic. In numerous respects he is exactly that, in the final section, "At Sea." His heroism, though, in no way redeems him. Toward finding out why, I suggest that we re-examine Hemingway's conception of heroism.

This I have tried to do elsewhere. Yet so far as I know, most readers of my general interpretation of Hemingway's writings did not quite get at what I regard as fundamental to my central arguement.[29]   I refer to *Death in the Afternoon*, a pivotal work very revealing and indispensable if we are to grasp Hemingway's view of, and his various characterizations of, manhood. (I should point out here that, subsequent to the appearance of my own book, there have been published two other book-length studies which demonstrate how crucial is *Death in the Afternoon* for comprehending the ethical qualities and psychological quiddities of Hemingway's heroes. All three of us students arrived at substantially the same views, quite independently of one another.)[30] However, with your indulgence, to recapitulate my understanding of that curious volume: Along with his discourses on bullfighting, life, love, and art, Hemingway pushes far his meditations on the certainty of death and the possibility of heroism. Singling out Goya's *Los Desastros de la Guerra*, he reserves his greatest admiration for that painter—in no small part because of Goya's adventurous, rambunctious, and self-assertive life and because as a man devoted to art Goya was reassuringly hard in his maleness. By contrast, what he takes to be homosexual elements in the canvases of El Greco makes Hemingway uneasy.[31]   The logic goes like this: a great artist can be effeminate; as such, he must be cowardly; ergo, greatness in art is no proof of manhood. If we prize manhood, the indubitably male hero is the great matador. For he has supreme courage, skill, and honor. Nor is his profession merely a dangerous way to provide an exciting spectacle. Bullfighting is a genuine art. In fact, declares Hemingway, if it were not "impermanent," like singing and the dance, "it could be one of the major arts."[32] He calls the great matador a "genius" in art. All the other arts are inferior: "Bullfighting is the only art in which the artist is in danger of death and in which the degree of brilliance in the performance is left to the fighter's honor."[33]

Hemingway goes on to make greater claims for bullfighting. It is not merely an art. In both its ethic and its esthetic it is a "tragedy": a tragic art of spiritual significance which can bring us a sort of "religious ecstasy."[34] How does the great matador do this? "He is performing a work of art and he is playing with death, bringing it closer, closer, closer, to himself. . . . He gives the feeling of his immortality, and, as you watch it, it becomes yours. Then when it belongs to both of you, he proves it with the sword."[35] One might suppose that in responding to, or surely in creating, a great work of non-*tauromaquial* art, one might have similar, even more nearly genuine, intimations of immortality. But not for Hemingway. The immortality the great matador shares with us is not so much through his graceful and perilous skill with cape and muleta as in the manner of killing. For the highest perfection of this art is in "the beauty of the moment of killing."[36] So, the great matador "must love to kill . . . . he must have a spiritual enjoyment of the moment of killing."[37] When you kill, you somehow triumph over death:

> Once you accept the rule of death thou shalt not kill is an easily and naturally obeyed commandment. But when a man is still in rebellion against death he has a pleasure in taking to himself one of the Godlike attributes; that of giving it.[38]

These metaphysical lucubrations are, I submit, worse than ridiculous. They are sick. To put it bluntly, the Hemingway idol here is a man who gets a perverted satisfaction from killing because at the moment of the kill he feels like a god in his power to destroy life. This is not metaphor, nor transcedance, nor primitivism nor heroism. This is criminal pathology. And insofar as such morbidity lies near the heart of the Hemingway hero, we had better protect ourselves against him. For any sadist, any twisted little egomaniac, can get this "Godlike" satisfaction when he murders. As if hysterical to make an affirmation out of the fact of death, Hemingway has concocted a mystique of killing and being killed.

Nor was he aware of the befuddlement he had gotten himself into. With bravado and doubtless accuracy, he itemizes gorings and dyings and specifies tuberculosis and syphilis as "the two occupational diseases" of bullfighters.[39] Weirdly, he makes self-destructiveness concomitant with virility. For the glory of the brave bullfighters is that they "lead lives in which a disregard of consequences dominates."[40] What is most curious about *Death in the Afternoon* is the way the author concludes it. He tells us—or tells himself?—that "the great thing is to last and get your work done and see and hear and learn and understand."[41] An impeccable prescription for the artist. But it collides head-on with Hemingway's notion that the matador is superior to other artists because he damns the consequences and is indifferent to "lasting."

From this conflict Hemingway never found an exit. It runs through his life. It remains unsolved in his writings. And the conception of heroism derived from his apotheosis of the bullfighter provides the mould for all his subsequent protagonists. It does not wholly determine the character and deeds of Robert Jordan because in *For Whom the Bell Tolls* the novelist sought to be affirmative in the war against totalitarianism.[42] Granted also, the heroic matador motif is sweetened and mythicized in old Santiago, but at the cost of Hemingway's almost simplistic rendering of his materials.[43] In Harry Morgan, Colonel Cantwell, and Thomas Hudson such a conception of heroism dominates exclusively. In these portraits it is the old *aficionado* studying the gorings so that he can capture "the feeling of life and death I was working for."[44] Can not Hemingway imagine any artist or thinker as manly enough to be heroic? Is there anywhere in his writings admiration for a Socrates, a Thomas More, a Michelangelo, a Milton, a Beethoven, a Thoreau? Rather, a virile man might feel almost ashamed to practice art. So Hemingway felt—and all too often, I suspect. To cite one instance: in a funk he wrote to his close friend, General Charles T.

Lanham, that without war his life was empty and meaningless;
another time he wrote the General that he wished he were a
soldier like him instead of a "chickenshit writer."[45] Dedication
to his art did not enough engage Hemingway to satisfy his
deepest hungers. So it is with the painter Thomas Hudson.
Hudson must reject any hope of a woman's love and must
get away from his sons—hence they are killed off in this story—
because he cannot resist the compulsion he is not conscious of:
to get himself into a kill- and be-killed jeopardy. So, we find him
"At Sea."

It is too long drawn-out; but this final section is the best-
structured, the surest in its mastery of techniques. Though his
plunge into violent action abets Hudson's program of not-
thinking, he cannot at times help doubting the value of his
military service. It might be "extremely useful" if he and his
crew could capture a German. "Then why don't you care
anything about anything? he asked himself. Why don't you
think of them as murderers and have the righteous feelings that
you should have? . . . Because we are all murderers . . . on both
sides." (p. 335) He drives himself ruthlessly, with too little
sleep, too many hours at the wheel of his Q-boat. His crew members are concerned about his self-destructiveness. " 'Take it
easy,' " one of them tells him. " 'I never felt better,' " Hudson
replies. " 'I just don't give a damn.' " (p. 338). He will, though,
do his duty. Encountering an "obscenely white" land crab
scavenging on the charred cadavers of some massacred islanders,
Hudson, before he kills the creature, greets it: " 'You still have
a chance. . . . Nobody blames you. You're having your pleasure
and doing your duty.' " (p. 316) At a weary moment when he
wishes someone else were chasing the Germans, he tells himself:

> Duty is a wonderful thing. I do not know what I would have
> done without duty since young Tom died. You could have paint-
> ed, he told himself. Or you could have done something useful.
> Maybe, he thought. Duty is simpler. (p. 391)

Such sentiments externalize and then, in effect, would abolish
the inward self.

Hudson's love-longings compound his confusion. Troubled
sleep brings pathetic dreams, of his sons still alive and of Tom's

mother sleeping beside him. In the jumble of dream-images, the pistol holster between his legs becomes a phallus; one of his crew, then hearing Hudson talk aloud in his sleep, covers him with a blanket and says, " 'The poor son of a bitch.' " (p. 323) Of the *Liebestod* motifs in this dream-passage, Arthur Waldhorn points out how it reveals Hudson's uncertainty about his sexual identity: "He seems appallingly helpless . . . to separate cruelty from tenderness, or to choose between aggressive control and passive submission, between a desire to destroy and a desire to be destroyed."[46]

The combat zone somewhat assuages these love-longings. The very enemies he is hunting down cause Hudson to reflect: "I have a sort of fellow death-house feeling about them. Do people who are in the death-house hate each other? I don't believe they do unless they are insane." (p. 353) What is better for these longings is the homoerotic bonds among soldiers killing and facing death together. One flippant reviewer of *Islands in the Stream* put it this way: "The members of the crew go about their tasks in a positive ecstasy of interdependence. Every heave of a line is heavy with the quasi-homosexual mystique of teamwork. The very engine throbs with *machismo*."[47] We need not go in for psychoanalysis or go so far back as Achilles' raging grief over the death of his buddy Patroclus to acknowledge the homoerotic ties among men in combat. In the remarkable scholarship of his latest volume, *The Great War and Modern Memory*, Paul Fussell provides us an amplitude of evidence in his accounts of the British on the Western Front.[48] Anyhow, in the final section, Thomas Hudson's closest emotional link is to Willie, the hard-bitten, one-eyed ex-Marine sergeant, the best, bravest, and most competent of his fighters. Significantly, Hudson knows that Willie "loves" to kill.(p. 420) As Hudson lies mortally wounded, he hears from Willie perhaps the sweetest words he has ever known: "I love you, you son of a bitch, and don't die." (p. 435)

The irony of the shoot-out at the finale is that the mission fails. Its purpose was to capture at least one German for interrogation. Instead, Hudson, for all his expertise in tactics and his responsible-mindedness, leads his boat into an ambush. We are left with corpses, Hudson's evidently to be included among the German varieties. When he is hit, Hudson expresses a dark fatalism: "Don't worry about it, boy, he said to himself. All your life is just pointed toward it." (p. 433) But he sticks to his post as long as he can, directing the operations, remembering to order the deactivating of a booby-trap which now could kill friends or innocent non-combatants—ruefully considering this the one "useful" thing accomplished. (p. 433) Sensing death's approach, "Hold it tight," he tells himself. "Now is the true time you make your play. Make it now without hope of anything." (p. 434)

On the last page, admittedly, Hudson is still alive. But that he should reach medical help and survive is not only unlikely; it also would undercut the whole thrust and theme of the story.[49] If his body is not lifeless, his creativity is dead. As he suffers his fatal wound, he tries to encourage himself:

> Think about after the war and when you will paint again. There are so many good ones to paint and if you paint as well as you really can and *keep out of all other things and do that, it is the true thing.* You can paint the sea better than anyone now if you will do it *and not get messed up in other things.* (pp. 433-434)

This resolve he should have made before he started on the heroics of submarine-chasing.[50] The end is plain enough when in the final sentences we read: "He looked up and there was the sky that he had always loved and he looked across the great lagoon that he was quite sure, now, he would never paint. . . ." (p. 435)

True to the code, Hudson dies well. Yet his is the posture, not the reality, of the tragic hero.[51] Under the guise of duty, he follows his obsessive drive to destruction and death. As to why Hudson-Hemingway was so in the grip of a death-wish, we can let the psychiatrists debate among themselves. Philip Young has offered his psychological explanation, and I have mine; and there are others.[52] Anyhow, Hudson's moral malaise comes from his dim and fumbling sense of what we can see clearly; he has failed in his duty to his art. That is the "honor" he feels he has betrayed and lost. Carylyle's view that there can be no great art without something heroic in the soul of its creator evidently never occurred to Hemingway. There was something else Hudson and Hemingway cared about more than dedication to art, an elation and gratification overriding perhaps even those of the supreme matador.[53]   What this something else is Hemingway publicly announced as far back as the spring of 1936: "Certainly there is no hunting like the hunting of man and those who have hunted armed men long enough and liked it, never really care for anything else thereafter."[54]

What is the meaning of *Islands in the Stream*? Personally, I was glad to see the hero out of his misery, felt no split-second of release through the violent action, only a sickening sense of waste. Yet our question here is legitimate. For this book, whatever its shortcomings, is at least one man's testament on the human condition—the witness, however limited, of a man and a writer who has always been a moralist on "how to live in it." To be sure, the work lacks an architectonic theme, the shaping power of a central idea. Thus, in *Islands in the Stream* Irving Howe sees Hemingway struggling desperately "with both his need for some concluding wisdom . . . and his habitual tough-guy swagger in all its sodden mindlessness."[55]   Or, as Philip Young puts the question: "In relating all the experiences the book deals with he [Hemingway] had never, it seems to me, discovered its meaning."[56]

No, Hemingway never discovered the meaning here. He has left it for us, though, implicit in nearly every one of these pages. The heroic code does not work. It is finished. Willy nilly, *Across the River and into the Trees* reduced it to absurdity. Certain abstractions from it, rendered with cunning simplicity, could give us a fisherman hero in *The Old Man and the Sea*. But this posthumous work, with an artist the protagonist, has laid bare all the strands of the code to prove it leads only to *nada*.[57]   Hemingway has here exposed the morbid and sinister elements which went into its shaping from the start. Its cult of manliness is no mere "boy's idea" that we can smile away.[58]   It is worse. This assertion of the *machismo*-matador-death notion is an evasion of inwardness. As such, it destroys the manly selfhood it claims to support.

If we hold the Nietzchean view that art ought to enhance life, then on the bases of both our own biology and the ethical contents of *Islands in the Stream*, we might call it a bad book.

I mean, it says no to life.[59] Its hero's agony is that he deserted his duty to art and to life. Yet, to take a different view—to return to my epigraph from Henry James—the "deepest quality" of this work is "the quality of the mind of the producer." On this score, whatever its failings as art, whatever our ethical objections, *Islands in the Stream* needs no apology. In a way distinct from the rest of the canon, it gives us the quality of the Hemingway psyche. For he made the effort here, as Edmund Wilson remarked, "to deal candidly with the disorders of his own personality."[60] The integrity we take for granted. What inspirits us is Hemingway's courage to put himself and his code to such an extreme test. Win or lose, that is heroism.

NOTES

[1]A convenient start is William R. Anderson, Jr., "*Islands in the Stream*—the Initial Reception," *Fitzgerald-Hemingway Annual* (1971), pp. 326-332. Anderson digests thirty of the more important reviews and appends a checklist with full publication data on each.

[2]See ch. XV "Islands in the Stream" in his *Hemingway: the Writer as Artist*, 4th ed. (Princeton, New Jersey: Princeton University Press, 1972).

[3]Philip Young provides these figures in his "Posthumous Hemingway, and Nicholas Adams," *Hemingway in Our Time*, eds. Richard Astro and Jackson J. Benson, (Corvallis: Oregon State University Press, 1974), p. 22.

[4]The label is Arthur Waldhorn's. See his ch. 15 "Islands in the Stream," *A Reader's Guide to Hemingway*, (New York: The Noonday Press, Farrar, Straus and Giroux, 1972), p. 211.

[5]*Ibid.*, p. 201.

[6]His review "Great Man Going Down," *Harpers* 241 (October, 1970), p. 120-125.

[7]Page references to all quotations from the novel itself will be cited in my text within parentheses. The edition used here is the paperback *Islands in the Stream* (New York: Bantam Books, 1972), 3rd printing.

[8]The phrase is Irving Howe's (note 6), p. 121, who remarks that the characterization· and behavior of the protagonist can lead readers to "a series of illicit speculations."

[9]Carlos Baker (note 2) gives an account of the composition and history of the manuscript, pp. 379-384.

[10]*Ibid.*, p. 266. Baker has written: "Even as late as 1949 . . . the traumatic effects of his life in the second world war still rankled in his mind. The story of Colonel Cantwell emerged as a way of exorcising what for Hemingway still had the aspect, and the terrorizing atmosphere of a recent nightmare." My speculations about the bad effects the war had on this writer are in *Hemingway: The Inward Terrain* (Seattle: The University of Washington Press, 1968), pp. 274-276. The fullest account of Hemingway's experience in World War II is of course in Carlos Baker, *Hemingway: A Life Story* (New York: Charles Scribner's Sons, 1969).

[11]In my book (note 10), pp. 176-190.

[12]In "Fathers and Sons" Nick Adams, recalling his father's suicide, explains—in behalf of his creator?—"If he wrote it he could get rid of it. He had gotten rid of many things by writing them." *The Short Stories of Ernest Hemingway* (New York: Charles Scribner's Sons, 1953), p. 491.

[13]Carlos Baker (note 2) uses the term but limits its significance more than I do: "Yet it is possible that Hemingway meant Davis to stand as an *alter ego* for himself, not as he was in 1946-1947, married to his fourth wife Mary and taking up his writing where he had dropped it when the war began, but rather as he had been in the middle thirties, socially truculent, full of hatreds, including that of self, not at all certain he had made the best use of his talents, and often masking his doubts beneath the outward manner of the roaring boy." pp. 393-394. Needless to say, I regard Baker's very apt description as applying every bit as much to the Hemingway of the post-World War II decade as to the man and writer of the Depression years.

[14]Baker (note 2) uses the Latin tag, p. 396. Regarding Roger Davis' removal from the novel, Arthur Waldhorn is insightful: "A continuing dialogue between them [i.e., Hudson and Davis] . . . throughout the rest of the novel might have led Hemingway to confrontations with himself that would have been psychologically as well as dramatically intriguing."(note 4) p. 208 For an interesting interpretation of the thematic and symbolic meanings of Roger Davis' participation in the episodes where Hudson's middle son, David, is nearly attacked by a shark and where he puts up the long and losing fight to land the big fish, see Francis E. Skipp, "Metempsychosis in the Stream, or What Happens in 'Bimini'?" *The Fitzgerald-Hemingway Annual* (1974), pp. 137-143. Skipp argues that Roger might have "felt his old sin redeemed by David's struggle." It is true that Roger irrationally blames himself for the near death of David; true that his own drowned brother had the same name, David; true also that Hudson's David thanks Roger for something the man had said to him after he lost the fish. Hemingway never tells us what Roger said to the boy, but remarks that "he understands him better than his own father did." (p. 135) Hemingway might have aimed at some sort of redemption for Roger in this way. If so, the novelist never makes it clear or intelligible. And Mr. Skipp's argument is a bit too mystical to convince me. More important, the next day (Chapter X, following the loss of the big fish), Roger is still so depressed he talks about his possible suicide.

[15]Waldhorn (note 4) is perceptive—and to me wholly convincing—in his discussion of Hemingway's handling of the father-sons relationship. See especially pp. 205-208.

[16]But John W. Aldridge has a sympathetic word about this episode: ". . . here is a dimension of Hemingway one has seen before but perhaps not often enough, that side of his nature which was capable of responding not merely to bluster and bravado but with admiration for bravery in the weak and with tenderness toward weakness in the brave." His essay-review, "Hemingway Between Triumph and Disaster," *Saturday Review* 53 (October 10, 1970), pp. 23-26, 39.

[17]"Cheering section" is Carlos Baker's phrase; his complaint is the same as mine. (note 2), p. 392 Anatole Broyard is more stringent: ". . . Hemingway blows up this scene into a cosmic struggle. It is intended to be a puberty rite, but it comes off more like a couvade, in which the husband suffers labor pains along with his wife." See his review "Papa's Disappointing Big One," *Life* 69 (October 9, 1970), p. 10.

[18]The Dantesque figure of speech is not mine but Hemingway's p. 185.

[19]During the first period of his work on *Islands in the Stream* Hemingway's two younger sons were in fact in an auto accident; the youngest boy was slightly injured; the other Patrick, sustained a concussion which kept him in serious condition for some weeks in the spring of 1947. See Baker (note 2), p. 380 and 388-389. During World War II Hemingway's oldest son was reported missing in action for several months.

[20]See his review, "A Double Life, Half Told," *The Atlantic* (December, 1970), pp. 105-106 and 108.

[21](Note 3), p. 16.

[22]"At Sea with Ernest Hemingway," *The New York Review of Books* 15 (October 8, 1970), pp. 17-19.

[23]Carlos Baker (note 2) writes of Hemingway: ". . . his cabin cruiser had never managed to close with a German craft during all his months of patrolling, and had certainly never given chase, as Hudson does, to the survivors of a U-boat destroyed by a plane." p. 403. Baker gives an account of these subhunting activities in his *Ernest Hemingway: A Life Story* (note 10), pp. 373-380.

[24]"Hemingway's Unstill Waters," *The Times Literary Supplement* (October 16, 1970) pp. 1193-1194.

[25]Baker (note 2), p. 400.

[26]As to "this implausible exchange"—the phrase is Waldhorn's (note 4) p. 203—here is the relevant dialogue:

"You don't want to talk about him," she said.

"No."

"Why? I think it's better."

"He looks too much like you."

"That isn't it," she said. "Tell me. Is he dead?"

"Sure." (p. 300)

[27] Evidently in their anger their voices rise—enough to upset the house-boy: "He had unavoidably seen and heart quarrels in the living room before and they made his brown face perspire with unhappiness. . . . He thought that he had never seen such a beautiful woman and the caballero was quarreling with her and she was saying angry things to the caballero." (p. 304)

[28] I cannot agree with Arthur Waldhorn's statement that Hudson and his ex-wife "understand why their marriage has failed." (note 4), p. 203.

[29] I refer to *Hemingway' the Inward Terrain* (note 10), where on pp. 92-110 I comment on *Death in the Afternoon*. In this paper my discussion of Hemingway's views of bullfighting-and-heroism are a digest of those pages.

[30] The two books are: Jacobus Bakker, *Ernest Hemingway: the Artist as Man of Action* (Assen, the Netherlands: Van Gorcum & Co., 1972) and Lawrence R. Broer, *Hemingway's Spanish Tragedy* (University, Alabama: The University of Alabama Press, 1973).

[31] Hemingway's remarks on El Greco's possible homosexuality are on page 205 of *Death in the Afternoon*. He writes here: "Viva El Greco El Rey de los Maricones." *Maricon* denotes both coward and homosexual.

[32] *Death in the Afternoon*, p. 99.

[33] *Ibid.*, p. 91.

[34] *Ibid.*, p. 206. When an *aficionado* sees a great matador perform, he participates, Hemingway tells us, in something "that takes a man out of himself and makes him feel immortal while it is proceeding, that gives him an ecstasy, that is, while momentary, as profound as any religious ecstasy."

[35] *Ibid.*, p. 213.

[36] *Ibid.*, p. 247.

[37] *Ibid.*, p. 232. The extravagant passage from which I quote contains self-contradictions like these: ". . . unless [the great killer] feels it is the

best thing he can do, unless he is conscious of its dignity and feels that it is its own reward, he will be incapable of the abnegation that is necessary in real killing. The truly great killer must have a sense of honor and a sense of glory far beyond that of the ordinary bullfighter. . . ."

[38]*Ibid.*, p. 233.

[39]*Ibid.*, p. 100.

[40]*Ibid.*, p. 101.

[41]*Ibid.*, p. 278.

[42]My quarrel with the interpretations of Robert Jordan's character by Jacobus Bakker and Lawrence Broer (note 30) is not that there are no matador elements in Jordan's make-up; but that in certain directions these two critics over-schematize his characterization, situation, and conduct.

[43]By "simplistic" here I do not refer to the characterization of Santiago, which in a number of respects I regard as quite complex in his consciousness. I mean that the hero of *The Old Man and the Sea* is for the most part uninvolved with any person other than himself. He has no wife, children, family, no intricate relationship with any group or community.

[44]*Death in the Afternoon*, p. 3.

[45]See Irvin D. Yalom, M.D. and Marilyn Yalom, Ph.D., "Ernest Hemingway—A Psychiatric View," *Archives of General Psychiatry*, 24, no. 6 (June 1971) pp. 485-494. The doctors Yalom quote from and refer to General Lanham, who cooperated and gave them "counsel" in the preparation of this essay and who for many years was a close friend of the novelist. Morley Callaghan quotes Hemingway in a relevant matter: "But my writing is nothing. My boxing is everything!" See Callaghan's *That Summer in Paris* (New York: Coward-McCann, 1963), especially ch. XV.

[46](Note 4) pp. 210-211.

[47]Anatole Broyard (note 17) p. 10.

[48]See especially his ch. VIII "Soldier Boys" (New York: Oxford University Press, 1975).

[49] A rather different view is held by the writer's widow. On Hudson's wounding she remarked, in an interview with Henry Raymont, in *The New York Times* of September 12, 1970, that "there is a chance that he will receive medical attention and be saved." Quoted by Arthur Waldhorn (note 4), p. 254.

[50] The italics in the quoted passages are mine. That Hemingway himself had conflicts over goint to war as against staying with his art is indicated in his remark, from London while the Nazi buzz bombs were falling on that city: ". . . sometimes it doesn't seem the right man in the right place and I have thought some of leaving the whole thing and going back to writing books." See *By-Line: Ernest Hemingway; Selected Articles and Dispatches of Four Decades*, ed. William White, (New York: Charles Scribner's Sons, 1967) p. 360. Later, in 1956—when perhaps it was too late—Hemingway promised himself: "You will never again interrupt the work that you were born and trained to do until you die." *By-Line*, p. 470. Henry Slater, who painted three portraits of Hemingway, declares that the author was dissatisfied with the first, complaining he looked "too literary." Slater adds: "He always rather repented that part of himself, the perfectionist artist, which made him a great writer. He wanted to be a real tough guy." Quoted by Emily Stipes Watts, *Ernest Hemingway and the Arts* (Urbana: The University of Illinois Press, 1971) p. 198.

[51] My phrasing is indebted to Arthur Waldhorn (note 4) p. 209.

[52] For the article by the Yaloms, see note 45. Some of the others are these: Richard Drinnon, "In the American Heartland: Hemingway and Death," *Psychoanalytic Review* 52 (1965), 5-31 [149-175] ; David Gordon, "The Son and the Father," *Literature and Psychology* 16 (1966), nos. 3 & 4, pp. 122-138; and Leo Schneiderman, "Hemingway: A Psychological Study," *Connecticut Review* 6 (1973) no. ii, pp. 34-49.

[53] Mary Hemingway has described this hero as "that thoughtful, complicated submarine hunter Thomas Hudson" in her "Note" to *The Enduring Hemingway: An Anthology of a Lifetime in Literature*, ed. with an introduction by Charles Scribner, Jr. (New York: Charles Scribner's Sons, 1974). This collection includes *in toto* the final Part III of *Islands in the Stream*.

[54] "On the Blue Water," *Esquire* 5 (April, 1936) 31, pp. 184-185. It is reprinted in *By-Line* (note 50).

[55] In his review (note 6) p. 125.

[56] (Note 3) p. 16.

[57] It is curious that in her interesting and valuable book, *Ernest Hemingway and the Arts* (note 50), Emily Stipes Watts does not stress in the characterization of Thomas Hudson his conflict between the vocation of art and his call to be a man of action. She is content to write: "Hudson is an artist who becomes an amateur fighting man. . . . With Thomas Hudson, life and art become blended. Throughout the novel, Hemingway is careful to balance physical activities with Hudson's aesthetic consciousness, with his painting, and with references to art." p. 189

[58] Writes Irving Howe (note 6): ". . . the cult of manliness which dominates this book, though with much less self-assurance than in his earlier books, is finally a boy's idea." p. 121

[59] For an affirmative interpretation, see Joseph DeFalco, "Hemingway's Islands and Streams: Minor Tactics for Heavy Pressure," in *Hemingway in Our Time* (note 3) pp. 39-51.

[60] In his review, "An Effort at Self-Revelation," *The New Yorker*, 46 (January 2, 1971) 60.

Art and Order in *Islands in the Stream*

by Gregory S. Sojka

The revaluation of Ernest Hemingway's writing presents a fitting occasion for a reconsideration of *Islands in the Stream*. Despite the editing controversy surrounding its publication, this posthumous book has its own artistic integrity, and my discussion proceeds on that assumption. Some critics have been so preoccupied with autobiographical connections that they fail to perceive the value of this work's narrative progression and thematic continuity within the Hemingway literary corpus.

Despite its 1970 publication, *Islands in the Stream*, in both its date of composition and its content, is actually a fictional transition between the Nick Adams short stories and *The Old Man and the Sea*. The "Bimini" section was written in 1946-1947, and "Cuba" portion was finished in 1950. After completing *The Old Man and the Sea* in early 1951, Hemingway finally concluded "At Sea" in May of that year.[1]

William R. Anderson suggests that reviewers "might have been better occupied had they attempted to comprehand and explain what Hudson, and thus Hemingway, was saying about the loneliness of the tough-minded first rate professional artist."[2] But, Edmund Wilson, Hemingway's oldest and most reliable evaluator, perceived the merits of the novel and placed it accurately in the context of previous work. Wilson wisely dismisses the myth-perpetuating autobiographical critics to pursue the thematic concerns that mark Hemingway's most "compelling" works.

> It was the strain they conveyed of men on the edge of going to pieces, who are just hanging on by their teeth, and just managing to maintain their sanity, or of men who know they are doomed to real inexorable defeat or death. The real heroism of these charac-

ters is their fortitude against such ordeals or the honor they manage to salvage from ignominy, humiliation. It is this kind of
theme in Hemingway that makes his stories exciting and stimu-
lating. Will the hero last? How long will he last?[3]

Wilson's comments focus upon the tension between the Hemingway hero who seeks a well-ordered life and the chaotic condi-
tions that hamper his quest. Thomas Hudson, like Nick Adams,
is beset by traumatic memories that periodically surface to his
consciousness. Of primary importance, however, is not the
nature of these troubling remembrances, but how the character
responds in his present life to a disconcerting past. The hero's
response determines whether he will be able to survive with
respect or wallow in shame. Thomas Hudson's attempts to
order his life against the imminent confusion of his fears consti-
tute the subject of this paper.

Hudson's ultimate success or failure depends upon his
discovering a coherent activity that provides therapeutic order
and aesthetic satisfaction lacking in ordinary life. Painting
and fishing offer discipline and principles that lend Hudson
and his sons the means to achieve dignity in a fictional universe
that often strips the strongest men of self-respect. Read as a
discussion of the "aesthetic of contest," my term for the Hemingway code demeanor, "Bimini" makes a convenient transition
between the early Nick Adams stories and the later *The Old
Man and the Sea*. "Fathers and Sons," which offers us the last
glimpse of Nick Adams, provides a restatement and complication
of the typical Hemingway dilemma: a man's quest for order and
his added obligation to supply his son with a viable moral and
social legacy. This situation reappears in Thomas Hudson's
situation; his great artistic self-discipline in painting, like Nick's
fishing, serves to preserve his confidence in the face of doubts.
A divorce, however, complicates Hudson's paternal duties. When
young David Hudson battles a huge swordfish, his father prepares
his boys for their future by using this fishing battle as a metaphor
for a world where the winner takes nothing and victory must
somehow be integrated into defeat. At the end of this novel
Thomas Hudson must rediscover his squandered self-respect
while leading a crew in pursuit of a German submarine crew.

II

Thomas Hudson's isolated house, conceived of as a ship that rides out the toughest of storms, provides a psychological as well as physical protection from the surrounding domestic turbulence. The artist's conception of his house as a worthy sea craft compares with Nick Adams's Two-Hearted River campsite as a shelter and refuge against outside forces. Hudson's house cannot, however, function as an Edenic escape from domesticity. So he reconciles his loneliness with the artistic self-discipline of his vocation, the "work and steady normal working life he had built on the island."[4] This stability has not always been an intrinsic part of Thomas Hudson's entire life. Although he had been a painter for a long time,

> learning how to settle down and how to paint with discipline had been hard for him because there had been a time in his life when he had not been disciplined. He had never been truly irresponsible; but he had been undisciplined, selfish, and ruthless. He knew this now, not only because many women had told it to him; but because he had finally discovered it for himself. Then he had resolved that he would be selfish only for his painting, ruthless only for his work, and that he would discipline himself and accept the discipline (pp. 8-9).

Knowledge of self, an important part of Hudson's severely ordered existence, parallels Nick Adams's emotional diet while trout fishing near Seney. If Hudson's past domestic difficulties have resulted from the lack of control and order, this self-imposed artistic self-discipline is the means and the end to a meaningful existence and satisfactory life. Hudson wants to "enjoy life within the limits of the discipline that he imposed" and works hard to achieve this end.

Thomas Hudson's painting creates order as it exorcises chaos. Like the mature Nick of "Fathers and Sons," who hopes to write away his painful memories, Thomas Hudson hopes to pour out the turmoil of his life upon a canvas. Mr. Bobby's proposal to Hudson for an "End of the World" canvas mirrors the fantastic chaos of the best Hieronymous Bosch apocalypse, with Hell's hatch opening and devils forking the protesting holy-rollers, supine blacks, stumbling rummies, and a few stray dogs and cats into the fiery pit. "The Garden of Earthly Delights" is the specific Bosch triptych to which Hudson comically refers, and Emily Stipes Watts notes the relationship between Hemingway's general treatment of love and Bosch's painting. The paradise, the sensual delights, and the suffering sinners of the three panels show that "there is indeed a danger in paradise, that there is fleshly pleasure, but there must also be suffering."[5] Man's Edenic happiness is only temporary and must be lost. Thomas Hudson's loss of marital tranquility stimulates his paternal responsibility. Only by following his regimen can this artist keep his life from falling into the debilitating disorder expressed in Bosch's third panel of suffering.

When Roger Davis appears on the scene his function as a contrast to Thomas Hudson soon becomes clear. Unlike the painter, Davis leads an undistinguished life of self-indulgence and emotional messiness. Carlos Baker observes that Davis has "demeaned his talents by writing for the films, entered into an incredible series of maladroit sexual adventures, and behind everything else is tortured by the guilty remembrance of a boyhood canoeing accident in which his younger brother was drowned."[6] The unstable writer is guilty about his aimless existence; when he explodes in a physical rage, literally destroying the face of a drunken yachtsman who penetrates his thin veneer of patience with verbal taunts, the truth hurts more than the insults themselves—"faker," "cheap phony," and "rotten writer" (p. 39). Davis' fists counter this attack upon his fragile dignity in a scene parallel in action and significance to Robert Cohn's assault upon Romero; Davis and Cohn win their fights but lose their tempers and thus their self-respect. Afterwards, there is nothing to show that Davis had been in a fight except for a tattered sweatshirt, and he sinks into self-pitying laments about "wicked people" and "bad times." "I'm ashamed of the fight on the dock," he explains, and resolves to give up fighting, to "quit writing junk," in order to "write a good straight novel as well as I can write it" (p. 76). Thomas Hudson suggests that the proposed novel should become a physical exorcism of Davis' troubled past; Roger should start by describing the canoe that tipped and drowned his brother. Davis replies:

I'm so corrupted that if I put in a canoe it would have a beautiful girl in it that young Jones, who is on his way to warn the settlers that Cecil B. de Mille is coming, would drop into, hanging by one hand to a tangle of vines that covers the river while he holds his trusty flintlock, "Old Betsy," in the other hand, and the beautiful Indian girl says, "Jones, it ess you. Now we can make love as our frail craft moves toward the falls that some day will be Niagara" (p. 77).

Roger comments sarcastically on his romantic screenwriting "pollution" and his tendency to move from basic facts to spectacular fiction. Tom Hudson, speaking for Ernest Hemingway, champions the sanctity of basic facts with advice that parallels Bill Gorton's attacks upon Jake Barnes's irresponsible expatriate affectations. He tells Roger that "canoe, and the cold lake and your kid brother" are the necessary elements (p. 77). If writing is Roger Davis' salvation, we do not witness his artistic redemption in this novel. The example of a "rummy" who functions well under pressure, a young boy who fights a huge fish with the resolution of a grown man, and the appearance of a young lady who carries the possibility of a new domestic start, are Roger Davis's potential sources of redemption.

In an earlier manuscript of over two-hundred pages, no.98-18 in the Hemingway collection catalog at John F. Kennedy Library, Roger Davis, (then called Hancock), is actually the central character in the novel and father of the boys. In one section, labeled "Book Two—Miami," Hemingway follows Roger Hancock as he travels across Florida with Audrey. He feels "the old hollowness comeing [sic] inside of him," when at locations associated with good times with his old family. He also talks about "whoreing" [sic] as taking money for "something that was not the absolute best he could write. . . . Now he had to atone for that and recover respect by writing as well as he could and better than he ever had." His present attempts to get back into writing shape include exercises in describing the countryside in a notebook; "to get [the] feel of country and in the notes to write accurate complete sentences in good prose. Mabe [sic] as sound and good as the ride from Bayonne to Pamplona in the Sun [sic]." Roger vows to "write so carefully and so well that you make the emotion with the country, . . not feeling emotion, but noticing the details that produced it." These interesting autobiographical ruminations were wisely excluded from the "Bimini" revisions. The eighteen existing manuscript stages of this novel suggest an immense amount of revising and rewriting—more editing, in fact, than is evident in any of the other surviving manuscripts. Hemingway's dimmed artistic vision, and not a lack of effort, caused the ultimate shortcomings of *Islands in the Stream*.

Eddy, Thomas Hudson's chief cook and bottle-washer, heroically defends his employer's honor in a bar. And when Thomas Hudson cannot shoot the hammerhead shark threatening his son, Eddy stops this killer in his wake. His salvation from drunken obscurity derives from his daily duties; as Hudson explains to his boy, "Eddy's happy because he does something well and he does it every day" (p. 161). This ordered work schedule is exactly what Roger Davis needs to save his life from undistinguished oblivion. At Roger's final exit he resolves to write "well and truly," which leads Tom Hudson to ponder the fate of his friend and fellow artist:

> So now he was going to start again and how would it turn out this time? How could he think that wasting his talent and writing to order and following a formula that made money could fit him to write well and truly? Everything that a painter did or that a writer wrote was part of his training and preparation for what he was to do. Roger had thrown away and abused and spent his talent. But perhaps he had enough animal strength and detached intelligence so that he could make another start. Any writer of talent should be able to make another start. Any writer of talent should be able to write one good novel if he were honest,. . . But all the time that he should be training for it Roger had been misusing his talent and how could you know if his talent still was there?. . . . How could anyone think that you can neglect and despise, or have contempt for craftmanship, however feigned the contempt may be, and then expect it to be at the service of your hands and of your brain when the time comes when you must have it. . . . Roger must start now to use what he has blunted and perverted and cheapened and all of it is in his head . . . if he could write the way he fought on the dock it could be cruel but it would be very good. Then if he could think as soundly as he thought after that fight he would be very good (pp. 103-104).

Hudson's thoughts on Davis incorporates Hemingway's own

aesthetic theory of art; the artist must write honestly and practice his craft.   Painters and writers must also keep in mental
shape in order to avoid messy emotional attachments that
spoil the integrity of their work.   Roger Davis' faults also remind
Tom Hudson of the fate that awaits him if he should misuse his
talent or neglect his craftsmanship.   Hudson's schedule, "a
pleasant routine of working hard," is built around the most
important regulating activity, his painting (p. 95).   The long
hours and hard work enable him to control his emotions just
as Nick Adams's preparatory camping and domestic duties
allow him to withstand the excitement and shock of hooking,
then losing a trout.   While his sons provide Hudson with an
enjoyable break from his solitary existence, their departure
creates a new vacuum.   "There was nothing to do about that,"
he thinks: "that would all come later and if it was coming
there was no good derived from any fearing of it now" (p. 96).

The best piece of sustained writing in the entire novel is
David Hudson's fight with a large broadbill, his *rite de passage*.
Hemingway's description of this fight is a stylistic and thematic
analogue for Santiago's titanic struggle to be written three
years later.   Unfortunately, since Hemingway chose to dispose
of David and his two brothers in the "Cuba" section of the
novel, we see only the boy's immediate reactions to the fight.
These reactions and those of the witnesses to his struggles il-
lustrate the "aesthetic of contest."

From the very beginning of his fight David is coached
by Roger and Eddy, while his father pilots the boat and speaks
to Tom Jr. about what is taking place.   Eddy comforts the
boy, and Roger ("a great fisherman"), serving as the sole technical advisor to David, assumes the role of surrogate father.
Hudson's unique ability to provide only the circumstances of
contest and to remain aesthetically uninvolved explains this
rather peculiar objective stance.   Again, Hemingway's own
substantive changes in narration and character also leave their
mark on the finished product.   Initially the narrator was George
Davis, a painter who tells the story of Roger Hancock, a writer
fallen upon hard times and also father of the three boys.   Therefore in the early draft Roger appropriately instructs his own son
while George Davis steers the boat and relates the action.   Perhaps fear of autobiographical identification of Roger as himself

prompted Hemingway's changes in narration and character focus. In either case, the final artistic arrangement establishes a greater dramatic tension between the two male characters: a self-disciplined painter and an emotionally confused writer. Thomas Hudson shows great self-restraint and wise judgment in allowing Roger, who "was as beautiful and sound in action as he was unbeautiful and unsound in his life and in his work," to coach young David, "a well-loved mystery" to his father (p. 143). Hudson does not lose face as a father, but rather gains respect as a man who realizes when *not* to interfere for the ultimate benefit of his son. He also gains stature because he is capable of providing a worthwhile legacy to his son, a legacy that Nick Adams of "Fathers and Sons" can not provide to his boy. Thomas Hudson realizes that deep-sea fishing, despite its dangers, provides the best educational mode for his son. David's success in fishing extends to all worldly endeavors. An inspired Roger Davis vows to write "straight and simple and good," and hopes that this artistic honesty will restore his old "sureness" (p. 156). Audrey's refreshing beauty and winning honesty presumably can assist Roger to lead an honest life and write an honest book.

Roger advises the novice angler; "You can't bull him a-round," but "lead him and try to convince him where he has to come" (p. 114). The veteran fisherman offers the same persuasive tactics that Hemingway preaches in his non-fictional articles and that Santiago employs in his marlin fight. David vows to follow Roger's advice "until [he] dies," an oath that matches Santiago's resolute gravity. Eddy also realizes the importance of David's fight as a test of manhood. "That's natural," Eddy responds to David's shoulder and arm pains; "That'll make a man out of you" (p. 116). When young Tommy Hudson voices surprise at David's skillful fishing since he can't play games," his father responds "the hell with games," to emphasize the importance of this character-building test (p. 118).

His brothers learn about fishing and, most importantly, life, from David's example and from the illustrative comments of their elders. For instance, Mr. Hudson tells son Andrew about the proper demeanor to display while fighting fish, He and Roger, used to suffer and act as though everybody was against us. That's the natural way to be. The other's discipline or good sense when you learn. We started to be polite because we found we couldn't catch big fish being rude and excited. And if we did, it wasn't any fun. We were both really awful though; excited and sore and misunderstood and it wasn't any fun. So now we always fight them politely. We talked it over and decided we'd be polite no matter what (p. 120).

Whether in fishing, painting, or writing, discipline, the key to aesthetic enjoyment, is always preferable to emotional indulgence. Although mere spectators, Hudson's other sons realize the importance of the event they are witnessing. Andrew tells his father, "I know this must be good for him or you wouldn't let him do it." (p. 125).

Eddy also provides an inspirational example; a "grown man, strong, shoulders like a bull," who "yellowed out and quit" on a fish because of the pain (p. 128). Mental toughness rather than physical bulk and age distinguishes this character-building sport. Tom Hudson Sr. explains his rationale to Tom Hudson Jr.: "there is a time boys have to do things if they are ever going to be men," and adds "that's where David is now." "I would have stopped this long ago except that if David catches this fish he'll have something inside of him for all his life and it will make everything else easier," he continues (p. 131). Eddy tells David to ignore his raw, bleeding hands and feet, which "look bad" but actually are "all right." For "that's the way a fisherman's hands and feet are supposed to get and next time they'll be calloused protection against future hardships.

At the height of this physical battle David temporarily loses control of his emotions and curses the fish; "I don't care if he kills me, the big son of a bitch," he says wildly. But he quickly changes his tone. "Oh hell. I don't hate him. I love him." He apologizes for this outburst; "I don't want to say anything against him. I think he's the finest thing in the world" (p. 134). The educational effect of this struggle is evident in David's movement from wild emotional outbursts of hate, to calm controlled professions of admiration. Although David loses his fight with the fish, he wins his quest for maturity. Afterward, his comments match Santiago's reactions in respect for a worthy opponent. "In the worst parts, when I was tiredest I couldn't tell which was him and which was me," he tells Roger. This parity of bondage transcends into a unified love: "I began to love him more than anything on earth" (p. 142). The young boy is not bitter about his personal loss of a handsome trophy; such records are meaningless and no animosity remains. "I'm glad that he's all right and that I'm all right," he simply states (p. 143). David learns early the lesson that comes later to men like Roger Davis. His ordeal serves as an example of un-selfish grace under pressure to both older men and reinforces their will to discipline their own lives.

Young David's fishing performance sets the stage for the humorous parody the boys and men enact at the Ponce de León. Hudson and Davis portray two drunken artists who allow young Andy Hudson to drink gin in a cruel exhibition of the breakdown of all parental responsibility and restraint. This surface humor is actually the ritualistic pantomiming of both men's worst fears. What appears as "horrible" and "tragic" to the spectators actually provides an exorcistic relief from ominous reality, as Roger Davis's intoxicated performance requires mini-mal theatrical talent.

With all the people and excitement suddenly thrust into his lonely ordered life, Thomas Hudson "was having a difficult time staying in the carapace of work that he had built for his protec-tion." "Work," he told himself; "keep your habits because you are going to need them" (p. 190).

His instincts for self-preservation are sound, for Hudson soon learns of David and Andrew's deaths. When Eddy curses the bad news, the painter verbalizes his will to continue life in fitting competitive metaphors. "We'll play it out the way we can," he says. But, "now he knew he did not have much interest in the game" (p. 196). Hudson's grief at the loss gnaws at his determination to structure his life and work. While drowning his sorrows in alcohol is a possible escape, he realizes that "drink-ing would destroy the capacity for producing satisfying work and he had built his life on work so long now that he kept that as the one thing he must not lose" (p. 197). He tells himself to "write off" and "give up" his ex-wife and two boys as dead and gone; thinking about this loss will only make him sloppy in self-pity. Yet, drinking corrupts his strict routine; alcohol offers the "simple happiness of breaking training" (p. 200). This respite from severity is, however, a lowering of defenses that are not easily resurrected. The sad results of this momentary indulgence are clear when Thomas Hudson reappears in the "Cuba" section of the novel.

III

The Thomas Hudson whom we encounter in "Cuba" is only a distant relative of the man we admire in "Bimini." Replacing the stoic, hard-working artist is an idle, self-pitying, pill-popping rummy. Large Seconal capsules dull the ache of his lost happiness, as the "aesthetic of alcohol" replaces the aesthetic of hard work, and a "quest for suicidal oblivion" in the Floridita Bar replaces the desire for the sanative Bimini refuge.[7] The sleeping pill, called "medicine" by Hudson, becomes an artificial defense and physical crutch to ease the pain of traumatic losses.

The sea, a primary source of artistic inspiration and physical relaxation in "Bimini," now plagues Hudson's conscience as a reminder of boring standby duty. The subchaser's thoughts reflect his revolt against static, trivial routine: "Now you take a bath, . . . Then you dress for Havana. Then you ride into town to see the Colonel. What the hell is wrong with you? Plenty is wrong with me, he thought. Plenty" (p. 237). Without artistic goals or paternal obligations Hudson's life is devoid of meaning. While riding into Cuba, assailed by the misery and poverty of slum-dwellers, he tries to justify his drinking as a guilty self-defense against "poverty, dirt, four-hundred-year-old dust, the nose-snot of children. . . , the shuffle of untreated syphilis, sewage in the old beds of brooks, lice on the bare necks of infested poultry, scale on the backs of old men's necks" and other miseries (p. 246). These self-pitying laments can no longer function, however, as excuses, for "lots of times," he tells himself, "you are just drinking." His chauffeur must remind this disappointed man "to take things with calm and patience" (p. 256).

The immediate reason for his grief becomes clear in a conversation; Tom Jr., his only surviving son, was killed in battle. This reminder summons other hidden sorrows to the surface of his memory: "He could feel it all coming up; everything he had not thought about; all the grief he had put away and walled out and never even thought of on the trip nor all this morning" (p. 263). Hudson is desperately close to the same breaking point that Nick Adams once approached. Unlike Nick, the once-disciplined painter of "Bimini" no longer has a physical means of therapy to help ease painful memories. Honest Lil, the gold-hearted Floridita whore, senses Hudson's problems and tries to get him to recount happy stories of past times. "Who isn't sad about the whole world?" she asks. "It goes worse all the time. But you can't spend your time being sad about that," she adds. Hudson rejects these "ethical discussions" in favor of "various palliative measures," especially drinking (p. 282).

Even the surprise appearance of his ex-wife fails to shake Tom Hudson from this physical lethargy and mental torpor. Up to this point Tom Hudson searches unsuccessfully for non-existent answers to problems in the bottom of a daiquiri glass. A call from the lieutenant with an assignment shakes Hudson from this tangled despair and in typically sparse but forceful Hemingway prose, he faces reality and reflects a new will to continue a purposeful existence: "Get it straight. Your boy you lose. Love you lose. Honor has been gone for a long time. Duty you do" (p. 326). His return to the Gulf Stream in "At Sea" marks a rediscovery of dignity and new-found resolve to make the best of his remaining talents; duty constructs a new carapace against melancholy. The key to Hudson's sea-search assignment is discipline, and the result is integrity with the affirmation of man's responsibility to himself and his fellow men.

IV

In "At Sea" Tom Hudson reaffirms Hemingway's consistent

code, which Mr. Bruccoli succinctly summarizes as "the avoidance of shit, the necessity for balls and the difficulty of love."[8] These common concerns link this piece of writing and *The Old Man and the Sea* written during the same year.

The "two novellas could have been placed side by side in the same book as a pair of pursuit stories, one in war, the other in peace," says Carlos Baker, who perceives the common bond between Santiago and Thomas Hudson as "a determination to endure to the end, to do what they set out to do, no matter what it takes, even to try to think their way into the heads of their respective quarries so as to anticipate whatever moves they make."[9] From the first pages of *The Old Man and the Sea* Santiago's will to succeed in his mission is never in doubt. Thomas Hudson's ability to lead the search for the German submarine crew is less evident. We never read about Santiago's eighty-four unsuccessful quests for marlin. Yet Thomas Hudson's debilitating drinking and sloppy self-pity, so fully displayed in "Cuba," are the distinct memories we carry into the final section of *Islands in the Stream*. We hope for a return of the same pride, respectability and self-discipline that Hudson exalted as a painter. We are not disappointed; for the once shaky drunk is transformed—off-stage, in the interstices of the novel—into a competent commander whose will to succeed enables him to transcend traumatic memories and face present difficulties. Thomas Hudson is reborn in his command with responsibility to duty and to a crew that replaces his lost family.

Hudson feels "glad to have something to do and good people to do it with" (p. 348). His duties keep his "mind off things" that would start his skin prickling again with foreboding. "I don't have to be proud of it," he says. "I only have to do it well' (p. 356). One of his men, however, reminds the Captain that:

> All a man has is pride. Sometimes you have it so much it is a sin. We have all done things for pride that we knew were impossible. We didn't care. But a man must implement his pride with intelligence and care. Now that you have ceased to be careful of yourself I must ask you to be, please. For us and for the ship (p. 358).

This call for pride awakens a concern for crew and self in the commander, who swears "to be very good" and work with the dedication he once showed for his painting (p. 361). Thus Hudson can admire a brave German who dies "with much style" (p. 362). "CONTINUE SEARCHING WESTWARD"—Hudson's order for this particular mission—also carries a larger connotation for this man whose personal mission is to search carefully for self-respect before death (p. 368).

Captain Hudson constantly practices precision maneuvres with his sea craft to keep his reflexes sharp.

> He must take the highest tree on the head of the island and fit it squarely into the little saddle on Romano. . . . He did it for practice and when he found his tree, . . he eased along the bank until he fitted the tree carefully into the slot of the saddle, then turned sharp in. . . . Then he steered straight in on his bearing. He was tempted not to look at the banks but to push it straight through. But then he knew that was one of the things of too much pride Ara had spoken of and he piloted carefully on the starboard bank and made his turn to starboard when it came by the banks and not by the secondbearing that he had (p. 373).

Hudson maneuvres his craft skillfully, yet without unnecessary chances, like a veteran matador who does not allow foolish pride to expose him to unreasonable risks.

As long as Thomas Hudson concentrates on practical tasks, careful observations, and pragmatic thinking, he retains emotional equilibrium. The facts of life—not the reason for their existence—are his salvation. Hudson "traded in remorse for another horse that he was riding now" (p. 384). The name of his mount is competence. In a series of questions concerning the German quarry, he switches mental gears from emotional memories to present practical problems that show his discriminating intelligence at work.

> I wonder how many dressings they have for that other wounded character? If they had time to get dressings they had time to get other stuff, too. What stuff? What do you think they have besides what you know they have? I don't think much. Maybe pistols and a few machine pistols. Maybe some demolition charges they could make something out of. I have to figure that they have the

machine gun. But I don't think so. They wouldn't want to fight. They want to get the hell away and on a Spanish ship. If they had been in shape to fight they would have come back that night and taken Confites. Maybe no. Maybe something made them suspicious and they saw our drums . . . and figure there was something around that burned plenty of gas. Then too they probably didn't want to fight with their wounded. But the boat with the wounded could have laid off at night while they came with that other sub. I wonder what happened with her. There's something very strange about that (p. 385).

His analytic mind explores the real possibilities of his present dilemma as a therapeutic exorcism of lingering emotional scars. Hudson illustrates the artistic strategy of thinking from the opponent's point of view, a similar move to that which Santiago uses against his fish. The "thinking about the problems had made him feel better and he slept without dreaming;" these mental exercises provide restful sleep without restless dreams (p. 386).

When the Q-boat chase takes Hudson out of the sea and into a labyrinth of inland channels, his scalp prickles in nervous anxiety at one very narrow key. Just before he runs his ship aground, he experiences a *déjà vous* of calamity. Although frequently experienced in bad dreams, this emotion "was happening with such an intensification that he felt both in command and at the same time the prisoner of it" (p. 414). Like the *nada*-like nightmares that plague Nick Adams with insomnia in "Now I Lay Me" and "A Way You'll Never Be," this possibility of a failed mission in a claustraphobic channel holds the possibility of mental relapse for Thomas Hudson.

The grounding itself is, however, followed by a "feeling of reprieve that a wound brings" (p. 389). This temporary setback does not render the Captain's entire mission a failure; rather, the physical and mental strain of this mission provides him with a duty, a "useful" and "wonderful thing," that replaces past responsibilities (p. 418). While sweating in the hot sun, Hudson contemplates a more comfortable alternative: "We could have just gone up the open sea with this breeze and made Cayo Frances and Peters would have answered their blinker and we would have cold beer tonight." Such possibilities would and we would have cold beer tonight." Such possibilities would be a direct avoidance of responsibility. "Don't think about it," he dutifully reminds himself. "This is what you had to do" (p. 432). The surroundings become reminiscent of the (p. 445). The boy's death is not mourned, but accepted, for Hudson finally realizes that "death is what is really final" (p. 449).

Mortally wounded in duty, Hudson demonstrates true courage under the imminent specter of death. He "tried to hold his pain in control," refusing a morphine injection because he "might still have to think" (pp. 462-463). This pain reawakens the competitive aesthetic and artistic integrity of the past. For

> if you paint as well as you really can and keep out of all other things and do that, it is the true thing. You can paint the sea better than anyone now if you will do it and not get mixed up on other things. Hang on good now to how you truly want to do it. You must hold hard to life to do it. But life is a cheap thing beside a man's work. The only thing is that you need it. Hold it tight. Now is the true time you make your play. Make it now without hope of anything. You always coagulated well and you can make one more real play (p. 464).

In appropriate athletic metaphors Tom Hudson tenaciously grips his reborn pride from the clutches of ignoble death. His dignified demeanor during his last moments is his greatest artistic accomplishment. Lapsing close to death, he feels free from past worries and present obligations.

> He felt far away now and there were no problems at all. He felt the ship gathering her speed and the lovely throb of her engines against his shoulder blades which rested hard against the boards. He looked up and there was the sky that he had always loved and he looked across the great lagoon that he was quite sure, now, he would never paint and he eased his position a little to lessen the pain. The engines were around three thousand now, he thought, and they came through the deck and into him (p. 466).

The boat provides a physical reassurance against any emotional vacuum in Hudson's moment of death; man, nature, and machine are in equilibrium. Hudson's devotion to duty regains a lost sense of pride and earns his place with the bravest of Hemingway's matadors, soldiers, hunters, and fishermen. Discipline breeds integrity and another Hemingway hero earns his existential salvation. While Thomas Hudson can come to terms with his life only in death, the task of survival and salvation remains for an old fisherman plagued by bad luck, who not only endures life's hardships, but prevails in spite of them.

[1] The dates are provided by Carlos Baker in *Hemingway: The Writer as Artist*, 4th ed. (New York: Scribner's, 1972), pp. 379-382.

[2] William R. Anderson, Jr., in *Islands in the Stream*—The Initial Reaction," *Fitzgerald/Hemingway Annual 1971* (Washington, D. C.: Microcard Editions, 1972), pp. 326-332, surveys thirty critical reviews and provides a bibliography.

[3] Edmund Wilson, "An Effort at Self-Revelation," *The New Yorker* 46 (2 January 1971), p. 59.

[4] Ernest Hemingway, *Islands in the Stream* (New York: Scribner's, 1970), p. 5. All subsequent references from this novel are from this edition with page numbers in parentheses in the text.

[5] Emily Stipes Watts, *Ernest Hemingway and the Arts* (Urbana: University of Illinois Press, 1972), p. 129.

[6] Carlos Baker, *Hemingway: The Writer as Artist*, p. 393.

[7] Joseph DeFalco, "Hemingway's Islands and Streams: Minor Tactics For Heavy Pressure," in *Hemingway In Our Time*, ed., Richard Astro and Jackson J. Benson (Corcallis: Oregon State University Press, 1974), p. 48.

[8]Matthew J. Bruccoli, *"Islands in the Stream:* A Review," *Fitzgerald/ Hemingway Annual 1970* (Washington, D. C.: Microcard Editions, 1970), p. 246.

[9]Carlos Baker, *Hemingway: The Writer as Artist*, p. 402.

Contributors' Notes

DONALD R. NOBLE, the editor of this volume, is Associate Professor of English at the University of Alabama. He is the co-editor of *The Rising South* (1976), the editor of *A Century Hence; Or, A Romance of 1941* (1977) and the author of articles on Singer, Roth, Faulkner and others.

JACKSON J. BENSON is Professor of American Literature at San Diego State University. He is the co-editor, with Richard Astro, of *Hemingway In Our Time* (1974) and *The Fiction of Bernard Malamud* (1977). He is the editor of *The Short Stories of Ernest Hemingway: Critical Essays* (1975) and the author of *Hemingway: The Writer's Art of Self-Defense* (1969). He is currently writing a biography of John Steinbeck.

ALFRED KAZIN is Distinguished Professor of English at the State University of New York at Stony Brook. His books include *On Native Ground* (1942), *A Walker in the City* (1951), *The Inmost Leaf* (1955), *Contemporaries* (1962), *Starting Out in the Thirties* (1965), *Bright Book of Life: American Novelists and Storytellers from Hemingway to Mailer* (1973) and *New York Jew* (1978).

LEO GURKO is Professor Emeritus of English, Hunter College and John Crawford Adams Professor of English at Hofstra University. He is the author of *The Two Lives of Joseph Conrad* (1965), *Ernest Hemingway and the Pursuit of Heroism* (1968) and many other books and articles.

ROBERT O. STEPHENS is Professor of English at the University of North Carolina at Greensboro. He is the author of *Hemingway's Nonfiction: The Public Voice* (1968), *Ernest Hemingway: The Critical Reception* (1977) and many articles on Hemingway.

CHARLES GEORGE HOFFMANN is Professor of English at the

University of Rhode Island. He is the author of *The Short Novels of Henry James* (1957), *Joyce Cary: The Comedy of Freedom* (1964) and *Ford Madox Ford* (1967).

A. C. HOFFMANN is Professor of English at the University of Rhode Island. She has published articles on Anthony Burgess and Virginia Woolf.

MICHAEL S. REYNOLDS is Associate Professor of English at North Carolina State University. He is the author of *Hemingway's First War: The Making of* a Farewell to Arms (1976) and several articles on William Faulkner.

SCOTT DONALDSON is Chairman and Professor of English at the College of William and Mary. He is the author of *The Suburban Myth* (1969), *Poet in America: Winfield Townley Scott* (1972), *By Force of Will: The Life and Art of Ernest Hemingway* (1977) and many essays on American Literature.

W. CRAIG TURNER is Assistant Professor of English at Texas A & M University. He has previously published articles on Robert Browning.

F. ALLEN JOSEPHS is Associate Professor of Spanish at the University of West Florida. He has published on various Spanish writers and on Hemingway in periodicals in Spain and in the United States.

PHILIP YOUNG is Research Professor of English at Pennsylvania State University. He has published *Ernest Hemingway* (1952), *Ernest Hemingway: A Reconsideration* (1967), *Three Bags Full: Essays in American Fiction* (1972), *The Hemingway Manuscripts: An Inventory* (1969) and over two hundred other pieces on American writers.

RICHARD B. HOVEY is Professor of English at the University of Maryland. He has written *John Jay Chapman: An American Mind* (1959) and *Hemingway: The Inward Terrain* (1968) as well as many articles on American Literature.

GREGORY S. SOJKA is Associate Professor of American Studies at Wichita State University. He has published articles on Philip Roth, Stephen Crane and Ernest Hemingway.